Cultural Intimacy

Cultural Intimacy
Social Poetics in the Nation-State

Michael Herzfeld

ROUTLEDGE
New York • London

Published in 1997 by
Routledge
29 West 35th Street
New York, NY 10001

Published in Great Britain by
Routledge
11 New Fetter Lane
London EC4P 4EE

For permission to reprint materials published elsewhere, the author would like to
thank the following: Walter de Gruyter & Co. for "The Poeticity of the Commonplace"from *Semiotic Theory and Practice* (Vol. 1), eds. Herzfeld and
Melazzo; Stauffenberg Verlag for "On Some Rhetorical Uses of Ionicity in Cultural Ideologies" from *Ionicity: Essays On the Nature of Culture*, eds. Bouissac,
Herzfeld, and Posner (1986); Royal Anthropological Institute for "Pride and Perjury: Time and Oath in the Mountain Villages of Crete" from *Man* (n.s., Vol. 25);
L'Homme (Vol. 121) for "La Pratique des Stéréotypes"; Smithsonian Institute
Press for "Of Definitions and Boundaries: The Status of Culture in the Culture of
the State" from *Discourse and the Social Life of Meaning*, ed. Chock and Wyman
(1986); and *Anthropologie et Sociétés* (Vol. 19, no. 3) for "Les enjeux du sang: la
production officielle des stéréotypes dans les Balkans. Le cas de la Grèce."

Library of Congress Cataloging-in-Publication Data

Herzfeld, Michael, 1947–
    Cultural intimacy : social poetics in the nation-state / Michael
Herzfeld
        p.   cm.
    Includes bibliographical references and index.
    ISBN 0-415-91778-6. — ISBN 0-415-91779-4 (pbk.)
    1. National state.   2. Minorities.   3. Group identity.
4. Ethnicity.   I. Title.
JC311.H525   1996
320.5'4—dc20   96-28864
                                                    CIP

for Ann and David

Contents

Preface and
Acknowledgments

Smashing huge numbers of cheap china plates across the feet of inebriated dancers is a practice that many a foreign visitor, prompted by popular films, happily anticipates on a trip to Greece. Under the military dictatorship, this practice was prohibited as both dangerous and demeaning in the eyes of foreigners; small printed notices everywhere announced, with mysterious inexplicitness for the uninitiated, "Breakage is forbidden." But this turned out to be not just some arbitrary caprice of the colonels. Some years after their overthrow, the ban was revived. And a Greek friend assured me categorically that plate-smashing was absolutely not a "Greek custom."

This book has grown out of my increasing fascination with the desire for control over the external images of a national culture that these denials and prohibitions express. Such evasive action often flies in the face of all the evidence, but it is sustained by what, to the outsider, can be an infuriatingly imperturbable air of total conviction: if we tell you that these things do not exist, then, as far as you are concerned, they do not exist. But the visitor is still left wondering why so much vehemence should be invested in denying what all the senses affirm.

In this book I explore the grounds of this defensiveness. I examine the contrasts that the visitor to many a nation-state encounters between the presentation of the national culture—what nationalist discourses personalize as "national character"—and the presentation of individual selves within the intimacy of the national space. Smashing plates is a personal performance of high spirits and unconstrained independence; the Greeks describe their national character in terms of individualism and disregard for arbitrary authority; yet both the law and the cultural establishment decry the idea that smashing plates should represent Greekness to the rest of the world. What are the political forces that cause this strain between the creative presentation of the individual self—what in this book I call *social poetics*—and the formal image of a national or collective self?

The issue is one that has become increasingly important for anthropologists and other students of culture. While we still study society and culture ethnographically—that is, by describing the minutiae of everyday life at a fairly microscopic level—our work is done in the context of far larger dynamics in which we ourselves are willy-nilly cast as the representatives of powerful and sometimes hated external forces. Nor can we ignore these entailments as our predecessors sometimes did with such blissful ease. To many people throughout the world we are both the signs and the agents of an intrusion, not just into private lives, but also into the privacy of nations—an intrusion into the collective space I have chosen to call *cultural intimacy*.

Many dismiss what we study as trivial, as mere anecdote, and as irrelevant to the large concerns of the nation. But if these matters are so unimportant, why do people invest so much energy in dismissing them? Clearly these reactions are diagnostic of a politics of significance in which much hinges on what is deemed important and what is relegated to the limbo of mereness. Anthropologists face such charges often, taxed with excessive interest in mere anecdote, mere hearsay, mere minorities, mere marginals and eccentrics. Arguments about the validity of anthropological scholarship take on the character of defenses put up by majority or elite forces against the violation of cultural intimacy. In these pages, I have brought into the common framework afforded by the concept of cultural intimacy several attempts to define and understand the sore zones of cultural sensitivity.

Inevitably for some readers this investigation, like any probe, risks irritating those tender spots even more. But if scholars are to think constructively about how far their responsibilities entail avoiding certain topics, or what kinds of political considerations their responsibilities to host communities and countries entail, they must ask some of these questions. They know from their field experiences that consensus is rare and, when it does fleetingly appear, an unreliable guide to future reactions. Consequently my first acknowledgment in the long list that follows must be a generic one. It is to all those who have so warmly accepted me as a virtual insider while knowing that the range of my subsequent conversations would not be confined to a narrow circle of knowing cultural intimates, but could easily become quite public. Since I began to push the compass of my field research beyond the permissible boundaries of officially sanctioned folklore in Greece over two decades ago, I have been increasingly grateful to all those friends, far from few in number, who willingly tolerated and even encouraged such repeated trespasses. I can only reassure them in the language that is often used to defend the ramparts of cultural intimacy: this is not a peculiarly Greek problem. In fact this book is not specifically about Greece. While for obvious reasons it is heavily grounded in examples from my fieldwork there, I have made every effort to present the issues in terms of their global implications. My focus here is primarily comparative and analytic.

I have become increasingly grateful over the years to those mentors and peers who shaped my first approaches to many of these issues. I continue to treasure critical advice: some colleagues read earlier versions of segments of this book in other incarnations and contexts and are recognized again here in the notes to the relevant chapters. I would like to offer specific thanks here to those who read some of the newer materials (especially chapters 1 and 5) and commented on their appropriateness for the overall perspective: Marc Abélès, P. Nikiforos Diamandouros, Jill Dubisch, Davydd Greenwood, Stephen Gudeman, Sally Falk Moore, Peter Pels, and Rosalind Shaw. None of the kind people who have offered their gentle criticism over the years should be held responsible for my own peculiar uses of it, but my gratitude to them, equally, should not be in doubt.

I am also deeply indebted to Luisa Passerini, whose invitation to address her seminar on European identity at the European University Institute in February, 1994, led me to formulate the ideas laid out in chapter 5. Chapters 4 and 5 also received considerable impetus from Margaret Alexiou's warm invitation to deliver the 1991 Christopher Lecture at Harvard University, while chapter 8 was originally developed in the context of a

Council for European Studies–sponsored workshop organized by Susan Carol Rogers and Marc Abélès.

Portions of this book have appeared elsewhere in various forms. I wish to thank the publishers for permission to make use of the following materials:

"Of Definitions and Boundaries: The Status of Culture in the Culture of the State," from Phyllis Pease Chock and June R. Wyman, eds., *Discourse and the Social Life of Meaning.* 1986. Washington, D.C.: Smithsonian Institution Press, 77–93, now incorporated into chapter 3;

"On Some Rhetorical Uses of Iconicity in Cultural Ideologies," from Paul Bouissac, Michael Herzfeld, and Roland Posner, eds., *Iconicity: Essays on the Nature of Culture.* 1986. Tuebingen: Stauffenburg, 401–19, now incorporated into chapter 3;

"Les enjeux du sang: la production officielle des stéréotypes dans les Balkans. Les cas de la Grèce," *Anthropologie et sociétés* 19 (1995): 37–52, now incorporated into chapter 4

"Pride and Perjury: Time and the Oath in the Mountain Villages of Crete," *Man* (n.s.) 25 (1990), 305–22 (published by the Royal Anthropological Institute, London), now incorporated into chapter 6;

"The Poeticity of the Commonplace," from Michael Herzfeld and Lucio Melazzo, eds., *Semiotic Theory and Practice*, vol. 1. Berlin: Mouton de Gruyter, 383–91, now incorporated into chapter 7;

"La pratique des stéréotypes," *L'Homme* 121 (January–March 1992): 67–77 (published by the École des Hautes Études en Sciences Sociales, Paris), now incorporated into chapter 8.

Some further expressions of appreciation are very much in order here. Alexandra Molnar was a quick-witted and sensitive research assistant whose efficiency, computer skills, and ready understanding made the task of bringing the initially disparate segments of the book together both feasible and fun. At Routledge I am fortunate to have worked with a remarkable series of editors: Ronda Angel, William Germano, Marlie Wasserman, and Eric Zinner; all, at various times and in various ways, brought unexpected excitement to the task of building a new entity out of the detritus of old thoughts and discarded confusions. Warm thanks go to them, to three anonymous reviewers who made generous recommendations regarding the organization of the book, and to a patient in-house copyeditor who dealt carefully and efficiently with the technical problems created by my stylistic vagaries over the many years of writing that have converged here.

I dedicate this book to my sister and brother-in-law, Ann and David Ussishkin, whose deeply affectionate skepticism has so often goaded me to seek better ways of testing and explaining the received pieties of my disciplinary world.

Chapter One

Introducing
Cultural Intimacy

The provisionality of the permanent

In recent years, anthropological interest in the state and in nationalism has belatedly taken on focus and intensity.[1] Anthropologists have hitherto largely shunned the state as a hostile and invasive presence in local social life and have seen nationalism as an embarrassing first cousin to the discipline itself, one distinctly prone to public excesses of essentialism and reification. Now they have at last begun to do what most appropriately falls within their competence, directing their interests to the experiences of citizens and functionaries rather than to questions of formal organization. Even so, they have often seemed to take official ideology as an accurate account of what the nation-state is actually about. This is very peculiar, since talking about "the state" in this way, as I have certainly done myself, reproduces the essentialism against which most of us rail with such predictable piety. Few are entirely innocent of this particular inconsistency.

In practice, however, most anthropologists eventually discover that some citizens accept officially sanctioned cultural and legal norms less willingly than do others. Yet the nonconformists are often the most loyal of all citizens in moments of crisis. The current challenge for the discipline, one that I shall articulate in this book, is thus to probe behind façades of national unanimity in order to explore the possibilities and the limits of creative dissent. It is to stop treating both the nation-state and essentialism as distant and unreachable enemies, and to understand them instead as integral aspects of social life.

That challenge is formidable. National harmony displays a deceptively transparent surface; it does not reveal the underlying fissures easily. The easy option is thus to ignore these fissures altogether, and many social scientists are consequently impatient with the anthropological interest in local-level detail. One can easily see how this scholarly complaisance with official perspectives develops. Even citizens who claim to oppose the state invoke it—simply by talking of "it" in that way—as the explanation of their failures and miseries, or accuse "it" of betraying the national interests of which it claims to be both expression and guardian. In the process, however, they all contribute, through these little acts of essentializing, to making it a permanent fixture in their lives. Few ever seem able to manage completely without it. Except, perhaps, in times of quite exceptional turmoil, most citizens of most countries thus participate through their very discontent in the validation of the nation-state as the central legitimating authority in their lives.

In this book, I try to get inside that engagement. I ask what advantages social actors find in using, reformulating, and recasting official idioms in the pursuit of often highly unofficial personal goals, and how these actions—so often in direct contravention of state authority—actually constitute the state as well as a huge range of national and other identities. I am especially concerned with the uses of cultural form as a cover for social action. This leads me to attempt to show how the control of cultural form allows significant play with cultural content. In the process, I shall argue that state ideologies and the rhetorics of everyday social life are revealingly similar both in how they make their claims and in what they are used to achieve.

Like social actors who use "the law" to legitimize self-interested actions, the state, conversely, uses a language of kin, family, and body to lend immediacy to its pronouncements. It thereby converts revolution into conformity, represents ethnic cleansing as national consensus and cultural homogeneity, and recasts the sordid terrors of emergence into a seductive immortality. Because it is grounded in an idiom of social immediacy, however, this historical streamlining never quite succeeds in concealing a residual sense of contradiction. That sense may provide opportunities for critique, and eternal truths can have surprisingly short lives.

The approach described here might be presented as exploring the relationship between the view from the bottom and the view from the top. I prefer, however, to treat "top" and "bottom" as but two out of a host of refractions of a broadly shared *cultural engagement* (a more processual term than the static *culture*). Simplistic talk of "elites" and "ordinary people" conceals that common ground (as well as the fact that these terms are often themselves instruments in the negotiation of power) and so inhibits analysis. Comparable polarities, such as that between colonized and colonizer, may similarly obscure complex processes of creative cooptation in economic, political, and administrative practices—an issue now amply illustrated by the vicissitudes of both colonial and postcolonial régimes in Africa (Mbembe 1991; Pels 1996). We would do better not to privilege either angle of vision.

What is the common ground that ultimately dissolves the possibility of clearly defined, immutable levels of power? Here I want to argue for the centrality of *cultural intimacy*[2]—the recognition of those aspects of a cultural identity that are considered a source of external embarrassment but that nevertheless provide insiders with their assurance of common sociality, the familiarity with the bases of power that may at one moment assure the disenfranchised a degree of creative irreverence and at the next moment reinforce the effectiveness of intimidation. Cultural intimacy may also reinforce the hand of power when its display becomes a sign of collective confidence, as in upper-class and colonial affectations of modesty. It consists in those alleged national traits—American folksiness, British "muddling through," Greek mercantile craftiness and sexual predation, or Israeli bluntness, to name just a few—that offer citizens a sense of defiant pride in the face of a more formal or official morality and, sometimes, of official disapproval too. These are the self-stereotypes that insiders express ostensibly at their own collective expense. Among a minority population, their use rests on finding common ground with the encompassing society, as in the self-deprecating Jewish diaspora humor that exerts ironic moral pressure on audiences that understand and so can respond. I suggest that the model of cultural intimacy is a particularly apt concept for anthropologists to contribute to the study of nationalism (as well as to other idioms of identity formation), because it typically becomes manifest in the course of their long-term fieldwork, a site of *social intimacy* in the fullest sense. Anthropologists are in

3

an unusually good position to know the forms of rueful self-recognition in which people commonly engage.

Central to the several themes developed in this book is the proposition that the formal operations of national states depend on coexistence—usually inconvenient, always uneasy—with various realizations of cultural intimacy. In the intimacy of a nation's secret spaces lie at least some of the original models of official practice. People recognize as familiar, everyday phenomena some of officialdom's most formal devices, and this generates active skepticism about official claims and motives. Moreover, most citizens may agree that since the state is staffed by rapacious bureaucrats, too much obedience to the law is merely silly. That is hardly the stuff of which the rhetoric of national unity is officially made, yet it informs the mutual recognition that one finds among a country's citizens everywhere—even among its state functionaries.

For its part, a government may try to coopt the language of intimacy for its utilitarian ends of commanding loyalty under what seem to be the most unpropitious conditions. Indeed, in the face of globalizing processes, defensive domesticity can acquire a persuasive appeal. Domesticity is a common image in this strategy. Faced with the disruption of its authoritarian control of information by the arrival of the Internet, the Vietnamese government reacted in revealing terms: "'When we start to open our door, we find that fresh air and dust come in,' said Pham Dao, director of the state-run Vietnam Datacommunications Co., which is establishing the Internet link. 'We would like to keep the fresh air and prevent the dust'" (Wilhelm 1996). The image of a tranquil, old-fashioned domesticity not only covers a serious intent to suppress dissent, but also attempts to make it palatable both at home and abroad. In an even more egregious example, Hastings Banda, the former president of Malawi, attempted to mitigate the seriousness of human rights abuses during his tenure of office by saying that he had been "selflessly dedicated . . . to the good cause of Mother Malawi" (*Boston Globe*, 6 January 1996, 7).

In an earlier work (Herzfeld 1992a), I developed the thesis that bureaucrats, as citizens themselves, participated in a symbolic universe that furnished convenient explanations (a *secular theodicy*) for the obvious failures of democracy in a less-than-ideal world; and I suggested that this universe and its legitimating cosmology were grounded in social experience at the most intimate levels—hence the frequency of bodily and familial metaphors as well as the everyday idiom of explaining defects in the system. Here I examine further the direct mutual engagement between the official state and the sometimes disruptive popular practices whose existence it often denies, but whose vitality is the ironic condition of its own continuation.

Specifically, I treat the conceptual separation of state and people, so pervasive in academic and popular writings alike, as a symbolic construct, deserving of study in its own right. Why do people continually reify the state? Behind every such invocation lurk the desires and designs of real people. Paradoxically they blame this ill-defined but all-important presence in their lives for their failures as they would a living human being and at the same time appeal to its impersonal "thingness" as the ultimate guarantee of disinterested authority.

Conversely, and no less paradoxically, the sometimes suffocatingly formal ideology of the state lays claim to intimacy and familiarity in a series of rather obvious metaphors: the body politic, "our boys and girls," mother country and *Vaterland*, the wartime enemy as the (sometimes actual) rapist of mothers and daughters, and the tourist as a family guest. Moreover, like any person, the state—actually a shifting complex of people and roles—conceals its inability to live strictly by its own superordinate rules behind a blustery rhetoric of "national honor."[3] In that rhetoric is the clearest evidence of what this book is largely about: that the nation-state's claims to affixed, eternal identity grounded in universal truth are themselves, like the moves of all social actors, strategic adjustments to the demands of the historical moment.

This insistent parallelism with a community of familiar faces is the basis of Anderson's (1983) image of the nationalist goal as an "imagined community." But this justly celebrated formulation requires at least two modifications. First, the metonymic extension of "those we know" to include a huge population is not confined to nation-states; they are not the only imagined communities.[4] Perhaps people everywhere use the familiar building blocks of body, family, and kinship in order to make sense of larger entities. This may indeed be the most purely social demonstration of Fernandez's (1974) renowned definition of metaphor as "the predication of a sign upon an inchoate [human] subject."

The second modification of Anderson's thesis concerns its top-down formulation. That *Imagined Communities* has been warmly received by most anthropologists is largely due to its recognition that understanding the appeal of nationalism requires us to ask how and why individual citizens respond to it. Why should people be willing to die for a formal abstraction? Sometimes, as conscripts, or even as taxpayers, for example, they may feel that they have no real choice. But still the question remains: why the uncoerced enthusiasm that this form of self-sacrifice often seems to inspire? Anderson took a major step forward by pointing out that nationalism offered citizens a means of converting their own deaths into a shared immortality. But he does not tell us why this works so well and so often, nor does he tell us whether the actions of the converted exert a reciprocal effect on the cultural form of the evolving nation-state.

This is the classic point of demarcation for the concerns of the anthropologist, and Anderson does not cross that line. He does not ground his account in the details of everyday life—symbolism, commensality, family, and friendship—that would make it convincing for each specific case or that might call for the recognition of the cultural specificity of each nationalism. In that regard, like Gellner (1983), he seems to assume that nationalisms are fundamentally alike in their debt to a common (European) origin and that they represent the imposition of an elite perspective on local cultural worlds; to the extent that local idioms are used, they have often been recycled beyond recognition. The irony of this position is that it reproduces the very ideology that it purports to question. It says, in effect, that ordinary people have no impact on the form of their local nationalism: they are only followers. In addition, it usually overlooks the fact that, like the personal selfhood and family membership that provide the models, national identity comprises a generous measure of embarrassment together with all the idealized virtues. It is this rueful self-recognition, this inward acknowledgment of cultural intimacy, that all the top-down accounts of the nation-state miss.

Simulacra of sociality

Embarrassment, rueful self-recognition: these are the key markers of what cultural intimacy is all about. They are not solely personal feelings, but describe the collective representation of intimacy. The less literally face-to-face the society we inhabit, the more obviously cultural idioms become simulacra of social relations. This is less usefully described as a displacement of the real by empty signs, as Baudrillard (1988: 167) has argued,[5] than as an attempt to project familiar social experience onto unknown and often potentially threatening contexts. The marginal communities that used to be almost the exclusive focus of anthropological study are often the sources of the national-character models entertained by the very nationalists who are most disconcerted by the anthropological gaze—a point to which I shall return below (and, in more detail, in chapter 5).

Those marginal communities are face-to-face societies. For international political and economic audiences, national leaders portray them as atypical of the new, modern reality embedded in a complex nexus of global communications. For the often humiliatingly self-abasing tourist trade, however, and in the romantic folklore of the urban elite, they embody the national quintessence. This disjuncture creates a perennial embarrassment: how is tradition to be recast as modernity, and rebelliousness as a love of (national) independence? For, as the state appropriates for its own purposes the local idioms of morality, custom, and the solidarity of kinship, it dismisses the local renditions themselves as conservative survivals, picturesque tradition, and familism, respectively—all serious obstacles to the European nation-state's rationalist vision of modernity.

Indeed, transnational modernity stretches the social metonyms based on face-to-face relations to the breaking point. In the United States and elsewhere, the packaging of politeness no longer tries to hide its nonliteral status; instead, it intensifies awareness of it, thereby further accentuating the ambiguity of the social relations that ride on it. This is the source of that frightful politeness with which the airline flight attendant or restaurant employee breathlessly announces an individuating personal name that denies any actual social identity: "Hi! My name's Leslie and I'm waiting on you tonight." Imagine the awkwardness that must arise when some unsuspecting cultural novice responds in kind. Advertising slogans like "USAir begins with you" and "Fly the Friendly Skies of United" exude fabricated sociability. Like state ideologies that derive their reality from everyday bureaucratic encounters, these cookie-cutter social relations are sustained by an impressive forest of symbols in the form of false indexicals in daily practice ("How are you today?" "Bye now"). These indexicals are patently false: they show how thinly the image of sociality has been stretched by what Hochschild (1983: 11, 19) has aptly called the *"emotional labor"* involved in the "transmutation" of private sentiments into public acts.

7

They are not simple falsehoods, however, but act out a pervasive nostalgia for "real" social relations. Such evocations of a balanced and conflict-free past are as common in social theory as they are in popular discourse: Mauss's image of an age when money had not yet corrupted pure reciprocity clearly rests on stereotypical assumptions about "the West" as much as about an orientalist "rest" (Carrier 1995b, 1995c) and exhibits a similar yearning for a time of pure structure. But social theory here seems merely a specialized case of what is, in fact, a widely popular notion. Thus Cretan sheep-thieves similarly bemoan the necessity of bringing in the legal processes of the state where once, they say, the word of honor sufficed to establish guilt or innocence (chapter 6). But it is also precisely those who bewail the passing of the old ways who find in that process justification for adopting the new: accusing others of violating the ethic of reciprocity opens the way to nonreciprocal acts such as recourse to law. There is a curious symbiosis between the state's argument that it must intervene to prevent a final collapse of civic morality and the rebellious Cretan sheep-thieves' view that the collapse of *their* morality is what has necessitated the intervention of the state. Both are engaged in a symbolism of purity, and it is this common ground that makes loyal patriots in wartime out of citizens who in times of peace show rich inventiveness in tweaking the nose of the state.

Pervasive essentialisms

Because the sheep-thieves embody such an extreme position in the argument about representativity, this limiting case is especially central to my thesis that nationalism and cultural intimacy are caught up in a mutual dependence. Ethnographic accounts (e.g., Gupta 1995)—intimate views of the nation-state in action—show that the realism that most citizens bring to their encounters with officialdom, far from undermining the conduct of state business, renders it comprehensible. Such insight comes, however, at a certain cost to democratic and administrative ideals: citizens (including many bureaucrats) treat rules as though they existed primarily in order to serve particularistic interests.

But I do not intend a variant of the equilibrium model here: to say that graft actually helps to keep the state functioning may sometimes be true, but only in the sense that corrupt officials have already made sure that it will be true. But it is also the case that the moralistic ideology of a national culture appeals to people in part because it is usually coupled with the relief of knowing that even (or especially) officials do not always adhere scrupulously to its austere principles but may use those principles exactly as other citizens do: as a strategy of self-interest. This is not an issue of determinism but of the practical constraints of social life: cultural intimacy is above all familiarity with perceived social flaws that offer culturally persuasive explanations of apparent deviations from the public interest. These flaws may even be used to explain the actions of those who obey the law or work to strengthen its institutions. In the midst of the great anticorruption drive in Italy, for example, even those who risked their lives to clean up the country's political life were often suspected of a particularly devious form of *furberia* (a socially respected idiom of cunning [see Bailey 1973: 183–184; Schneider and Schneider 1994: 253]), and the prosecution of ex-premier Silvio Berlusconi—elected in part for his promises of clean government—as well as the deep suspicions expressed against members of the anti-Mafia movement have only intensified such ambivalences. Serving the public interest, even with the most civic-minded intentions, may confer both specific and diffuse personal benefits as well. Most countries have countless honest and even altruistic citizens. The apparent overdetermination of official moralism, however, may in practice offer an enormous range of play to individual social actors regardless of their individual motives.

Methodological individualism—treating the nation as merely the aggregate of its citizens' individual wills—is thus not an adequate description of these processes. It is in fact a reverse essentialism, politically expressed in Ronald Reagan's voluntarism and Margaret Thatcher's attempt—"there are only individuals"—to argue the social out of existence altogether. Certainly, citizens engage in the ceaseless business of shaping the meaning of national identity, often in ways that contravene official ideology: politicians, civil servants, professionals, and intellectuals are "ordinary people" too, and anthropologists have been increasingly willing to treat them as ethnographically interesting.[6] But they, no less than the subjects of classic ethnographies, are also constrained by the sense of collective identity, however evanescent, that they help to create. It was not mere whimsy that led Marc Abélès (1989) to treat French politicians as a "tribe."

Here the tribe of politicians is a collectivity that consists of different people doing a variety of things. Similarly, the state is not a monolithic, autonomous agent. I have often been tempted to treat it that way, following exasperated local friends who blame "it" for all their ills. But during fieldwork I also came to know and like a host of officials (including police officers), bureaucrats, academic and artistic celebrities, and politicians, and I came to realize that they usually worked with the same assumptions and experienced the same constraints. The point is worth making because some readers have mistakenly interpreted my insistence on recognizing the cultural force of cynicism as a comprehensive endorsement of that cynicism.[7] But it is important to recognize that bureaucrats who blame the system—whether to avoid responsibility or because they are genuinely dismayed by their inability to help—participate in the same reification of the state as their most disgruntled clients. Like these citizens, officials both contribute to the creation of standardized views of the state and experience the constraints on action that result from this constant process of reification. The option of blaming the state gives definition and authority to its shadowy power.

An anthropology of nationalisms and nation-states must get inside this ongoing production of static truths. To do so means looking for it among all segments of the population, for all are implicated. The approach is thus neither "top-down" nor "bottom-up": except in a narrowly organizational sense, there is neither a discrete "top" nor a discrete "bottom." This is far from the perspective of most authorities on the theory of nationalism. Outside anthropology only Hobsbawm stakes out a critique of the top-down perspective, arguing against Gellner on this point (Hobsbawm 1990: 10–11). This seems to represent a substantive departure from Hobsbawm's early work on social banditry (1959,1969), in which he explicitly denies the possibility that "primitive rebels" might develop an ideology of their own, and from his introduction to an earlier volume on the study of the "invention of tradition"(Hobsbawm 1983b).

For Gellner (1983), the ideologies of particular nationalistic leaderships were uninspiringly similar, cut from the same European cloth, and utterly disconnected from the thoughts and actions of the people each purported to unite under a single banner. While that view may be historically accurate for the original formulation of some European national ideologies, it fails to explain what happens thereafter: the continuing appeal (and ceaseless reformulation) of nationalism in public discourse, and its shaping by the actual people whose values it claims to invoke. To argue, as Gellner does, that massive education creates the common culture does not account for the predisposition that makes such a process possible.

Here the historian Hobsbawm, with his construct of "popular proto-nationalism" (1990: 46–79), comes closer to the anthropological emphasis on local-level values. Unfortunately, however, the range of models he elects to categorize in this way is, as we should perhaps have expected from his earlier writings, restricted to those in which a self-aware form of ideology building can be detected. This emphasis on conscious intellectual activity eventually leads to a despairing conclusion: "We know too little about what went on, or for that matter what still goes on, in the minds of most *relatively inarticulate* men and women, to speak with any confidence about their thoughts and feelings towards the nationalities and nation-states which claim their feelings" (Hobsbawm 1990: 78, my emphasis). But innermost thoughts are never accessible, despite the rhetoric of hearts and minds, and so the role of local values is once again elided in a Marxist-derived, top-down understanding of ideology not so very different, in this regard, from the strongly anti-Marxist Gellner's. Pragmatically, it is true, Hobsbawm is right: written records are rarely a promising source for popular, "relatively inarticulate" social ideologies.[8]

The focus on cultural intimacy works against this static, elitist, and conflationary reading. Its data are ethnographic and are of a kind often summarily dismissed as mere anecdote. But who sets the boundary between importance and mereness? There is a suspiciously close convergence between the refusal to take ethnographic detail seriously and the homogeneity enjoined by nationalist ideologies. In chapter 5, I address in greater detail the political logic that animates such criticisms of anthropology, which in turn, through its resolute insistence on the significance of the particular, is thus able to document how nationalism is understood (and sometimes recast) by living social actors. There is no doubt that many nationalist ideologies are externally alike, as Gellner and others have claimed, but that is no reason to ignore the highly localized specificities that sometimes give nationalism distinctive meaning in an enormous range of cultural and social settings.

The recognition that local actors may not always agree with official renditions of history has taken a surprisingly long time to come into focus. Edwin Ardener's (1975) notion of "englobing" did, however, suggest the possibility of a reading that could symbolically subordinate state authority to local concerns. Studies of archaeological sites such as Masada in Israel (Bruner and Gorfain 1984; see also Handelman 1990) and Colonial Williamsburg in the United States (Gable, Handler, and Lawson 1992), and of historic conservation in Greece (Herzfeld 1991a), all suggest the possibility of the subtle recastings of official discourses that we might call counterinventions of tradition, in which local and minority groups variously (and often discordantly) propose a host of alternative pasts. Oral memories of the Spanish fascists' attempt to incorporate the population of Galicia through forced labor on a massive road construction program (Roseman 1996), or of events mythologized by the historians of civil strife in both Greece and Spain (Collard 1989; Hart 1996; Mintz 1982), tell a new set of stories. Rethinking the tangle of multiple pasts often happens in the intimate spaces of culture.

The fact that such processes often use bodily and kinship metaphors is not evidence of some cultural inability to think beyond immediate social experience but simply shows that members of local communities think about the state through much the same categories as those through which state officials woo local opinion. If public officials adopt familistic rhetoric in order to command loyalty or court votes—the current debate about family values in the United States offers a striking case in point—it is because that rhetoric demonstrably works. But it also has its price: as many European and American politicians have discovered, they become answerable to the demands of this simulacrum of moral family leadership.

In other cases the image of domestic harmony becomes exposed to its concomitant logic of fraternal strife—as in Lebanon, for example (although King Hussein's farewell to "my brother" Rabin showed that even the bitterness of metaphorically internecine feuds can be reversed). Indeed, Greek peasants explain civil and international strife in terms of embattled siblings, whose intense mutual affection can all too easily be transmuted into an equally intense struggle over the division of their parents' property, represented by territory in the case of the nation-state's relationship with countries like Turkey[9] and access to resources in the case of class struggle. David Sutton (1995) has argued that the passions stirred in Greece by the struggle over the name Macedonia only become comprehensible in light of the tight mutual association of affect, land, and personhood in the traditional transmission of names.[10] Greek politicians have certainly both exploited and been swept along by the resulting tide of popular sentiment.

These familial metaphors show that conceptually the nation-state is constructed out of intimacy; and intimacy can also recompose its geopolitical claims. Three superficially very different cases illustrate the principle. First, for the Wakuénai of Venezuelan Amazonia the very idea of nation-states whose borders cut across their own territorial boundaries is both immoral and dangerous. By treating Brazil, Colombia, and Venezuela as merely three additional named groups that came, logically and morally, after the Wakuénai's own sibs and even those of neighboring tribes (Hill 1990: 127, 1993: 37é38),Wakuénai incorporate all three nation-state names into their own kinship format, treating them as nothing more than a set of subunits of a local entity, and so symbolically invert the power relations between themselves and the intrusive nation-state entities historically grounded in European domination and a European model of the nation-state. In my second example, from New Zealand, some Maori traced national origins to the Jews who escaped from Egypt; this not only furnished a parable of deliverance from subjugation but also, by transforming analogy into genealogy, relegated the colonial Christian missionaries to the status of "younger brothers" (Schwimmer 1990: 29–31). While this kind of inversion does not provide an effective means of resistance in itself, it may furnish the requisite first step in that direction; in the Maori case, it appears to have done so.

Sometimes, to turn to my third illustration, this kind of reformulation can appear right in the heart of Europe, where its more direct articulation with the dominant political idiom gives it the real potential to make a difference in the struggle for self-determination. Here cartography is a potent weapon, turning linguistic and religious groupings into new national entities—a visual rhetoric of acknowledged efficacy. Thus, Basque cartography of Southern and Northern Basqueland works "in symbolic defiance of the Spanish/French border, which has divided the Basque provinces into separate states, separate juridico-administrative entities, and separate histories since the 16th century" (Urla 1993: 825). These tactics deny the legitimacy of dominant state powers. Again their actual effectiveness may be constrained by demographic, economic, and institutional limitations, but they do furnish emergent ethnic solidarities with expressive force and direction within the carefully guarded spaces of cultural intimacy from which they may later emerge in resplendently militant and public form.[11]

Disemia and the coding of intimacy

I offer the concept of cultural intimacy as an antidote to the formalism of cultural nationalism. It expresses in more directly political terms the dynamic that I had earlier sought to clarify through the more formalistic notion of *disemia*—the formal or coded tension between official self-presentation and what goes on in the privacy of collective introspection. While the official aspect is a legitimate (and indeed necessary) object of ethnographic analysis, the intimacy it masks is the subject of a deep sense of cultural and political vulnerability.

The tension between official and vernacular cultural forms has long been familiar to sociolinguists under the name of "diglossia," a situation in which a national language is split between two "registers" or social dialects: a formal and often deliberately archaic idiom used mostly for official purposes, and the ordinary speech of everyday life (Ferguson 1959). In diglossic situations, the so-called "high" register often requires access to scarce educational resources. It becomes a device of social, political, and economic exclusion; in Greece, the *locus classicus* for this phenomenon, peasants sometimes used to need interpreters in courts of law. In time, however, these arcane languages increasingly merge with vernacular forms, in which formal archaisms may indeed become a source of popular irony at the expense of the powerful—a reversal that illustrates my central theme.

The concept of disemia, however, expands the narrowly linguistic frame of diglossia. It does not ignore language, but contextualizes it as part of a semiotic continuum that includes silence, gesture, music, the built environment, and economic, civic, and social values. Architecture may well be its most obvious expression: stylized stucco Ionic columns may mask the simple intimacies of a Turkish-style domestic space or the more bodily and gendered ones of a lingerie shop. And while this model may still superficially appear to support a binary split between elite and ordinary people, that division is part of the code itself, not of the social world that uses it: anyone can claim elite or humble status, but these attributions are always being contested in the play of social interaction. The binarism belongs to the code itself; it does not describe the heterogeneous and shifting social world in which people nevertheless use it to establish their own claims to power and distinction.[12] Above all, its very formality makes it capable of conveying the most exquisite irony;

literal readings often compound that irony by falling into the traps it sets.

A historian of China, Charlotte Furth, has made the point that not all binarism arises from the imperial project of orientalism, but that binarism may in fact prove useful for describing the consequences of that project: "Binaries come with the necessary activity of making distinctions, and narrative strategies give linguistic distinctions entitivity" (Furth 1995:998)—a point that demonstrates the material significance of the symbolic. Within a political structure defining the shape of cultural identity, people are constantly and ineluctably drawn into binary choices. Nation-state ideologies tend to divide the world into Manichaean pairs and to coerce or seduce their citizens into adopting the same rhetoric for the moral organization of their own everyday social relations. But people's actual uses of that rhetoric may be deliberately irreverent or even subversive.

Binarism often is, in fact, a key ordering principle of political inequality.[13] Gelles (1995) has recently argued that the dualistic systems of Andean societies, long associated by structuralists with ritual and with marriage rules, actually derive from indigenous ideas about political hierarchy, possibly even reinforced in the colonial period by similar features in Spanish social ideology. Political relations are in any case oppositional virtually by definition. Political identities, including nationalisms, are contrastive with regard to each other; this, as Spicer (1992) and others have argued, is the basis of ethnogenesis. Concomitantly, such identities also become contrastive in the tension between self-promoting and introspective stereotypes. The content of these stereotypes is unstable. This is because what gives them their significance is not so much their actual form—what Gellner mistook for the uniform content of nationalist ideologies—as the social uses to which they are put. The confluence of stereotypes, their use in social interaction, and their necessarily unstable evocation of competing histories is the defining object of a social poetics, especially of a social poetics concerned with life in the context of the nation-state.

The disemia concept may work best for countries with an ambiguous relationship to ideal images of a powerful culture, in which both formalism and irony provide important resources for political negotiation. The foreign-dominated Greek state adopted the glorious name of Hellenes, as a more powerful evocation of great power interests than the more intimate and little-known

Romii.[14] State formation often gives rise to this Janus-like adoption of a dual identity, balancing foreign-directed display against sometimes rueful introversion. Spicer (1992: 32) notes examples of Native American peoples whose self-designations (ethnonyms), hidden from the supercilious inspection of encompassing state structures much as the identity of the *Romii* was concealed from the "philhellenic" great powers of western Europe, evoke precisely this sense of intimate self-knowledge. Such categorical shyness mocks the failure of the powerful to penetrate the innermost lives of the dominated.

These pairings of external and internal ethnic names signal an important consequence of conquest and other forms of domination. Put quite simply, it is that the denigration of the culture of the conquered may become a source of secret pride. This may lead to the adoption of once derogatory group names during a period of collective regrouping, as has happened with several of the designators for African Americans (notably Black) and with the term *Türk*, adopted as a matter of state policy in the aftermath of the overthrow of the Ottoman rulers of Turkey.[15]

Subnational strivings for greater autonomy may give rise to other, related articulations of disemia. Bretons, rejecting both French state control over their persons and the authority of the official medical establishment, turn for the curing of a wide range of ailments to New Age formulations that combine arcane local knowledge with the scientistic rhetoric of rays and waves (Badone 1991). These are practices that make interior knowledge a mark of intimacy as well as security. In Sicily, as Jane and Peter Schneider (1994) have argued, the widely approved cultural doctrine of *sicilianismo* rejects the national (Italian) denigration of Mafia values as peculiarly Sicilian and tries to reframe these as a trenchantly local moral response to domination by the manifestly corrupt Italian state. This is a defensive posture vis-à-vis the central authorities, but, very much like "interior ethnonyms," it is proactive in promoting a sense of local cultural and moral autonomy and dignity.

Such devices disturb externally imposed models of cultural superiority. Yet they may also long outlast the force of arms or wealth that elevated those models to dominance in the first place. In the Balkans and southern Europe generally (see Maddox 1993: 14), the Caribbean, and parts of Latin America and the Middle East (see Orlove and Bauer 1996)—places where the once monolithic authority of northwestern Europe has lost much of its practical force—the touchstone of cultural hierarchy is still commonly a generalized notion of Europe. In Greece, Romania, and Spain, the idea that these countries are today supplicants for European identity is a raw expression of international cultural politics supported by powerful local elites.

The allure of "Euro-style" imports (including Parisian intellectual fashions) follows a similar logic even in the former colonies of the United States, demonstrating how tenaciously hierarchies of style may survive the collapse or inversion of hierarchies of military and economic power. Globally reproducing the dynamic described by Friedl (1964) as "lagging emulation"(which for her meant peasant imitation of city fashions), the changing global meanings of disemia may thus show great sluggishness through time. In England the defeated Anglo-Saxons gave their name to a cultural ideology of blunt common sense and four-letter words, set against the elegance and formality of its imperial Latin precursors and soon-to-be-aristocratic French conquerors: as with the Greek play of Hellenic and Romeic, the Saxon *Kuh-* and *Schwein*-herds who assured their Norman masters a plentiful supply of *bœuf* and *porc* serve as metaphors for ideologically contrasted cultural identities, *both* of which all social actors internalize and selectively deploy.

In the American example, again, the poles of disemia are an almost sycophantic adulation toward the cultures of the European *anciens régimes* on the one hand, and contempt for Europeans' alleged stuffiness and rigid sense of hierarchy on the other. Context determines which side of this uncomfortable ambiguity predominates. Any European who too eagerly or literally accepts American friends' cultural obeisance soon learns due caution. While American admiration for "Europe" is often couched in terms of nostalgia for a time of cultural finesse—the Old/New World doublet nicely conveys the conversion of historical time into cultural space[16]—it is matched by an equally powerful nostalgia for the communal simplicity emblematized by the paintings of Norman Rockwell and the artifacts of near-defunct groups such as the Shakers.[17]

Such ambivalences may also appear in countries, such as Portugal and Russia, that are simultaneously recent colonial powers and impoverished members of the global community of nations. Russians are often ambivalent about the European aspect of their identity, while their neighbors in Finland have challenged their claims to civilization itself (see Wilson 1976: 132). In Spain, too, the proximity of "Africa" has sat uncomfortably with local class ideologies—not to speak of a long colonial history—and remains an issue in debates about the cultural respectability of bullfights and other emblematically national institutions (Douglass 1995); tourism and parochialism can lead to morose reflections on more localized identities as well (see Fernandez 1988; Greenwood 1977). These examples complicate another dualism, that of colonized and colonizers, in two ways: by reminding us that a European colonial power may also be marginal within Europe; and by highlighting the internal regional inequalities that may—as in the case of Scotland (Nadel-Klein 1992)—provide a practicing ground for the global version. In that global context, however, for obvious historical reasons "Europe" still provides the richest and most exigent model of cultural dominance.

Perhaps the most striking case of a disemia grounded in the ambiguities of "Europe" is the predicament of Greece, at once the spiritual ancestor and the political pariah of the European Union. But there are other products of the same broad historical dynamic. In a mirror image from the opposite shore of the Aegean Sea, Dorn's ethnomusicological probings of the play between "Turkish" and "Frankish" styles in Istanbul points up an enduring ambivalence rooted in the tensions between Islamic and Kemalist visions of Turkey's future (Dorn 1991). In Romania, self-declared island of Roman identity in a Slavic sea, European identity is a two-edged sword, wielded by both sides in a contest over the future evolution of the national polity (see Verdery 1996:104–29)). Here, too, as Kligman (1989: 326–327, n.4) has pointed out, the tension between Orthodox east and Catholic west surfaces as a peculiarly reversed "religious disemia," in which older practices associated with Catholicism pervade most of the intimate spaces of everyday life despite a surface adherence to formal Orthodoxy.

Kligman's example in fact illustrates the instability and negotiability of the disemic extremes. In Greece, Orthodoxy has had a distinctly uncomfortable relationship with the neo-Classical vision of Europe, from early fulminations against the perceived threat of a pagan revival in the early years of the state to the current anti-Western and largely left-wing "neo-Orthodox" movement of today. In Romania, by contrast, the Orthodox faith appears to have represented cultural orthodoxy as well, even under the officially atheist Ceauşescu régime; that government's perceived favoritism toward the Orthodox church has led citizens from formerly Catholic communities to claim Orthodox identity as a matter of self-presentation. The result is an intensi-fied public-private dichotomy marked by contrasting religious at-titudes and ritual habits—Kligman's "religious disemia."

It is important to note here that while disemia can be treated as a pairing of codes, what matters socially is how these codes are actually used; and that use is often affected by historical processes of which the actors may be only partially aware. The Ceauşescu régime's pro-Orthodox stance decided the public face of religious disemia, but use and choice of these now "overcoded" symbols (see Eco 1976: 133) would depend on particular actors and could perhaps influence future events. In much the same way, the origi-nal Greek nationalist binarism—Classical Greece as the fount of Europe and the official face of the modern nation—ran into some opposition after the huge influx (nearly a quarter of the existing population) of refugees from Asia Minor after the disastrous 1920–22 war with Turkey. Although the refugees

> maintained close contact with the West as well, they were quick to dismiss the mainland Greeks' bond to the West as arising from in-feriority and subordination to the European powers. Furthermore, the refugees noted with disappointment what they perceived to be a serious cultural anachronism within Greek society. In pursuit of Western ways of modernization, mainland Greeks neglected their more recent Byzantine heritage and sought to restore the secular ideals of the distant pre-Christian classical past. Moreover, native Greeks projected . . . a very unfavorable image as narrow-minded, parochial, and unsophisticated people (Giannuli 1995: 277; see also Hirschon 1989: 22–35).

Further complicating the static West-East formulation of Greek identities was a strong element of modernist occidentalizing among many nonelite Greeks, as Bakalaki (1994: 76–77, 97–102, and passim) has argued in a persuasive modification of my own earlier argument. Since Greeks could always internalize images of Europe as their own, Bakalaki points out, we may find that, for example, the apparently localist preoccupation of women with handicrafts actually masks their absorption of fash-ions from Western Europe, while informal dress—easily read as a mark of domestic introversion—may in fact signal, perhaps even simultaneously, the desire for European comfort and the pervasive presence of a culturally and politically powerful model of the self.

These shifting locations of binary tension are not always easy to spot. Because they appeal to notions of eternal verity, their strategic uses are well concealed: this is what invests the binarism of the code with a spurious sense of social actuality. Architectural arrangements, in which physical permanence easily overshadows the significance of variable use, share with the idiom of morality the semiotic illusion of invariance: constant signifiers mask shifting signifieds. The more fixed the semiotic forms, the greater is the play of ambiguity and the more surprising are the possibilities for violating the code itself. Skilled actors use the appearance of rigidity to get what they want (Herzfeld 1983). Unskilled (or simply unsuccessful) actors blame the system; this is the worldview whereby they also blame the state and so confirm its power.[18]

The most permanent-seeming devices are perhaps the most literally physical. In societies where the architectural screens that divide the intimate from the public are gendered, as in much of the Islamic world, these moral imperatives may reappear in local practice as gender and body metaphors of the contrasted ideologies of national identity. Even in societies where that separation is less palpable, however, women often bear the brunt of self-knowledge, men of self-display. In practice, however, these symbolic roles are strategically reversible, and this may constitute a further dimension of cultural intimacy: there are aspects of their actual roles that men may prefer not to reveal to strangers except under highly formalized or ritualized conditions (Almeida 1995: 229).

But the official use of gender stereotypes still has quite remarkable staying power. In the United States, where sensitivity to gender bias in public contexts is at least formally well articulated, nationwide patterns exhibit an arresting conservatism. Among the airline crews whose conventions I discussed earlier, the frequent practice of introducing the cabin crew (usually overwhelmingly female) by first name and the pilots (usually male) by rank and surname serves as an additional prop for the commercial charade of domesticity in the passenger cabin. Here, official organization uses the intimate side of disemia for public purposes.

At the other end of the scale, the human body may endure the greatest disemic tensions. There it is sometimes expressed through the somatization of embarrassment as pain, especially where state brutality leaves few private spaces uninvaded and so makes the self the only available refuge for any sense of intimacy (Kleinman 1995: 106–107). The body is exposed to such extremes because it is the primary site of both privacy and display.

Sometimes, too, shame can also be fought back through the ambiguities of embodiment. Thus, for example, colonized peoples may resort to sign languages in which external form remains obdurately indecipherable to those for whom verbalizing is the highest, and often the only, mode of communication (Farnell 1994, 1995b; Kendon 1995). Silence and irony, too, both provide a shield for subversive mockery and set limits to its capacity for generating change (Chock 1987; Herzfeld 1991b; Norman 1994). Whether anything actually does change as a result of such subtle performances—whether, for example, the balance of power between genders or classes shifts—is an empirical question to be asked of the social poetics to which I now turn.

Social poetics

The nation-state is ideologically committed to ontological self-perpetuation for all eternity. While it may seek to embrace technological or even social change ("modernizing states"), it maintains to the semiotic illusion of cultural fixity and may well try to impose a static morality on others ("moralizing states" [Moore 1993:4]). The technology for the construction of this timelessness pragmatically connects a mythological notion of pure origins with respect for perfect social and cultural form; innovations are coopted by being treated as the realization of an eternal essence. Yet in practice they are often debated: Americans' "rights" to health care are pitted against their supposedly inherent self-reliance, for example. On the other hand, attacks on the essentialism that grounds these debates are less easily tolerated: they disrupt moral purity, temporal seamlessness, and cultural homogeneity. The nation must always be one and indivisible. National history, like Lévi-Straussian myth, retroactively elides (experiential) time in the name of (generic) time.

This adherence to a static cultural ideal has a surprising and presumably unintended consequence: not only does it ground certain permissible forms of debate but it also permits and perhaps even encourages the day-to-day subversion of norms. This comes about because the very rigidity of outward forms provides some actors with a mask with which to conceal a variety of messages, just as a strict morality may sometimes enable—through the mastery of its codes—remarkable freedom of individual action. This is why official ideologies generally deny semantic lability: acknowledging that lability would lead to the realization

21

that official meanings were themselves unstable. Perhaps the most dramatically paradoxical demonstration of the state's self-generated predicament is the *structural nostalgia*—the longing for an age before the state, for the primordial and self-regulating birthright that the state continually invokes—that citizens can turn against the authority of the state itself, along with all the other similarly vulnerable symbols of official fixity (chapter 6). In the United States the so-called militias' appeal to primordialist notions of frontier justice and self-reliance, for example, has already significantly embarrassed the U.S. federal government. And populist appropriations of nationalist rhetoric about the ancient glories similarly embarrassed the Greek government when it wanted to exhibit Cretan antiquities abroad (Hamilakis and Yalouri 1995:126).

A critique of state ideology should render this sleight of temporality visible. Fixity of form does not necessarily entail a corresponding fixity of meanings and intentions; exaggeration, parody, and other deforming practices both perpetuate the sense of enduring cultural form and cause substantive change. The analogy in language is with poetic diction, which, as Jakobson (1960) recognized, permeates everyday as well as "set-apart" usage: the sometimes disconcerting ambiguity of language-in-use as well as the shock of brilliant metaphor may equally unsettle the semiotic illusion of a culture and a moral universe that claim never to change.

It is crucial not to mistake this move toward ambiguity for the romantic mysticism of seeing poetry in social life (see chapter 7). It is not about *poetry* (except as a special case), but *poetics*—not the mystically endowed semiosis of a genre, but the technical analysis of its properties as these appear in *all* kinds of symbolic expression, including casual talk.

Social poetics, however, can all too easily be conflicted with the aestheticizing of social relations (Gilsenan 1986; Vidal 1988). In *The Poetics of Manhood* (Herzfeld 1985a), I clearly slipped into an aestheticizing idiom when I contrasted the poetics of swashbuckling masculinity with the "more prosaic vision" of sedentary, law-abiding modernity (272)—a formulation that conflicts with the claims I was making for the approach, and one that I would not now endorse. But it is not central to the main argument; on the contrary, it misuses that argument.

Several critics (e.g., Damer 1986) have argued that the poetic approach appears to celebrate only the politically successful; in the context of highland Cretan masculinity, for example, I said little about the situation of women or of politically weak men. I have made partial attempts (especially Herzfeld 1991b) to correct this imbalance. But a suitably deromanticized notion of aesthetics, as of poetics, does not automatically entail the whitewashing of unpleasantness, brutal power, or the small and large agonies of oppression. If I have been guilty of ignoring some of the more grossly material aspects of inequality, this may be due to my initial, too narrow application of the approach, rather than to the approach itself. Moreover, the conventional alternatives of symbolism bashing and economic reductionism do at least as much violence to people's lived experiences.

The idea that symbolic activity is irrelevant to material analysis is pernicious. This Cartesian division of labor underlies serious gaps in earlier ethnographies: the absence of narrative, gestural (see Farnell 1994a, 1994b), musical (Feld 1982), and many other supposedly nonmaterial aspects of social life shows what sanctimonious nonsense the holistic ideal of ethnographic research has always been. It is itself the product of an ideologically laden binarism opposing anthropology-as-"morality" to anthropology-as-"science" (D'Andrade 1995). The positivistic illusion of an unbiased and comprehensive description necessarily ignores the highly charged binarism that undergirds it. Often those who—in defiance of the vast indeterminacies of social life—claim that their ethnography is comprehensive are the most hostile to the inclusion of lengthy passages of narrative, informant exegesis, and what they contemptuously dismiss as folklore in ethnographic accounts. It is easy to be holistic when one has predetermined the parameters of the "whole."

For that matter, the writing of ethnography itself is both a social and a poetic act. Kenna (1992) correctly notes that my ethnography of the Cretan highlands was a performance, but one must ask whether any ethnography is not a performance, as I pointed out in an earlier response (Herzfeld 1992b). That a written text is more permanent than a spoken utterance is no more relevant in this context than that architecture is an ostensibly less ephemeral social gesture than a wink or a nod. Like the shepherds I was studying, I deformed a social and cultural convention: this was the ethnographic style of my own intellectual lineage, that of my teacher (Campbell 1964), who had in effect deformed Evans-Pritchard's (1940) model, designed for the presentation of an African society, by applying it to a European one.

Performance is always embedded in "real" events: every performance has antecedents. Victor Turner articulated the embedding of present social life in the experiences of the past in his concept of "social drama" (Turner 1974). This can be grand theater, as when the actions of public figures feed on glorious pasts or central religious myths. It is no less suggestive, however, for the analysis of humbler moments—of the stuff of the stories ethnographers tell, "mere anecdotes" that reveal what moves people to action. A social poetics recognizes that people deploy the debris of the past for all kinds of present purposes. No less than the Mexican revolutionary Hidalgo or the medieval cleric Thomas à Becket, whose respective personal trajectories evoked, according to Turner (1974: 60–155), the worship of the Aztec gods and the drama of the Passion of Christ, the grieving Greek mother who finds solace by identifying with the bereaved Mother of God is reproducing, if on a smaller social stage, a universalizing drama through which she transcends her own immediate grief (see Alexiou 1974: 77).

In the outpourings of nationalist historiography, moreover, ordinary people find the materials to construct a potentially infinite range of personal and collective pasts, some of which may run counter to the intentions of their nationalist exemplars. The repeated reuse of masonry in towns of great antiquity—as when the remnants of a pagan temple reappear in the most important national pilgrimage site of Greek Christianity[19]—is a telling metaphor that embodies this semiotic bricolage, and is all the more so when, as so often happens, such reuse is actively prohibited by state and civic conservation authorities. For them the practice of a living history, as opposed to rhetoric, is a threat to their most treasured as well as their most concrete essentialisms.[20]

The state is caught on the horns of its own reification. To achieve at least an illusion of stability it must command the active involvement of ordinary people; and ordinary people reify, all the time, everywhere. They, too, invoke solidified histories, rediscovering in the official mythology some aspects that will serve their own cause. It is not only the postcolonial subject who, as Mbembe (1992: 25) observes, "by compromising with the corrupting control that state power tends to exercise at all levels of daily life . . . is reaffirming that it is incontestable—precisely in order the better to play with it and modify it whenever possible." Nor, as he observes, are obscenity and the grotesque simply sub-

24

versive "weapons of the weak," to use Scott's (1985) celebrated phrase; the play of power, while often oppositional, draws on shared symbols that are then differently used and interpreted according to the interests, resources, and desires of the actors. Like the commanding/grotesque body of the postcolonial despot—Mbembe's model is the West African state of Cameroon, but he insists that there is nothing uniquely African about what he describes—it is the signs of power "that have force, that get interpreted and reinterpreted, and feed back further significance into the system" (Mbembe 1992: 8). Given that virtually no polity is immune to some degree of power abuse, I would add, such ambiguities are also richly present in the humbler reaches of political life, where exaggerated displays of bodily might may be rendered still more contestable by the ridicule of intimate acquaintance. Thus the Glendiot shepherds contemptuously describe the bureaucrats and politicians whose patronage they enjoy as "eating," a common metaphor for rapacity and theft; yet each one of these lean, tough men wants his sons to acquire—and display—a paunch that signifies access to precisely the same sources of enviable abuse. The disreputable components of power that comprise cultural intimacy are drawn from everyday life; and, in dictatorships like those described by Mbembe (1992: 25–29), the state so fully adopts the cultural signs of that intimacy in order to permeate the oppressed citizens' every sentient moment that it exposes itself to greater day-to-day manipulation by these same citizens, who are familiar with the capacity of those signs to bear subversive interpretations.

Social poetics is about the play through which people try to turn transient advantage into a permanent condition in this socially comprehensive sense. It links the little poetics of everyday interaction with the grand dramas of official pomp and historiography in order to break down illusions of scale. I would not want to claim that this perspective replaced other approaches. Rather, it occupies a militant middle ground between the twin denials of social experience—the extremes of positivism and deconstructionism—allowing neither to elide the intimate concerns of ordinary people in the name of fatuously self-serving abstraction.

In this, it remains faithful to the poetic vision of Vico. He decried both the rejection of direct observation and the idea of pure literalness or permanent meaning. It was also Vico who pointed out the parallel stupidities of tyrants who forgot the fragile popular basis of their power, and of scholars who forgot that all their

language was derived from images grounded in bodily
edge and transmitted through the popular language of
ts.[21] Following this powerfully antireductionist lead, it is
the specific task of social poetics to reinsert analysis into lived
historical experience and thereby to restore knowledge of the social, cultural, and political grounding—the cultural intimacy—of
even the most formal power and the most abstract knowledge.

Practical essentialism: creating resemblances

One of the most common social poetic concerns is the use of
stereotypes in social interaction. Most anthropological discussions of stereotypes have addressed them from the perspective of
group boundaries and mutual hostility. But these approaches are
liable to the charge of static binarism unless they are contextualized as social action. Who uses stereotypes? Under what circumstances? How stable are the forms of stereotypes and the
meanings people attribute to them? Racial stereotypes offer a
particularly good illustration of how use can appear to convert
transient perceptions into self-evidence.

Such questions underscore a key point of this book: that social
life consists of processes of reification and essentialism as well as
challenges to these processes. This is the corollary to recognizing
the strategic character of essentialism. Distrust of essentialism in
social theory should not blur our awareness of its equally pervasive presence in social life. Essentializing essentialism is point-
less. At this point, too, the social sciences come under their own
comparativist lens. As Richard Handler and I have both argued,
recognizing the essentialisms shared by nationalism and anthropology provides both historical insight and critical distance.[22]

What I have just remarked about essentialism can also, *a for-
tiori*, be said about binarism. A social poetics makes no assumptions about the structure of human cognition but asks where
people find the binary oppositions that they actually deploy and
examines how they use them in their negotiations of power. Let
us recall Furth's observation, which if extended beyond the linguistic domain would virtually define what I mean by social poetics: "narrative strategies give linguistic distinctions entitivity"
(Furth 1995: 998).

All social performance reifies people in culturally coded roles
or identities. This is why the achievement of national statehood
constitutes perhaps the most dramatic example of the strategy of

26

essentialism, although some religions, those that proclaim both ecumenical inclusiveness and universal truth, can justly claim even greater success in terms of sheer scale. Recent work on critical media responses, however, suggests that such monopolies may now be outflanked. Writing of Basque youth culture, for example, Urla (1995) has suggested that alternative media can challenge the relentless production of unitary truth even within movements that are themselves conceived in opposition to—but therefore often initially assume the monolithic cultural logic of—nation-state systems.

The strategies of essentialism all hinge on creating the semiotic effect technically known as iconicity, the principle of signification by virtue of resemblance (see chapter 3). An icon is not, technically speaking, just a popular image that typifies a culture (as in the phrase "American icon"); indeed, that common misuse of the term suggests how muddled much public thinking about the creation of national identity continues to be.[23] An icon signifies something by virtue of a perceived similarity: a photograph is an icon of its subject, a Vivaldi flute passage of bird song. Iconicity seems natural and is therefore an effective way of creating self-evidence. But it is in fact culturally constituted in the sense that the ability to recognize resemblance depends to a large degree on both prior aesthetic criteria and the politics of the situation: people often indignantly deny any resemblance with their own portraits, with parents, or, indeed, with certain politicians. Perhaps because persuasive visual images possess a "redemptive power" by virtue of their reproducibility (Freedberg 1989: 440), they directly serve nationalism's twin preoccupations with infinite human reproduction and collective immortality. Visual and musical iconicities have been especially effective in rallying entire populations, but others—those of taste and smell as marshalled in national gastronomies, for example (Appadurai 1988)—may achieve to an even greater degree the surreptitious obviousness that the process of naturalization requires. Even where iconicity is explicitly foregrounded, as in the religious (and political) use of visual images, its immediacy "significantly democratizes their rationale" (Freedberg 1989: 401).[24]

Nationalism is directly predicated on resemblance, whether biogenetic or cultural. The pivotal idea is that all citizens are, in some unarguable sense, all alike; this is what Benedict Anderson's (1983) "imagined community" implies. Most nationalists fear variant cultural readings—minority self-determination, youth

27

nonconformism, cultural dissidence—that might undermine their universalist claims. In fact, not only do alternative readings coexist with the dominant interpretations, but most nationalisms would have a hard time keeping popular support without such disruptive familiarities. National embarrassment can become the ironic basis of intimacy and affection, a fellowship of the flawed, within the private spaces of the national culture.

That is why I wish to move the discussion of stereotypes to the realm of practice, bringing it to bear on the totalizing iconicity— citizens with a homogeneous national character—of nation-state ideology. This is closely related to Gellner's (1983: 37) perceptive observation that culture moves from being an "adornment, confirmation and legitimation of a social order" to the status "of a necessary shared medium." I have elsewhere argued that this ideological change—which, unlike Gellner, I regard as one of degree rather than of kind—entails reducing a set of relational (or indexical) signs, the recognizable fragments of the flow of social life, to the static and therefore timeless iconicity of national culture (Herzfeld 1992a). The metonymic extensions of intimacy are not so much transformed, as Gellner thought, as they are stretched beyond any serious possibility of literal meaning. In their ubiquitous triviality, the airline courtesies I briefly discussed above similarly exemplify this process, while Andrew Strathern (1996) has noted its salience for understanding the transformation of local exchange items (pigs, shells) into the iconography of the national currency in Papua New Guinea—a country where nationalism must constantly seek to overcome the perpetual tension among the huge variety of local cultural idioms competing to inform it (see also Gewertz and Errington 1995). In New Zealand certain art forms became a means of expressing an emergent Maori national identity grounded in the evocation of ancestors now claimed as common to all; as a result, a single form was then also emblematically expropriated by the New Zealand government to "express a joyous and comforting message—of just what it [the message] is not too clear: life in general" (Schwimmer 1992: 70–71).

Social relations on the ground disrupt these timeless fictions— or eternal images—of national culture. Margaret Thatcher recognized this when she sought to deny the very existence of the social, insisting instead that there were "only individuals" who shared a common culture on which she proposed to perform prodigies of streamlining. It would be hard to find a better ex-

ample of the way in which nationalism shifts emphasis from in-
dexicality to iconicity—from social relations refracting cultural
difference to a socially atomized cultural homogeneity.

The analytic challenge is to reverse the process, to see what indexical social ploys lurk behind the seemingly imperturbable
iconicities of an officially unified culture. I particularly wish to
take the useful concept of "orientalism" (Said 1981) beyond its
hitherto much too narrowly textual sense, as Carrier (1992) has
effectively done already for his parallel coinage of "occidentalism." Let us speak, then, of practical orientalism, practical occidentalism, and practical essentialism in general.[25]

The pragmatic reification of people as representatives of fixed
categories is in part what Althusser (1971: 162) has dubbed "in-
terpellation," of which the oft-quoted illustration is the hegemonic act of a policeman who stops a passer-by with a
peremptory "Hey, you!" According to Althusser, the policeman
acts as the agent of ideology, which at that moment constitutes
the passer-by as a "subject." But this formulation, concerned as
it is with the exercise of state power, is still top-down; it is also
explicitly atemporal in that the passer-by has in fact "always-al-
ready" been a subject of ideology, which Althusser represents as
existing outside history (Althusser 1971:150, 164). In this way
Althusser, for whom the only freedom is that granted by powerful institutions to accept their total control, reproduces and reinforces those institutions' power. He rejects the possibility that
such moments of social interaction might have palpable performative impact on the state ideology and culture in turn.

While this may be an empirically accurate account of specific
moments, it is too deterministic. In this regard it follows a long
anthropological tradition in which social actors seemed to be
locked into an ideational predestination, the possibility of independent agency all but precluded (see also Fardon 1985: 6).
Ethnographic evidence does not support such comprehensive determinism. In a recent study of Salvadoran politics and gender,
for example, Stephen (1985: 812) shows how the state empow-
ers a sixteen-year-old in uniform to "interpellate"—she does not
herself use this term—an old woman as subversive, although he
would have treated her with respect had he met her in his own
neighborhood and had he been out of uniform. Since the military
cultivation of the machismo ethos predicates women's social
identities on the "traditional" categories of virgin and whore,
Stephen's example shows that the state's power to exercise this

kind of control through its agents depends on the selective manipulation of stereotypes already in popular circulation. This familiar model, however, is "good to think" for both sides. The prominent role of women in some Latin American revolutions allowed them to seize on other selections from the repertoire of generally received gender stereotypes to reverse a long-standing pattern of collective abuse and to bring about substantive social and cultural change.

Stephen's description of how women are absorbed into a category fits the argument I have advanced elsewhere about the bureaucratic uses of categorical ascription (Herzfeld 1992a). She demonstrates, moreover, that the weak can fight back by recasting the original ascriptions by which they were consigned to the margins. In so doing, they challenge the prevalent interpretation and use of key categories. Consequently, their small acts of resistance may lead, at least incrementally, to some degree of change in the larger distribution of power. Because it is practice-oriented and performative, Stephen's demonstration is a welcome contrast to excessively textualist accounts of "resistance" currently in vogue. Female engagement in politics, which men at first strenuously resisted, led to a revaluation of gender roles; this in turn led men as well as women to new understandings of violence and power; and the resulting awareness may still further affect the state's ability to get away with injustice. Such is the provisionality inherent in all official forms of permanence: because national ideologies are grounded in images of intimacy, they can be subtly but radically restructured by the changes occurring in the intimate reaches of everyday life—by shifts of meaning that may not be registered at all in external cultural form.

Sometimes the effects of local reappropriation can be hilarious. Cretan sheep-thieves, drawing self-consciously on the flamboyant lawlessness of the revolutionary guerrillas of the War of Independence (*kleftes*, literally thieves!) and dismissing the Athenian authorities as virtual Turks, delight in treating the investigating policemen to ritualized hospitality, informing them afterward that they have now eaten the evidence (Herzfeld 1985a: 220–222). These sheep-thieves' ironic relationship to national historiography may not be as unusual as statist ideology has led us to think: many a "liberator" began under the label of "bandit" or "terrorist," only to face the embarrassments of real power and the need to curb erstwhile colleagues. Yasser Arafat springs immediately to mind.

Often such inversions of legal status have more obvious implications for the state's capacity to define the terms of incorporation, as when Wakuénai reduce to the intimacy of kinship units
those nation-state entities whose borders have arbitrarily violated their own territorial integrity. Nor should we forget that
those uproarious Cretan sheep-thieves' actions also have immediate political consequences, for they remind the hapless local authorities that these shepherds electorally command the protection
of parliamentary patrons who not only set up both the relevant
legislation and its implementation but also may achieve very high
office indeed—partially through their access to the bloc votes
controlled by client sheep-thieves belonging to the larger clans.[26]

In effect, such tactics call the bluff of formal power and its self-es-
sentializing strategies. They force recognition that essentialism is always the one thing it claims not to be: it is a strategy, born, no less
than these subversive tactics, of social and historical contingency.
The agents of powerful state entities and the humblest of local social actors engage in the strategy of essentialism to an equal degree,
if not always with the same visibility or impact. Social poetics can
be precisely defined as the analysis of essentialism in everyday life.

The essentializing strategies of state legislators and ordinary
citizens alike depend on a semiotic illusion: by making sure that
all the outward signs of identity are as consistent as possible,
they literally create, or constitute,[27] homogeneity. They produce
iconicities of both national culture and national law, the latter
exemplified by the kind of fundamentalist ethic that in the
United States is called strict constitutionalism and appeals to certain "truths" as so "self-evident" as to be beyond semantic or
political analysis—to be, in a word, sacrosanct.

Essentializing is thus not exclusively a state activity. Indeed,
"strategic essentialism" has entered our vocabulary through the
programmatic discourse of feminism (Spivak 1989). But state officials do have access to an exceptionally rich variety of devices
for essentializing: law, censorship, an immigration bureaucracy,
and so on. Iconicity is central to this endeavor because it backgrounds its own operation. That makes it the perfect instrument
for performative nonperformance—here the invisible historical
processes of local universalizing that underlie all so-called common sense. Stereotypes appear correct to those who espouse
them *because* they reduce all the members of a population to a
manageable iconicity, while those who apply stereotypes to
themselves may, as Chock (1987) suggests, be ironically ridicul-

ing the majority population's blithe assertions of superiority to those who are simply different and therefore stereotypically all alike—a classically Eurocentric view.[28]

Organization of this book

The chapters of this book did not all spring directly from the concept of social poetics. At times, I preferred to focus my investigations less on the day-to-day negotiation of status and identity than on the extraordinary claims of permanence that so many nationalist ideologies have made. In time, however, these interests converged. Greece was an ideal catalyst: in a country claiming at once to be the ancestor of Europe and yet also widely seen as one of the continent's newest and least European states, the paradoxes of permanence came easily into critical focus.

Thus, while many of the case materials presented here are drawn from my fieldwork and other research in Greece, the resulting models, including that of cultural intimacy, should be seen as heuristic in a more general, comparative sense. Their relevance to other cases is probably quite uneven. Many nationalists would argue that these models had no relevance at all to their respective countries, including Greece. That alone, however, should be reason enough not to dismiss them out of hand.

With the exception of this introductory chapter and the afterword, none of the essays that comprise this book was originally written for inclusion in it, and most were presented elsewhere in another form. In bringing these papers together, however, I intend something decidedly more than a retrospective collection. For that reason, I have taken the task of revision seriously. Instead of simply supplying bridge passages loosely linking the single chapters to a broad scheme of autobiographical rather than conceptual scope—a self-indulgence that became increasingly distasteful as this project took form—I have identified earlier and sometimes ill-defined echoes of the thinking now laid out in these introductory paragraphs and have reworked those echoes into a stronger, more explicit, and internally more consistent line of argument throughout the book. Like iron filings brought into alignment by a magnet, the several subthemes of the original formulations will now, I hope, work to support my central understanding of anthropology's task in moving from its once determinedly local focus to a perspective that can also convincingly incorporate the ethnography of nation-states.

Chapters 2 and 3 ("Of Definitions and Boundaries" and "Persuasive Resemblances") comprise a critical appraisal of the spatial and representational rhetorics of state nationalism. While these chapters are partly grounded in the ethnography of Greece, that specificity becomes more central to "The Dangers of Metaphor: From Troubled Waters to Boiling Blood." Here the reliance of nationalist rhetoric on local-level idioms of social solidarity is explored in relation to current Balkan conflicts, in order to make the key point that larger events draw sustenance from highly intimate and localized values. This, I suggest, is the distinctive contribution of anthropology to the understanding of the larger picture. For that reason, in the chapter that comes next ("Cultural Intimacy and the Meaning of Europe"), I respond to some nonanthropologists' testy dismissals of anthropological insights as irrelevant, pointing out that these attacks on the discipline are themselves symptomatic of the key problem: the discourse of foreign affairs rests heavily on the symbolism of stereotypes, and it is a symbolism that belongs more embarrassingly in the realm of cultural intimacy than its purveyors would ever want to admit. Nationalistic resentment of anthropology's concern with supposedly marginal populations forces an interesting and important ethical choice. Nationalist objections rest on the view that such groups are numerically insignificant and therefore atypical. While this view does not answer, for example, concerns over human rights, anthropologists must be aware that nationalists can point to great-power interest in minorities as yet another example of international bullying—of which foreign anthropologists then find themselves represented as the agents.[29] But those who make such arguments are often themselves elite conservatives whose modernist arguments about national homogeneity reproduce the same hegemony at the local level. By that token, recognizing national grievances over cultural and political marginalization would seem an oddly inconsistent reason to concur in the suppression of minority demands for self-determination within the nation-state.

To cite an example that concerns a major international dispute: it is indicative (if perhaps unsurprising) that those who most deeply resent any foreign recognition of a Macedonian or a Turkish minority in northern Greece are the most disposed to argue in the course of everyday conversation that the population of that area consists of "impure" Greeks—for such hierarchies of national purity are admissible within the spaces of cultural intimacy, if not in the public arenas of diplomacy and scholarship (and the importance of those casual conversations can be conveniently belittled with the usual dismissal of "mere anecdotalism"). There is an obvious parallel here in anthropology with the positivistic invocation of holism to exclude supposedly unscientific data (mere anecdotes again): symbolisms of purity operate in both cases. And I have already noted how, in the purity-based logic of structural nostalgia, the very people who most decry the necessity of state intervention are those who are most likely to have recourse to it. In all three cases we see a strategic move to essentialize pragmatically impossible ideals for pragmatically possible purposes. This is a perfect illustration of social poetics in action.

The next chapter, "Structural Nostalgia: Time and the Oath in the Mountain Villages of Crete," works from precisely this parallel between anthropology and its multiple objects. It deals with the kind of population whose prominence in my own and other anthropologists' writings has so irritated nationalists and other critics. In it, I explore the Cretan villagers' view of church and state as intrusive and demeaning. In so doing, I suggest that the symbolism of official history as well as that of modernist social theory is drawn from the same sources as their own rebellious inversion of official ideology. I thus use the chapter as a two-pronged probe of cultural intimacy: to explore the embarrassing practices of a marginal population, but also to investigate the elite values whereby that embarrassment and that marginality are constituted.

The villagers' view of the state is indeed a considerable embarrassment, for the state appears to them as the antithesis of trust and as an alien source of authority. The prominence of the state's legal institutions in their lives signals a fall from social harmony, and the state is itself the target of all sorts of criminality—tax evasion, bribery, perjury—that the villagers represent as fair revenge for its interfering rapacity. From the villagers' standpoint, however, these marks of sinfulness are an important part of what makes the state itself more human and the nation worth defending. Its formal face is merely the defensive posture, not what is actually defended. People do not fight for abstract perfection but for the intimacies that lie behind it; these unruly shepherds recognize the humanity of the politicians who seek their votes, the bureaucrats who expect to be bribed, the police who can be neutralized and turned into likable dupes by an act of sheer cheek thinly disguised as hospitality. Such creative mischief both subverts and sustains the authority of the state.

This contradictory duality, the defining ambiguity of disemia in social practice, is also the core proposition of social poetics: norms are both perpetuated and reworked through the deformation of social conventions in everyday interaction. At this point in the book, I lay out the technical features of a social poetics and, in order to flesh out its practical implications, illustrate its possibilities from the contrasted cases of Greek and American displays of gendered stereotypes ("Social Poetics in Theory and Practice: Regular Guys and Irregular Practices"). While this chapter is less immediately concerned with the nation-state as such, it may be helpful as a more precise description of social poetics and, more specifically, as a closer look at how both normative and subversive forms become incorporated into everyday social repertoires. It is also an examination and explanation of the relationship between cultural forms and social deformation, which, as I have indicated, provides the pragmatic means for official discourse to penetrate the intimacies of everyday life. This dynamic provides a model of the larger intimacies to be defended against the prying hostility of the nation's critics and enemies.

That play of images in everyday life is the subject of "The Practice of Stereotypes." Centrally at stake are the disemic confusions of conflicting self-ascription. Are we "European" or "Third World"? When do we claim which identity? In what contexts do these discriminations matter, and what larger geopolitical realities do they index? While these issues are perhaps unusually acute for the Greeks whose cultural predicaments form the bulk of my illustrations, they are indicative of more general issues concerning the relationship between international politics and everyday social life. It is this mutual reproduction of different levels of identity that gives the model of social poetics its distinctive analytic usefulness. In this chapter I particularly address the local consequences of the global—a complement to, and inversion of, the earlier discussions of how local values may impact global events.

Finally, in "Afterword: Toward a Militant Middle Ground?" I return briefly but practically to the issue of cultural intimacy and its violation. What are the ethics of anthropological reporting? Given the long-standing preoccupation of anthropology with gossip, are we simply to accept the role of the academic tabloid? I think not. For the moment, however, suffice it to say that nationalists' irritation with anthropology suggests a more serious ethical dilemma than whether to suppress the sensationalist aspects of ethnographic description to suit the demands of modesty. To pretend that anthropology escapes moral imperatives, as some advocates of "scientific" approaches desire, is a rejection of the discipline's engagement with socially experienced reality. But to pretend that the discipline can offer unequivocal solutions to such dilemmas is an equally poor substitute for taking responsibility for our own respective positions and for actions, including writing, that flow from those positions.

In compiling this book, I have gathered a set of texts, recast here as chapters, that emerged under quite varied circumstances. This has necessitated some rewriting. In any case, I was not interested in producing a reprint collection for its own sake. The exercise has permitted some reappraisal and a good deal of systematization. But it is still a performance, and it may well be a more self-conscious one than were the several short pieces out of which it has grown. Does this make it somehow more suspect? Or does it deliberately make it part of what it represents, the practice of social life?

That, at least, is what I hope has happened. For me the pleasures of writing have throughout sustained an absorbing tension between the essentialism entailed in giving shape to ideas and impressions, and the taunting vertigo of skeptical doubt without end. This has been the "militant middle ground" on which I have engaged with the conventions and assumptions of my profession. If I appear to want to turn everything, including that profession, into an anthropological issue, I can only reply that for me there is no anthropology separate from social life. Nor can I imagine any aspect of social life that does not partake of the social poetics I have tried to make central to the anthropological task. Even the silence of withdrawal is a performance: it has an audience, and that audience will pass judgment. Paraphrasing the Roman poet Terence, we might then observe that nothing human is alien to this perspective. Or, conversely paraphrasing Samuel Johnson, we might assert that when humans tire of the concerns that animate an anthropology so conceived, they are tired of life.

Chapter Two

Of Definitions
and Boundaries

In his autobiography, Giambattista Vico ([1728] 1977: 28) tells us that the only occasion on which he was awarded any kind of academic prize was for the presentation of a treatise, "full of Greek and Latin erudition and critical treatment," on the etymology of the term *stato*, "state." We do not know what Vico actually wrote in his disquisition, as the text has been lost. His pursuit of etymology in the search for hidden historical truths, however, invites speculative emulation.

Thus, for example, we could highlight the fact that in Italian, *stato* is used as the past perfect participle of the verb for "be" (*essere*, significantly, a cognate of the English word *essentialism*, but directly derived from *stare*, stand, be in a certain state or condition). Such an etymology represents the state as the ultimate eternal verity, that which "has [always] been," and as such an outstanding example of what we would today call *naturalization*. In that case, the transformation of a verb particle into a noun— *lo stato*, the state—bears witness to a process of reification. With their literalistic perception of reality, the academic representatives of formal culture who awarded Vico his prize would perhaps have taken such etymological imaginings at face value and assumed that they indeed validated the state's claims to the standing, or status, both words being cognates of *stare* as well, of an eternal verity—the political equivalent of a *statement* in language.

Vico's imaginative games with etymology were the very antithesis of that kind of literalism, however, and, even without further speculation about what he actually said in his long-lost essay, we can take our lead from him. The social world is suffused with "trailing clouds of etymology" (Austin [1956–57] 1971: 99–100) that give to social experience a range of meanings both allusive and elusive. Rendering these connections explicit and recovering their historical development entails what Deely (1982: 1) has appropriately called the "semiotic consciousness," that is, the awareness that all human knowledge is mediated by signs and that consequently description must always at some level be construction. Etymology can be (and most commonly is) used to validate rather than to undermine power, and popular consciousness may be so suffused with official etymological principles that it actually reinforces the messages emanating from official sources: Greeks often dismiss nonnormative acts or artifacts by pointing out that their names are "Turkish." But to whom do they address such declarations of adherence to official historiography? A critical study of etymology must inspect these processes in their social and political contexts, which was also the task Vico set himself.

The etymological hunt can thus be pursued against the grain of official interpretation by resurrecting a host of derivations from the "dead stretches of experience" (Ardener 1978: 111)—a recorded but now inert history. Far more than a mere punning game, the search for an etymological history of reification serves to remind us of processes that are constantly at work through language and other semiotic systems and that principally serve the interests of those political and ideological formations that have successfully established their respective legitimacies. In so doing, we will be doing in social theory what everyday actors do when they contest the "received wisdom"—a revealing phrase— purveyed by official sources of knowledge.

This tactic disturbs the synchronic order of things by restoring to it a sense of historical contingency, reminding us that the signs whereby we convey "self-evident truths" have histories of their own, and suggesting that the underlying self-evidence does also. In the linguistic sphere, for example, the *status* of the *state* and the *static* concept of meaning are supported by *statements*. The concept of the statement or constative utterance suggests, as Austin ([1962] 1975: 139–147) argued, a view of language that ignores the social conditions under which discourse is produced. Meaning is not a given, a datum. (The process whereby *data* seems to be in the process of becoming a singular noun illustrates this creeping reification: as people forget that it is a plural entity grounded in the verb *dare*, to give, they can relax in blissful ignorance of its complexities.) Meaning is created by the interaction between an intending and an interpreting actor and by the alternation of roles between them, and the force of a performative utterance lies in the immediacy of the social situation. A statement, by contrast, would be given its force by the a priori validity of its premise. All attempts to naturalize a contingent claim (for example, to the legitimacy of a new government) therefore purport to be statements, or representations of fact. By treating them as performatives, and by focusing on the constructedness of their factuality, one can challenge their legitimacy, opposing analytic tactics to the official strategy of essentialism.

Nationalists appeal to tradition because its alleged antiquity validates their claims by rooting them in a seemingly unassailable bedrock of historical fact;[1] its constructedness is suppressed, as is the performative force of its presentation, through the solemn medium of academe. Nationalists naturalize their concerns by rendering them as self-evident truths. We should not forget, however, that it is the very performativity of discourse, its strategic capacity to express a fiat, that makes such a transformation possible.

Nationhood, especially as conceived by the nationalists of early nineteenth-century Europe, was explicitly cultural; yet its claims to eternal validity rested on the authority of a culturalized nature. Thus, the concept of nation encapsulated a paradox, and in this regard it reproduced, or at least prefigured, what Alain Goldschläger (1982) has called "authoritarian discourse." This rhetorical mode has much in common with Lévi-Strauss's view of myth: mutually incompatible propositions are presented as mutually reinforcing statements, paradoxes as truisms (see Herzfeld 1985b: 199). The very concept of nationhood that undergirds all of Goldschläger's illustrative examples fits the pattern. The nation is conceived in the Romantic ideology as a natural entity that can only reach full self-determination through the acquisition of political statehood, a quintessentially cultural imposition of order on chaos. This process entails the privileging of the arbitrary; it thus provides a classic example of semiotic illusion, or literalism, in which the signifier is mistaken for the signified, the natural symbols of national statehood for nature itself. Here in the abstract is the logic of the passport office, a social institution that has the authority to "naturalize" human beings. It is a relationship that gives a political twist to Saussure's insistence on the *arbitrariness* of the sign (see Hawkes 1977: 25).

Nature, however, is not always or necessarily benign in relation to culture. In many societies, outsiders are "animals," or at least appreciably less human than ourselves. For the Greeks of today, the epithet *zoö*, "animal," is a grave insult, suitable for Turks and antisocial individuals, but not to be used in addressing (or even speaking about) one's compatriots except perhaps in obvious jest. Nature, or at least an important part of it, is here opposed to an exalted culture. Clearly, the concept of nature is employed in two quite divergent senses. On the one hand, it conjures up the supposedly bestial world of alien societies. On the other, culture is cosmologically a part of nature: it is natural, eternal, and therefore good. The underlying opposition is thus not solely between nature and culture, but between the more inclusive categories of nature-as-evil and nature-as-good, respectively. A moral distinction thus underlies the rhetorical framing of nationhood, and it is on this distinction that the state's claim to be the arbiter of morality ultimately lies: it is the procrustean moral formation upon which all other moralities may be modeled.

The absolute finitude with which such ideas are articulated can be seen in the definite article in *i Fili*, "the race," with which official Greek rhetoric refers to the Greek people. This is in contrast to the usage of the term in everyday discourse with either a specifier ("the *fili* of the Gypsies") or the indefinite article. The same is true of the term *yenos* (classical Greek *genos*, the "aristocratic conical clan" [Humphreys 1978: 194] of ancient times), which has come to mean "the [national] stock." Thus, the great prophets of national independence like Adamantios Koraes—the virtual creator of the official neo-Classical "high" register of modern Greek—are often called "Teachers of the *Yenos*." The term appears in classical Greek as an agnatic group, usually of noble status; significantly, it combines the resulting implication of aristocracy with a strong agnatic bias in its transmutation into official modern Greek: *yenos* is the term used to designate the bride's and bride's mother's respective surname groups for the purpose of completing the official registration of a marriage.

Nationalist rhetoric has turned the nation into a superordinate *genos*, thereby removing to the sphere of its own conceptual and legal control the potentially feud-prone agnatic idiom of kinship from the local level (although that idiom does still subsist on Crete and in the Mani, usually in situations, such as feuding, that quite explicitly pit local against state values). It has also absorbed the very similar (and historically related) popular perception of the term that we encounter in, for example, certain medieval and postmedieval poems that mention *ksantha yeni* (classical Greek *xantha genē*), "blond tribes"—in other words, the Russians who were expected to come to the rescue of their enslaved Orthodox brethren, the Greeks. "Racial" inheritance, nobility, and the male line have all been coopted and singularized by the discourse of the bureaucratic state. The resulting grammatical uniformity (singular noun, definite article) reproduces the conceptual reification of social and cultural experience in a unified form.

The term *yenos* has survived in the widespread dialect form *yenia*, usually meaning some kind of agnatic grouping. Thus, doubtless aided by a separate morphological formation, it has strayed from the homogenizing and singularizing statist discourse just discussed and has become associated with a plurality of social groups within the local community. Even where agnation is no longer significant, as on the island of Rhodes, one may still hear that a child's character is formed by the "seven patrilines" that contribute to its ancestry (Herzfeld 1983a: 162–163). On Crete, the *yenia* (a cognate of the Classical *genos*) is virtually a symbol of the local community's opposition to official norms, since it is the normative unit of blood vengeance; it is also a segmentary concept, which automatically places it in opposition to the reified concepts of social grouping necessary to any bureaucratic organization.

The idea of the *genos/yenia* is closely associated with concepts of nature and birth (*genesis*), just as *nation* and *nature* are related through a common Latin root, *natio*, meaning birth. Many villagers consider the patriline to be the channel for the transmission of the *fisiko*, character, but etymologically and more specifically a person's nature (*fisi[s]*) in the sense of inherited traits. The idea of the Greek nation as a single, unified patriline thus encapsulates, at least by historical allusion, the embedding of nationhood in nature, which is close to what the Latin roots of the English terms also imply. In short, nation is a metaphorical construction; it brings together two superficially unlike entities— genetics as nature and national statehood as culture—and insists on their commonality. It is for this reason that statists must be literalists: their entire rationale rests on the premise that both the nation and the state are "real" entities, not metaphorical ones. It is also for this reason that Greek journalists and other commentators commonly do not recognize a distinction between genetic and cultural definitions of national or ethnic identity—and, indeed, see no reason to distinguish between the national and the ethnic, which are conflated in a single term.

Nationhood thus represents both a naturalization of political centralization (in the sense of representing it as a form of logical entity) and a "culturalization" of nature (in the sense that political centralization is grounded in ideas of genetic inheritance). Moreover, these are secured through a semantically stable terminology. Signifiers (words, terms, legal pronouncements) often have invariant forms. The state would thus be hard pressed to detect the nonconformist implications of a popular discourse in which these verbal symbols are deployed in significantly different ways. Perhaps the most striking example of this divergence between the two kinds of discourse, which should nevertheless not be thought of as entirely discontinuous with each other, is in blasphemy, an unreflexive mode of ideological expression in which the doctrinally unitary figures of religious iconography are fragmented through the divisions of the social order; in the most dramatic example, a person swears against "*your* Virgin Mary," thereby implying that an enemy's Mary cannot possibly be the same as one's own (Herzfeld 1984a). But there are many more obvious examples of such divergence between definition and usage, including the play of precision and ambiguity in ethnonyms.

Morality and identity: the status of eternal verities

Nationalism treats national identity as a system of absolute values, in which the relativism of ethnic shifters has been transformed into a set of reified eternal verities: the state has always existed. This process of reification follows the fate of the more general class of moral-attribute shifters, but it does so within a specific and identifiable political context. Nationalism deprives the essentially moral terminology of identity of its relativity, imposing upon it a definitional fixity that sometimes creates genuine difficulties and embarrassments—as, for example, when the Greek state is forced to specify that Muslim citizens are eligible for police service because, although popularly known as Turks (indeed it has become rather dangerous for any Greek Muslims to call themselves Turks because of the official denial of ethnic minorities' existence), they are in fact Greek citizens. Here popular usage is so strong that the state's claim on the loyalty of all citizens is implicitly called into question and has to be reinforced by a very explicit official statement.

Thus, ethnic identity is a highly relative concept that the political morality of nationalism seeks to transform into an absolute one. Identity as a "style," something that "assumes choice and allows for change" (Royce 1982: 9), is transmuted into a presumed national character; ethnic shifters (Galaty 1982) become fixed designators. The terms for cultural identity assume a certainty hitherto denied them by the experiential exigencies of social life. Nationalistic reification of these terms reverses the contextual sensitivity appropriate and necessary to their use as terms of personal, moral evaluation; they become instead the technical vocabulary of a fixed political order.

Ultimately, the language of national or ethnic identity is indeed a language of morality. It is an encoded discourse about inclusion and exclusion. Like all such systems, it is subject to manipulation in everyday speech. For this reason, a semiotic critique of nationalism must examine the process whereby nationalism invests certain kinds of identity with a rigidity that they do not commonly possess in everyday discourse. Such an approach would resist the process of literalization—the process whereby bureaucratic organizations reify the language of social interaction as a set of eternal verities. Meeker (1979: 30) sums up the semiotic task appositely: "Values and ideals are interpreted in terms of their function in a particular form of discourse rather than as timeless truths which stand beyond a speaker or writer."

Statism, on the other hand, exploits the power of discourse to generate the semblance of timeless truths in two ways: first, by coopting morality itself as a function of the state, and, second, by inserting its own identity in the resulting canon of values. No more revealing or immediate example of this can be found than the use of the term *patriotis* in Greek. In everyday usage, this word simply means someone from the same local community as the speaker and is close to Italian *paesano*; in nationalistic discourse, by contrast, it exclusively possesses or is possessed by the meaning of citizen, with the added sense in which it has entered English as a cognate: patriot.

If all ethnic and national terms are moral terms in that they imply a qualitative differentiation between insiders and outsiders, all moral value terms are to some extent negotiable markers for the lines of social or cultural inclusion and exclusion. The close identification between moral and ethnic categories leads with inexorable logic to the state's institutionalization of moral authority—cultural rather than natural justice, as it were, but conscripted against the allegedly unnatural phenomena of immorality, miscegenation, and treason. (The now-defunct apartheid laws of South Africa exemplified the resulting bureaucratic logic in an extreme form.) Even in the most centralized nation-states, however, it seems that everyday usage continues to reflect the relativism of ordinary discourse rather than the presumed absolutism of the state—itself a rather misleading proposition that many bureaucrats perpetuate by blaming "the system" for the harshness of its laws, but one that their own sometimes remarkably flexible and inventive strategies—including that of blaming the system—therefore effectively belie. This suggests that for practical purposes people operate on the basis of a theory of meaning that conflicts with the lexicographical rigidity they attribute to the state. In societies where state control is weaker, it is easier to recognize this; in such societies, when interethnic contact occurs, for example, the parties concerned make different assessments of the situation and of the extent to which they share a common identity (see Shalinsky 1980: 279–280). But even in tightly controlled societies most people know how to adopt the rhetoric of normativity in order to achieve nonnormative ends.

Strategies depend on situations, and the choice of term does not depend on what group one belongs to but on what moral self-designator one invokes in the context of a particular level of interaction. To call a Greek town dweller a *Vlakhos*, for example, is scarcely complimentary. The literalist would expect that this meant simply that the addressee was a member of the Romanian-speaking pastoral Koutsovlach community and would assume that the distaste evinced for the term by many Greeks derives from nationalistic feelings of distrust toward a foreign group. According to this perspective, any other use of the term would be a metaphorical extension. This, however, is putting the cart before the horse: the nationalistic definition of both *Ellinas* (Greek) and *Vlakhos* (Vlach) does not precede, semantically or chronologically, the establishment of nation-states in the Balkan region, but has merely been coopted and subsumed by the latter process. To most Greeks, the context would be sufficiently well defined to ascertain whether the speaker meant Koutsovlach, Northern Greek shepherd, or simply country bumpkin. Such fluidity in the use of terms normally associated with clearly defined groups is often a response of marginalized populations—as, for example, Castilian as a term for Andalusian (as well as for the non-Spanish ethnographer) in relation to Gypsy (Brandes 1980: 13, 57), Israeli Arabs' use of Sephardi to describe *themselves* in contrast to all Jews (Cohen 1971), or the famous distinction between Catholic Jews and Protestant Jews (depending on the part of Ireland from which they come). These usages are inconsistent only if one adheres to the absolutist logic of official ethnicity rather than to the entirely different theoretical underpinnings of ordinary talk.

The meaning of an ethnic shifter depends on the relationships binding the social group in question (narrative event) to the salient social identity of the speaker (speech event). Terms of this kind conflate social identity with morality by implying that similar principles of morality apply to all of the discriminations made, regardless of the level at which they are made: outsiders remain inferior to insiders in any sense. Thus, in Afghanistan, Uzbeks and Arabs both justify their respective practices in terms of Islamic law (Shalinsky 1980: 280). Each group uses the seemingly fixed conceptual abstraction of Islamic law to define boundaries and symbolic objects according to its own needs and perceptions. Moreover, such shifters are not always verbal. In Glendi, photographs of Eleftherios Venizelos, a staunchly anti-monarchist early twentieth-century liberal politician, appear in most coffeehouses, including those of diehard conservatives. Since Venizelos was Cretan, every local politician claims him as a spiritual ancestor. Thus, the virtues that his portrait represents—those of the stereotypical Cretan—are of negotiable content. The image of Venizelos, no less than the equally divisible Virgin Mary invoked in blasphemous curses, is a shifter.

The use of moral-value terms represents social diagnoses of where the boundaries lie. Like all diagnoses, these are open to dispute. Moreover, the criteria themselves are negotiable. Two speakers may think they share a common understanding of what is meant by honesty, Islam, *onore*, or being a Vlakhos. The use of the phrase "un-American activities," for which there is an equally anticommunist equivalent in Greek,[2] illustrates how even statist rhetoric may seem relativistic; in fact, it represents an attempt to fix both the term and the reality in an unchanging relationship so that the national boundaries become inflexibly coterminous with the exclusion of communists. National and ethnic terms allow for a surprising amount of semantic slippage; their appearance of semantic fixity allows actors to treat them as though they were existential absolutes rather than counters in a game.

45

Within state societies, the shifters that have escaped with the least damage to their semantic lability are those that signify moral values not actively endorsed by the state's own peculiar version of national morality. Thus, for example, Gilsenan's (1976: 201) treatment of the term *makhlu'* in Lebanon deals with a concept of social identification so bound up with notions of revenge and the blood feud that it could not have served comfortably in any nationalistic canon. A young revenge killer was regarded as *makhlu'* after his release from jail, but not at the time he committed the deed. Moreover, when he was subsequently attacked by an outsider,

> his family's only concern . . . was whether one of the other families in the village had done it. Had it been so, there would have been little choice but to continue the cycle of revenge, since his being *makhlu'* defined him as socially anonymous within the defining group but not vis-à-vis outsiders, to whom he remained visible and a member of Beit Ahmad. (Gilsenan 1976: 201)

Gilsenan was sensitive to the fact that attributions of *makhlu'* (and other moral properties) might well be affected by the interlocutor's outsider status, whether the latter was an ethnographer or a "native insider" (1976: 202). Social boundaries between speaker and addressee as well as the relationship between actor and narrator mediate the attribution. The diagnostic signs of being *makhlu'* are rarely so self-evident as to permit absolute claims. The point to be emphasized is not just that moral standing can be, and is, negotiated but that the negotiability of the identity in question is made possible by both the seeming fixity and the actual lability of the terminology.

Returning to Greek material, the concept of barbarism provides a good illustration of this interplay of fixity and lability, in counterpoint to the equally ambiguous status of "civilization" (*politismos*) and of its geographical embodiment, "Europe" (*Evropi*). These terms are all derived from the nationalistic view of Greece as the continuation of ancient Hellas and therefore as the source of all European culture. In Classical times, barbarism characterized those whose foreign and therefore incomprehensible speech was thought to resemble the chattering (*bar-bar*) of swallows; modern Greeks similarly attribute oxlike dumbness to the Turks (Herzfeld 1980a: 297), whose language seems so different from their own. In the nationalistic discourse of modern Greece, barbarism sums up the Turks' supposedly inhuman and rapacious cruelty and their so-called lack of religion, where religion is defined as Christianity (see also Asad 1994).

Politismos, on the other hand, combines the meanings of "culture" (*qua* "high" culture) and "civilization,"[3] and is particularly associated with the ideal of European identity. For the nationalist, *Evropi* (Europe) has a fixed semantic field, combining geography with the concept of a common heritage derived from Classical Hellenism—with the ideals, in fact, that are ordinarily understood by the term *politismos*.[4] In everyday discourse, however, this fixity melts away. "Europe" includes the Greeks in situations where a collective display of cultural patriotism is called for (notably in conversations with foreigners), but often excludes them when the Greeks have occasion, among themselves, to dwell on what they perceive as national failings and weaknesses—in brief, as evidence of their erstwhile condition as the serfs of *varvari*, barbarians. All this argues a measure of historical consciousness; and it is indeed the sense of history that invests all the relevant terms with their special powers of evocation (cf. Elias 1978: 7). By the same token, the ambiguity of terms such as *Evropi* derives from the duality of that historical experience: tension has always subsisted between the idealized, Western-derived models of "high culture" and the often far less flattering self-recognition that Greeks associate with cultural intimacy.

Similarly, although barbarism is conventionally associated with the Turks and other supposedly unenlightened peoples, Greeks often treat it as a specifically Greek problem when they are talking in confidence among themselves or with friendly outsiders. Residents of the island of Nisiros (in the Dodecanese chain in the southeastern Aegean) complained in my presence that the practice of letting off firecrackers immediately in front of people was a "barbarous custom," yet one of them became incensed when, upset at having exploding firecrackers thrown at my feet, I foolishly thought I could put a stop to this teasing by adopting their own rhetoric. I was curtly and explicitly put in my place by a very drunk and extremely angry Nisirian. Who was I to say such things, after eating and drinking with the islanders and enjoying the generous time that they had devoted to helping a callow young man with his research?

Indeed, the irate islander's use of irony—a clearly tactical inversion of what Chock (1987) has so appropriately captured as "the irony of stereotypes"—highlights the strategically useful semantic fluidity of what at first sight look like fixed, negative self-stereotypes. My clumsy attribution of the "Turkish" quality of "barbarism" to Greeks—and local Greeks at that—threw cultural intimacy in the teeth of my hosts, thereby violating their hospitality; and hospitality itself is a major context for the negotiation of social relationships, affording plentiful opportunities for the symbolic inversion of encompassing power relations and for drawing the lines around intimacy both social and cultural (Herzfeld 1987b). Although a student at the time, I was also in some sense a representative of that West to which many Greeks felt obliged to calibrate their hierarchy of cultural values; I had thus failed to recognize my obligations of sensitivity as a member of the privileged world outside Greece.

The structural property of barbarism that made this ironic effect work so devastatingly is that the term, as a shifter, contextually tied Greek collective self-doubt to my status as a "European"; there may also have been other inequalities at stake, such as those between educated urbanite and illiterate peasant, or even between Athenian—given the style of my spoken Greek at the time[5]—and provincial. As a visitor I adopted the term from local speakers, only to discover the hard way that this act of appropriation had in itself been sufficient to change the term's meaning. The moral is clear: (Western) Europeans have a particular obligation to respect the semantically rigid mutual exclusion of Greeks and barbarians. Only those with privileged access to the intimacy of Greek culture may engage in the play of semantic fluidity that permits self-denigration and damaging assessments of local culture.

This complex response exemplifies the difficulty of pinning down the meaning of terms of moral evaluation. (Gilsenan [1976: 206–210] provides a related analysis, when he explores the way in which a "liar" can reveal "truth" by exposing another's failure to read the signs of the liar's own "lying.") Such terms do not make sense in the abstract; indeed, to attempt a decontextualized definition of them violates their semantics. Yet definition is precisely what the state (which benefits from the semiotic illusion that there exists an absolute or correct understanding) imposes on morality in general. In terms like *varvarotita* (barbarism), moreover, morality and national identity coincide, calibrated to an externally derived criterion of excellence. The foreign visitor treads this minefield at considerable risk.

Further ethnographic illustrations from Greece

A brief look at some related ethnographic materials can make these contextual properties stand out more clearly. In the example I have just given of the charge of barbarism, it is the foreigner whose presence provokes the semantic coalescence that marks effective exclusion. My Nisirian acquaintance shifted—in the technical sense of the semantic shifter—from a reflexive understanding of the concept to one more closely identified with the values of the nation-state, producing a stalwart defense against an invasion of cultural intimacy.

But such shifting implies an already existing dissonance between intimate and formal uses of the terminology. In a moment of patriotic anger the Nisirian acted, not as he would probably have done with a close friend from his own community, but as a representative of his entire nation-state. This was especially noteworthy in that in the Dodecanese, incorporated into the Greek state only in 1948, people still talk of "when Greece came [here]"—in other words, treating the state itself as the intrusive or foreign power. My presence and lack of tact contextualized the Nisirian as a Greek rather than as a Dodecanesian.

Such shifts are common and can even be reversed. On one occasion in the Cretan village of Glendi, two men of local origin who had lived in Athens and become very metropolitan in their personal styles began to berate me for all the crimes of the Anglo-American conspiracy against Greece. Almost immediately, one of the local villagers, a man who had especially delighted in haranguing me about the very same topic but who also had learned that I was sympathetic to Greek concerns, bristled at the visitors and offered to intervene. Fearful that violence might erupt on my behalf, I declined his help with appropriate expressions of gratitude; but the incident made it very clear that residence in the village and my still rather partial command of the local dialect had given me a situational edge over the deracinated visitors. My wife and I were, as someone commented, "our own outsiders"— virtual Glendiots in the context of Athenian-style affectations.

The self-reified state inevitably masks numerous shifting meanings, but the goal of territorial fixity and absolute ethnic identity create a model that does not easily tolerate open ambiguity. This is particularly true of any moral concept closely associated with national identity. This authoritative definition of moral values often contrasts starkly with the variety of interpretations that we meet in everyday speech. In statist morality, for example, *eghois-mos* (broadly, self-regard and self-interest) is usually a negative value. Even here, however, matters are not quite as unambiguous as the exponents of state morality try to make them seem; for this same concept can be represented as individualism—viewed as a stereotypically European virtue—and used as the basis for claiming the Western character of Greek small business and artisanship. Often these commentators then criticize the same occupations for their endemic resistance to any form of cooperation; at this point, *eghoismos* acquires the implications of a Turkish rather than a European value.

For the swashbuckling villagers of Glendi, where I conducted fieldwork for some sixteen months between 1974 and 1981, the term has a far more accessible ambiguity; indeed, the villagers are quite explicit about this. There are forms in which *eghoismos* is acceptable—some of them, notably systematic, reciprocal animal-theft—entirely contrary to the laws of the state. But villagers sometimes speak of "an *eghoismos*," intending through this use of the indefinite article to indicate that someone exhibits a specific—and usually not very admirable—version of this social value. In other words, they recognize its variability: in some contexts, such as that of small-scale capitalism, they consider a highly competitive stance to be morally right; a man who is *eghoistis* in this sense is defending his family, and that is as it should be. The usage of "an *eghois-mos*" demonstrates a significant measure of fragmentation in the villagers' social experience and shows that they recognize the situational character of moral definition. It is not a usage that one would expect to encounter in official writings.

For most Greek villagers, moral evaluations are not assessments of innate character—which they deny being able to read even as they try to do so—but rather of social inclusion. The boundaries of the state are fixed. Those of the moral community of covillagers, on the other hand, belong to a shifting and fragmentary social world and are therefore necessarily subject to continual readjustment and reevaluation. Rhodian villagers explicitly call the morally bad "those outside of here" (*i okso apodho*), and they explain that this phrase could mean equally the moral or the physical community: "here" is itself a shifter and can convey both the local community (village or district or region) and the larger community of Greek Orthodoxy (see Stewart 1991: 164). In the Rhodian agricultural community where I worked in 1973–74, and to which I have given the pseudonym of Pefko, villagers justify village endogamy by using a proverb that elaborates on another adage far better known as a dictum about the folly of marrying a non-Greek.[6] All moral terminology conflates moral disapprobation with group exclusion; when the definition of "the" group is itself ambiguous or variable, the relevance of moral prescriptions becomes negotiable in a way that directly contradicts the codified perspective of bureaucratic law.

We can summarize the Greek terminology in a few words that might help clarify the main point. Pefkiot villagers symbolically equate the physical exclusion of devils (through exorcism) with the social exclusion of the wicked. *Ghrousouzia*, the evil condition of flawed covillagers, is furthermore equated with a "lack of good fortune," so that fate and not the hapless covillager takes the brunt of the blame—an effective way, at the same time, of denying the existence of truly malign wickedness within one's own community, especially when talking to outsiders. By contrast, evil outsiders are *atimi*, without social worth. But the latter term can, under some circumstances, be used descriptively of a covillager, for example, in the context of an interfamilial or interclan dispute. By the same token, it may not be used of any Greek at all in the context of a discussion comparing Greeks with Turks, the definitive enemy. Similarly, *ghrousouzia* is applicable to animal theft in any form in eastern Crete; in western Crete, where animal theft is still partly endemic, the term can only be used to condemn intravillage animal theft, whereas intervillage theft is usually greeted with some approval.

In short, the moral content of "outsiderhood" is not geared to any particular level or realization of that condition, although its diagnostic traits may vary somewhat from level to level. When the traits do vary, however, they themselves become shifters. The wickedness of a covillager who is not a kinsperson is usually seen as very different from that of a Turk, although to both may be ascribed a subhuman lack of social worth. Women, too, are described as illiterate in comparison to Greek men, but they are never so described when the Greeks are collectively contrasted to the stereotypically illiterate Turks (Herzfeld 1980a: 296–297).

Thus, ethnic shifters emerge as above all evaluative terms, which nationalism reifies in much the same way as it generally assumes the control of ethical norms. The corollary is that those who regard themselves as good citizens may nevertheless talk of the national entity as an intruder, while those who see themselves as outside the law will speak of the state as the intruder. Even the most law-abiding Rhodian, for example, mindful of the recent date of the incorporation of the Dodecanese into the Greek state, will speak of "when Greece came here," thereby treating *Elladha*, Greece, as a term of ambiguous and to some extent outsiderlike standing. The more rebellious Cretans with whom I worked stated the matter more succinctly: "We're the free Greece here!" Such a statement truly challenged the authority of national (and ecclesiastical) law. On another occasion, confronted by an angry police official demanding respect for "the law" (*to nomo*), an equally angry Glendiot responded that he "had 'two shoulders' (*dhio n-omous*) too!" His pun poetically reinforced its own message: such wordplays challenge the authority of the official lexicon, by introducing dialect forms[7] and by poking fun at the solemnity of official language.

In fact, the contrast between the law-abiding Rhodian farmers of Pefko and the rebellious Cretan shepherds of Glendi illustrates more or less the extremes of semantic variation that one encounters in Greek moral terminology, as indeed occurs in the use of national and ethnic labels as well. The Glendiots have found a way of recasting themselves as the moral center of the nation, even though they complain frequently of being at its political periphery; the milder Pefkiots, on the other hand, committed as they are to at least an outward show of respect for the law, are unable or unwilling to make the same distinction between nation and state. It is noteworthy that the Glendiots found it far easier to explicate the segmentary properties of the insider/outsider distinction than did the Pefkiots, just as they had a much clearer sense of the ambiguity of *eghoismos* and other value-terms. To a Glendiot, there is nothing problematic about identifying Cretan pride with Greekness. For the Pefkiots, on the other hand, who claim Greek purity in contrast to the supposed bastardization of the mainland population, the business of being Greek is itself identified with loyalty to the state. And Glendiots were fully explicit about the segmentary implications of their blasphemy, recognizing that it differentiated one's own Virgin Mary from that of the enemy, where Pefkiots simply dismissed such blasphemy as a "bad habit" and seemed uninterested in exploring further what its syntactical and semantic properties might portend.

Meaning and the state: the status of definition

The foregoing examples suggest two quite distinct semiotic orientations on the part of informants. On the one hand, the relativism of informant usage argues a "use" or "action" theory of meaning as the organizing conceptual framework. The official representatives of the state, by contrast, maintain a much more lexicographical perspective on meaning. That this is so becomes abundantly clear when one considers legal terminology: Pefkiots, for example, use the terminology of inheritance in senses directly opposed to the meanings given in codified law, and their uses of the terminology are consistent only if one takes every definition in combination with the context of utterance (Herzfeld 1980b). This lability, moreover, matches their own concept of meaning, which corresponds most closely to an action theory.

Lability constantly threatens the semantic stability of the state's moral universe. It is an ever-present threat: not only are state functionaries themselves engaged in negotiating the meanings of legal and ethical as well as administrative concepts, but the timelessness of the state is itself an illusion, indirectly challenged in recent years by such events as the breakup of neighboring Yugoslavia. Moreover, the local communities on which the nation-state is so often modeled are themselves, as we have seen, hardly innocent of ambiguity.

Ambiguity itself becomes a defining characteristic of the cultural intimacy denied by official ideology. In states where a savage nature, opposed to the ordered culture of the national entity, is identified with a specific human enemy, this can have remarkable effects on local uses of etymology to explore issues of ambiguity. Thus, it is noteworthy that many of the Greek terms for extreme disorder—*alaloum*, total mayhem; *tourlou-tourlou*, running all over the place; and *koutourou*, without counting precisely—are not only of Turkish derivation but are also known to be so. More generally, this association seems to rest on a sound symbolism that itself promotes images of both phonetic and cultural purity (see Joseph 1992). The words in question are immediately recognizable as sounding sufficiently foreign to stand for admixture, plurality, and confusion.

In this way, popular understandings of the cultural order are aligned with official values. That Turkish-derived words are also used to express strong personal emotions—*kefi*, unbridled and relaxed pleasure (on this see further Cowan 1990: 106–112); *meraki*, enthusiastic absorption in an activity; and so on—does not undercut this argument. On the contrary, it indicates the extent to which cultural intimacy identifies personal with cultural privacy—spaces for the acceptable display of emotion and for release from formal social constraints. Even the terms for disorder that I have just cited are more often enunciated with affectionate amusement and perhaps even collective self-mockery than with a sense of real cultural alienation.

These emotions are aspects of the "natural-person" interior of human beings, just as the "Turkish" forms of disorder belong to the "nature" interior of the Greek national character—the very substance of cultural intimacy. In both cases, supposedly natural feelings and impulses have in effect been domesticated by formal culture, to be displayed only before intimates. On the exterior, not only has nature become culturalized but also culture itself is more sharply defined and naturalized. Context gives way to eternal verity.

Thus, what I have described here is not simply a process whereby an emergent state arrogates to itself the moral privileges that hitherto belonged to competing social groups, as Blok (1981) has suggested for "honor," although that is certainly an important part of it. It is also the process whereby public concepts of morality and identity are essentialized to harmonize with a uniform and unitary image of the nation. By recognizing the connection between morality and social or ethnic identity, moreover, we can perceive how difficult it would be for state officials to tolerate, in any open and self-conscious way, a use-theory view of morality or identity. Not only would it conflict with the image of invariant law but, by that very fact, it would also undermine their individual authority. Reference theory, by contrast, provides a prescriptive idiom of definition that serves the conceptual needs of those whose job it is—and in whose interests it lies—to promote territorial, political, and moral finitude all at once.

Even in popular discourse, people increasingly identify nation with culture, and thereby surrender the right of cultural definition to the agencies of state control: folklore gives way to folklorism. At the same time, however, the perceptions of actors engaged in such systems are attuned to the negotiation of social values and they often call the bluff of official rhetoric. In so doing they raise the possibility of an alternative, critical perspective, one that peers into the semantic intimacies that notions of pure referentiality conceal. Clearly, people do not think, act, or speak exactly as the schematized ideologies of statism would prefer.

Nevertheless, they do continue to serve their national entities with great loyalty and to move within the legal and political frameworks that the latter provide. By questioning the naturalization of culture in statist ideologies as well as the concomitant reification of nature, we can perhaps begin to understand how sensitive actors can negotiate the tensions of social identity and daily life within the turbulent context of the modern nation-state, and how they can be fiercely patriotic and just as fiercely rebellious at one and the same time. This perspective represents an epistemological militant middle ground; it entails recognizing agency rather than surrendering to either regress or reification. Brought to bear on the shifting shapes of the nation-state, it restores Vico's original vision of the human capacity for symbolic invention to an anthropology no longer restricted, one hopes, to the exotic and the marginal.

Chapter Three

Persuasive Resemblances

Iconicity and the backgrounding of rhetoric

Icon is a misleading word—and all the more so in a book where the emphasis on Greece and the Orthodox Christian world may already have created false expectations. In religious usage, the term—*eikon*, Greek likeness—conveys the imitation of the divine. But since we shall be concerned here with the secularist theology of the nation-state, perhaps the confusion is illuminating after all. For it is the rhetorical force of likeness that I explore in this chapter.

In modern popular usage, again, the term icon carries a potentially misleading significance. It often means little more than emblem: a cultural form, or more commonly a person who seems to embody the ideal traits of a faddish cultural ideology. In the more technical semiotic sense in which I use the concept of iconicity here, I mean instead the way in which meaning is derived from resemblance: as a portrait "means" its subject. Of course, one could argue that the popular usage is not entirely off base: to be "ideal-typical" in a national context is to reproduce one version of the "imagined community" envisioned by Anderson (1983), although not necessarily the one desired by the official state. But it is helpful to be clear about the specific meaning of the term used before we launch into an extended discussion.

Note that I write, not of icons, but of iconicity. This seemingly minor shift of terminology actually makes a large difference: it reminds us that we are speaking not of permanent things but of processes whereby permanence and thingness are achieved. A sign is only an icon because someone uses it that way, and because others agree to understand it as such. Of all signifiying processes, moreover, iconicity may be the one that most effectively hides from analysis. It would not be helpful to aid and abet that elusiveness by reifying as icons signs that from another angle do not resemble their alleged referents at all.

The decision to recognize iconicity always has potential political implications. Sometimes these have to do with the politics of taste and knowledge. Questions of plagiarism, creativity, and originality all hinge on iconicity: what in academic discourse is straightforwardly plagiarism, for example, might become originality in a culture much given to impromptu oral versifying, in which a different context of use creates a new text, as happens with the rhyming duels of Cretan mountain villagers. Was Canaletto a mechanistic precursor of photographic reproduction or a gifted observer? Sometimes the issues are more obviously political, and it is these that will concern us here. As an illustration, we may ask what happens to propositions of national linguistic unity when the speakers of what has been classified as a dialect insist that their speech instead represents a language. Or we may consider how systems of egalitarian citizenship address the complaint that some groups smell different, pollute food by sharing it, or practice unspeakable rites.

These are all questions about the uses of iconicity. They concern the issue of social and political context. Iconicity does not exist; it is called into existence. Because state bureaucracies are immensely powerful and command enormous resources, they often possess means—through the media, for example—to constitute iconicity out of a variegated cultural world. We must not lose sight of the fact that these agents are nevertheless still creating iconicity. While it is often their goal to create the impression that iconicity is beyond analysis—that it is totally "natural"—ours should be to challenge that stance and see official agency as constructing iconicity in a social field in which others have highly variable degrees of freedom to contest it. Whether perceived resemblances correspond to reality is less relevant than the fact that they are perceived: some ethnographic work (e.g., Forge 1968) suggests that basic assumptions about iconicity (that a photograph represents the object it shows, for example) do not work in all cultural contexts. But even when those concerned agree in principle on the criteria of resemblance, they may disagree about specific cases, and their disagreement will reveal something of the play of power among them. Much may be at stake in discussions about which parent a baby resembles (and to which it therefore in some invidious sense belongs) or whether a royal claimant has noble bearing. If such matters, which are about the very basis of classification, were unambiguous, they would not prompt such heated discussion.

In this chapter, I shall largely be concerned with the production of iconicity by official sources of ideological unity, especially officers of the bureaucratic nation-state. It is also important to remember, however, that the shift I have just signaled—from icons to iconicity and more generally from signs to sign use (see also Eco 1976: 191–208)—allows for a considerable play of alternative iconicities. Those who contest iconicity can also create it in other spaces, using other materials. Those who do not concur with the official view of how the community is to be imagined will find other connections out of which to suggest other imaginings.

Perhaps more than any other sign relationship, iconicity— meaning something by resembling it—"backgrounds" (Douglas 1975: 4) its own semiotic character for the human observer. From original to simulacrum is a short, often circular path. (That is why those who simulate intimate social relations, as I noted in the introductory chapter, can accuse rebellious consumers of bad manners and character.) According to Eco (1976: 6–7), the possibility of deception exists in all semiotic operations. In that sense, iconicity must be the most deviously employed of all semiotic principles, since, as every forger knows, it is often not seen as a sign at all. It is easy to routinize: we are all morally alike, equal, standardized, even within ideologies that recognize our personal idiosyncrasies.[1] Most social and political ideologies rely on this capacity for homogenization (see Eco 1976: 155).

Some cultural ideologies seek temporal depth for modern homogeneity. They articulate an idiom of structural nostalgia: they seek to reconstitute perfect archaic forms out of modern cultural idioms and genetic phenotypes. Appealing to the idea of a corrupted world, they rebuild original texts (the folklorists' *Urtexte*), racial ideals (as in ethnic cleansing and Nazi obsessions with racial purity), and national arts. They construct claims of similarity—imperfect but recoverable—between modern and ancient cultures. These claims, which are essentially appeals for le-

58

gitimacy on the basis of historical priority, are grounded in literalistic ideas about cultural content—that is, about the etymological, archaeological, genetic, and ethnological data out of which historical continuities can be constructed. The reliance of this type of ideological discourse upon the iconicity principle has so far largely eluded detailed analysis, a fact that in itself suggests how effective the backgrounding has been. Because resemblance looks natural, challenges to such projections of iconicity are profoundly disturbing to those who have learned to accept them. In this way, resemblance perpetuates itself.

Two decades ago, Umberto Eco (1976: 190–217) unleashed a massive critique of the concept of iconicity. His argument was simple: iconicity was in a sense a victim of its own logic; too much is conflated under a single label and the phenomena it subsumes are not usefully understood as all the same. If we take seriously Eco's own call for treating semiotic analysis as social criticism, the objection begs the important question: why is a presumption of sameness so important for ideological purposes? To argue that this is self-evident is to surrender to the iconizing logic of the idea of common sense: who says that such a sense must be common or (universally) sensible and what motivates these claims? It is the usual argument of nationalists to insist that the essential resemblance of the ethnically pure is beyond question; the usual defense of egalitarian communities—their concealment of the inequalities that a more intimate knowledge would reveal—is to deny the existence of difference, whether of viewpoint, moral quality, or economic status.

We must thus ask whether the ideological creation and use of resemblance constitute a unitary phenomenon in any useful sense. If racial and linguistic features are treated as isomorphic in their geographical or historical distribution, for example, our own ideological objections to such a methodology as racist should not blind us to its intrinsic interest as a form of discourse. (This is exactly the argument that I use elsewhere in these pages to insist on the importance of taking stereotypes seriously, however much we may disagree with them.)

We should, however, seek to ask critical questions about the uses of these procedures. Why are such distributions treated as isomorphic by the adherents and apologists of a given ideology? How persuasive did that treatment prove? Did critics of the prevailing order manage to unpack the iconic bundle, and what did they find? Those who argued in the early nineteenth century for or against a particular kind of national unity (see Herzfeld 1982a: 77) conflated racial and ethnographic forms of evidence, no matter which side the protagonists were on in a particular debate. They all fell into the same conceptual trap. But to deny that they were all arguing about resemblance makes it impossible to understand why the shared assumptions about cultural homogeneity should have proved so persistent.

One of the commonest fallacies about iconicity is that it must be visual (see Sebeok 1979: 117). By the same token, classification is frequently assumed to be exclusively verbal. Animals, lacking language, nevertheless clearly have taxonomic capacities; it would therefore clearly be absurd to insist that humans should be entirely dependent upon language for their classificatory needs. Thus, just as Gombrich (1961: 101–104, 178) writes of "visual classification," so, conversely, we may also recognize the iconicity of visual and other nonverbal correspondences. Smell, for example, provides a common basis for ethnic and class stereotypes, not only in the elite cultures of Western Europe and North America (Classen 1993: 7–10, 102).

Verbal iconicity is usually treated, in its synchronic and diachronic versions respectively, as folk etymology and philological, or academic, etymology. Folk etymology is further differentiated from its scholarly counterpart by being largely dismissed as the manifestation of unconscious error, as in Bolinger's (1975: 406) characterization of it as "a kind of auditory malapropism." This division, privileging as it does the perspective of the scholar, has been roundly criticized (Ardener 1971b: 224). Like the artificial distinction between myth and history (see Lévi-Strauss 1962; Feely-Harnik 1978; Drummond 1981; Hill 1988), it smacks of scholarly privilege: "folk etymologies" may in fact be ways of wresting ideological control from a powerful oppressor, perhaps even by deploying the cultural logic of the oppressor for the purpose. The animal-thief who argued with the law by saying that his community bore the weight of social understanding on its "two shoulders"—suggesting that as a community insider he had access to richer veins of knowledge than did the self-important representatives of the state—was hardly betraying ignorance.

The parallel between the folk-academic discrimination in etymology and the distinction between myth and history is close, and has similar political implications. Both discriminations are predicated on elite claims to the monopoly of truth. In both, moreover, we may discern a scholarly proclivity to see a fundamental similarity among the observed (the natives all look alike, make the same complaints, behave typically), while simultaneously forging discontinuity between them and the observer. This is an excellent example in scholarly practice of the ideological use of iconicity close to home.

Etymology and recognition

At the moment, however, I shall be concerned with more distant instances. The passage of time makes them seem more readily accessible to critical analysis. The element of reduction—of caricature even—that temporal distancing permits foregrounds certain aspects of the problem that depend for their effectiveness on remaining in the background. I have just mentioned etymology. This is the usual term for verbal iconicity; its usefulness for ideological purposes has long been recognized and exploited. Ironically, it was especially the work of Giambattista Vico—for whom the beauty of etymology was that it could be used to *discommode* established "truths"—that spawned a whole generation of ideological etymologists in Italy (Cocchiara 1952: 176–177, 239, 278–282), Greece (Herzfeld 1981, 1982a), and elsewhere, a generation whose insistence that the literal truth about cultural identity could be gleaned from etymological and other ethnographic evidence contrasted strangely with Vico's own celebrated axiom regarding the constructed nature of truth. With the advent of Saussurean linguistics in this century, the study of verbal etymology fell into some measure of disrepute, although there have been resurgences (see Lehmann 1975: 12–13, 18–19). Conversely, the academic production of etymologies of nonverbal cultural forms never weakened, especially in those countries in which the study of folklore was actively encouraged for political ends. It was not usually called etymology; its dissociation from academically *démodé* kinds of historical linguistics saved it from their fate, while its association with ruling power groups rendered it comparatively immune to overt criticism.

For the student of nationalism, officially sanctioned uses of iconicity are of compelling interest, since cultural continuity has repeatedly served as the primary justification for territorial claims. Where direct political advantage does not necessarily explain the particular framework of interpretation, ideological considerations may still be at work. Past cultural changes, for example, may be explicitly acknowledged, but interpreted in terms of a prevailing cultural morality. Thus, there is some evidence that earlier British archaeologists were prone to attribute all evidence of cultural change in the archaeological record in Britain to "invasions," apparently in accordance with a general reluctance to see the British Isles as a center for any kind of aesthetic innovation (Clark 1966). Apparently, this kind of thing did not sit well with self-professed Anglo-Saxons, whose academic nativism—a form of cultural intimacy operating at the level of scholarly discourse—preferred hardheaded common sense to the artistic genius of foreigners. Historical and ethnological facts are given significance by a present concern; as perspectives change, so too does the past (Collingwood 1965: 138–139; cf. Buttitta 1971: 10).

Historiography is a disturbing teacher, since it suggests that the concerns of the present may not be as immutable or as nearly eternal as their protagonists might believe. The very fact that we talk about "the past" illustrates the groping for a reified certainty to which we are all heirs. And it is easy to see how what Collingwood (1965: 127) has described as Vico's use of "systematic disbelief" about the claims of scholars and nations alike could be converted in a brief span of time into systematized nationalist dogma. When such dogma is allied to political interests, moreover, the incentives for renewed criticism may atrophy rapidly. The representation of cultural continuities, both geographical and temporal, cannot easily be subjected to analytical dissection in countries where territorial disputes with other nation-states impose a degree of internal solidarity. The sharing of cultural intimacy poses risks; why initiate what is in essence a critique of factuality itself, when the facts support one's case? (Wallis's [1975: 18] gentle rebuke that "not all scholars are yet aware that likenesses . . . are also signs" may be extended to the consumers of such signs, and has special force in those cases where the scholars themselves were both generating and consuming the resemblances.)

Students of culture often disagree about the attribution of a particular cultural link with the past. They are also often unwilling to confront the contingent nature of the resemblances in which such links consist. The list of scholarly concerns to which this applies is enormous and includes such diverse topics as etymology, evolutionary and developmentalist theories of culture, the study of so-called culture areas, archaeological distribution mapping, Urtext models of oral tradition, and various forms of anthropological diffusionism and comparativism. In all, "sameness" and "likeness" have virtually been given the status of primary data, not of problems worthy of investigation in themselves. Today, it is true, there are signs that valuable correctives are being generated in all branches of anthropological and historical inquiry, but the older trend has certainly not been halted.

There is at least a strong presumption that many of these so-called resemblances could more profitably be dismantled than perpetuated. In general, the value of any taxonomy is at its greatest at the moment of dissolution, even more so than at its point of constitution. This moment offers us a glimpse of the historical context that gave currency to the act of scholarship itself.[2] One might surmise, for example, that early twentieth-century diffusionism sprang in part from a desire to reproduce in the archaeological record something of the flavor of imperial mercantilism, just as the most prestigious British university education long insisted on the primacy of Classical learning in the formation of true imperial leaders (Symonds 1986: 31–34). Lacking any firsthand acquaintance with the events of ancient times (Collingwood 1965: 136; Goldstein 1976: 125–128), scholars instead constructed an icon of their own immediate experience in the archaeological record—iconic relations being fully reciprocal or reversible (Sebeok 1979: 118–120).[3]

It is when knowledge is invested with absolute authority—when a scholarly account, which is itself rooted in a particular social and historical context, claims definitive status—that we can most comfortably agree with Buttitta (1971: 10) in declaring that "to know is to deform." Just as the concept of social poetics may help us comprehend how norms become understood in a particular society through their creative deformation in social performance, this appraisal shows that authoritative knowledge can perhaps most critically be seen as a performance in the Austinian sense: as the creation of factuality by the creative and culturally effective use of discourse. Peirce's (1.384) call for "destructive distillation" recognizes this aspect of knowledge, the intellectual aridity of a closed taxonomy (see also Handler 1985). Any re-cognition of historical events must entail some sort of taxonomic straightjacket, or we could not know at all. Equally, however, knowing about that knowing works against the tendency for taxonomy to become a hypostatized datum in its own right.

Such insights are extremely dangerous to absolutist ideologies of ethnic or national identity. Tight boundaries on the conceptual map sit well with hermetically sealed and rigidly demarcated political borders. That is why maps are such an important icon of territorial integrity. The intense involvement of mid-nineteenth-century European political leaders in the encouragement of official ethnology is ample evidence of this concern; consider, more recently, the cold-war title of the nationalist Greek folklorist Stilpon Kyriakides's essay, "The Northern Ethnological Boundaries of Hellenism" (1955), in which territorial mapping was further enhanced by the iconizing of Slavophones as communists and vice versa. Such devices conflate what we would analytically regard as separate domains of identity. By mapping out several mutually reinforcing iconicities, ideologically motivated scholars produced a multidimensional image of their cultural theories. That is one reason for which anthropologists' insistence on separating the genetic from the cultural has been so fiercely resisted by advocates of extreme nationalism and totalitarianism.

But the more obviously manipulative examples of recent times should not lead us to assume that such conflations are always, or necessarily, made in bad faith. The burden of anthropological thinking in the nineteenth century did not suggest the importance of making clear distinctions at every turn between the racial and the cultural; the horrendous consequences of conflating the two became obvious only in our own century. Not surprisingly, non-specialist discourse remains relatively slow to incorporate this change of perspective. In addition, the desire for clear definition is often so great that people are willing to accept anything that produces that effect. When evidence from the two domains seems to converge, finally, the taxonomic imperative is such that acceptance often appears the most reasonable attitude to take.

The genetic-cultural distinction may be more easily made explicit in verbal than in other ways. The use of visual iconicity often works in the opposite direction. Here we are in the realm of a nonlinguistic taxonomy. The recent (1964) reprint of J. C. Lawson's (1910) survivalist study of Greek folk religion carries a frontispiece juxtaposing an archaic bas-relief of a shepherd with a photographic portrait of a modern shepherd from Arachova. Facial features, occupational stance, and an enigmatic smile are thus brought together as components of a visual statement about cultural continuity—one that probably needed no further explication unless we count the main text of the book itself. In fact,

there is a caption, claiming that the juxtaposition "brings this archaic sculpture to life *unknowingly* showing one on [sic] the
many similarities between ancient and modern life in Greece"
(my emphasis). The caption carries a certain persuasive force of
its own, but in practice the visual statement would have worked
very well without it. The emphasis on an unconscious—"un-
knowing"—connection is revealing: iconicity is a matter of self-
evidence. The verbal statement foregrounds, as it were, the
semiotic character of the iconic relation, but it also thereby poses
a risk: that someone may, as I have just done, question its assumptions.

Commitment to a particular taxonomy, however, is often
strongly resistant to critical erosion of this sort. That arch-
diffusionist, Grafton Elliot Smith, claimed to have discovered a
stone relief of an elephant among the Maya ruins of Palenque:
"Some cautious scholars, it was true, circumambulated the elephant by suggesting that the animal pictured might be a rendering of the tapir. . . . But Smith simply laughed at them" (Ceram
1957–58: 322–323). In this case, visual classification clearly
made an appeal to Smith that was far more forceful than any verbal argument. We should not forget that this scornful dismissal
of views different from diffusionist orthodoxy came at the height
of British mercantile hegemony, of which diffusionism was itself
a remarkably persuasive icon.

In nationalism, too, claims of iconicity in cultural relations con-
fuse resemblance with identity. Archaeological and ethnographic
evidence for a connection between ancient and modern cultures is
understood to signify an essential sameness, which is why claims
about the antiquity of fragile new states like Greece—especially
when they originated from the Western European countries on
which Greece's survival depended—appeared to be so threatening
to Greek national interests; and why any attempt to suggest that
cultural continuity may be mixed with discontinuities generally
meets unremitting fury. The presumed sameness of ancient and
modern is then projected back on to the data, so that the resemblance itself is conventionalized, taken for granted; its contingent
character is rendered invisible. Paradoxically, however, resemblance rests on the possibility of difference; a living continuity between past and present likewise rests on the concomitant
possibility of change. The effect is analogous to that of a dead
metaphor, which is the result of the collapse of the tension that
makes any effective metaphor work (see Richards 1936).[4] The

possibility of recovering that tension—of investing a tired metaphor with a new sense of freshness—is usually present. Thus, the confusion between resemblance and identity reproduces that between the metaphorical and the literal. Iconicity, like metaphor, is necessarily predicated upon a potential *absence* of equivalence. Were this not so, all iconic relations would be merely tautological; instead, there is always a risk that outsiders may unmask the cultural intimacy of difference that iconicity conceals.

In this, they resemble what is after all but a special case of academic taxonomy, as I have sketched it here. But some academic classifiers welcome that challenge. Absolutist ideologies, by contrast, require scholarship to confirm the validity of the iconicities upon which cultural and territorial claims rest and to furnish supposedly irrefutable taxonomic claims about the identity of the modern nation with its forebears. Continuity in this sense is really more a form of marking time—marking it, moreover, as one's own.

The central paradox of iconicity thus conceived always contains within itself the seeds of its own potential dissolution. People know perfectly well that they are not ancient Teutons or Aztecs. This is why we cannot simply dismiss nationalistic ideologies as spurious without becoming literalists ourselves: engaging in that kind of debate is classic top-down theorizing in that it ignores what ordinary people say or imply. And to assume that all the members of a given nation-state agree completely on the essence of cultural continuity is to suppress the agency of numerous populations and individuals.

Nonetheless, iconicity remains a powerful tool; its use works on the principle of Poe's "purloined letter": it is there for all to see, so no marauding critic (or "thief of history," as so many nationalists say) suspects its presence. The uses of script illustrate how the paradox is sustained in a particularly clear way. Script types are used in an allusory fashion to suggest continuities with earlier, more powerful political entities (Morison 1972; Wallis 1975: 61–63, 76). To take a case in point: the last Greek king, Constantine XIII, took his number from the Byzantine series, rather than from the national Greek series (in which he also figured, as Constantine II). The coins of his reign have Byzantine lettering, rather than the classical lettering used by both his father, Paul, and by the military junta that first restricted his powers and then, when he rebelled, supplanted him altogether. Both modes pointed back to historical glories with which the modern polity could claim some degree of continuity. Whereas scholars of culture who wished to make the same point might take artifacts of both the earlier epoch and the present one, and set them side by side in order to signify the nature of the cultural connections in question, the designers of these coins achieved much the same effect by means of an allusion. And allusion, being indirect, discourages critical dissection.

Both allusion and direct juxtaposition illustrate the paradox that makes iconicity so useful a tool for ideologies of the sort being considered here: juxtaposition, by positing at least two terms to be compared, logically denies identity. It states a contradiction that cannot be resolved in literal fashion: tension between difference and sameness underlies any claim to cultural homogeneity and thereby renders that claim potentially open to eventual disintegration. The ideologue controls the contradiction by encasing it in the rhetoric of a rigid taxonomy. In this, the exponents of nationalistic ethnology follow a familiar pattern: "The King is dead. Long live the King!"

All these devices are strong performative utterances: they reconstitute what may be an impossible condition in one sense as fundamental truth in another. They belong to the larger class of devices that ostensibly background the figurative character of an attribution ("So-and-so is a *real* shark"). Just as it would be merely silly to object to the reality of the shark, so too we stand to gain nothing from simply dismissing the claims of cultural ideologies as untrue. Their validity is subject to what Hanson (1979) has called a "double contingency," one side of which lies in the evidential rules within which the ideology itself is formulated.

Like all performatives, such devices are successful in varying degrees. The Nazis' use of Germanic folktales eventually failed to convince because it involved the removal of the tales from their current German context (Kamenetsky 1977: 178): in effect, the strain between idealized past and experienced present built up to critical proportions under the combined stress of external pressure and military and political failure. For foreign observers, the demands on credulity had in some cases become too great even before the outbreak of war, especially in the realm of archaeology, where they were challenged by German scholars as well (Clark 1939: 201–206). For the populace at large, however, they were embedded in a cynical reconstitution of "Indo-European" culture in terms of blood ideology and the pagan origins of

Christmas customs (Gajek 1990). Protoypes are always retrospectively created, although sometimes people catch the ideologues in the act.

More generally, we can say that the rhetorical force of such iconic correspondences resides in their being perceived as somehow natural. That the concept of natural symbols is itself a paradoxical formulation has not prevented its growing importance in cultural analysis (see, for example, Foucault 1966; Douglas 1973: 11–12). Once a cultural order can be represented as part of the natural order, the moral rejection of dissonant cases proceeds as a matter of course, and this is reflected in the scholarly literature by an often negative treatment of such themes as miscegenation, cultural and textual corruption, and demographic minorities. Minorities in particular appear as symbolic pollutants (see Herzfeld 1992a: 31). Not all scholars have adopted the official position, of course, but scholars have certainly played an important role in the development of modern nationalism through their authoritative control over the conceptualization of culture. More than that, they have in a sense been the agents of the conversion of cultural data into natural truths.

Not all uses of archaeology and folklore for nationalistic purposes have rested primarily upon iconic relations. Geographical distribution is also a key factor, and it has sometimes proved sufficient to demonstrate continuous habitation in a given region in order to stake a convincing territorial claim. The associated material remnant has a certain hardness, which, for example, etymological data seem to lack.[5] Yet the straightforward recovery of antique relics as a basis for irredentist claims differs from appeals to iconicity in one important respect: it is predicated on the complete absence of any recognition of cultural difference or change. This is why the enormous popularity of archaeological metaphors in the nineteenth-century survivalist literature (see Hodgen 1936) creates such an impression of overwhelming literalism. Yet there are many situations in which distributional studies rest upon resemblances rather than on the mere survival of material artifacts in situ. We have already noted the use of genetic data in conjunction with cultural evidence; while anthropologists and archaeologists have been generally critical of such conflations in recent years, their perpetuation in other domains of discourse such as journalism and political rhetoric is striking. Distributions based on different sets of iconic criteria tend to reinforce each other as a means of expressing cultural differentiation: "What is begun in one thread (language) is completed in another (spatial relations). . . . A boundary between two settlements may be a city wall or a piece of legislation, a disjunction in building materials, or in dialect" (Preziosi 1979: 59)—or, we might add, in discursively created cultural or "racial" difference.

Some illustrations

At this point, I would like to consider some specific examples of cultural etymology. I begin with an instance of what could be represented as folk etymology; my goal in so doing is to suggest that its historicity is essentially similar to that of many of the cultural claims made by literate ideologies. It is part of the cultural etiology of the Iteso of Kenya: "They state that they were originally members of the Karimojong tribe which migrated south. The Karimojong who remained behind told the younger men who were pushing on that they were going to their graves, *atesin*—hence, the Iteso. The people who stayed in Karimoja were called the 'tired old men'—*Ikarimojong*" (Karp 1978: 16).

Because statements of this kind are verbal, their validity seems especially vulnerable in the context of literate history. But the Iteso example shows that recourse to verbal iconicity is not the exclusive preserve of literate cultures. Etymologies of this kind provide compact instances of the differentiating character of origin myths (see Drummond 1981), and they legitimize the moral boundaries of culture in ways not altogether different from what we encounter in nineteenth-century European nationalism.

Even in Europe, moreover, the nationalisms of the nineteenth century were not the first ideologies to make use of verbal iconicity. Thus, for example, we learn that the Romans utilized etymologies of the local names of the Anatolian deity, Men, in order to conflate the god's homeland and the territory in Italy that included some homonyms of Anatolian place-names (Lane 1975: 239): "the cult of the god Men seems deliberately to have been fostered as a unifying force by the Roman rulers in Asia Minor, and a mythology deliberately created, which, through epithets laden with legendary lore and the clever use of word resemblances, underscored the cult of Men as an integral part of the supposed racial relationship between the subject Anatolians and their Italian masters." One sees here a remarkable anticipation of the twentieth-century Italian claims to the Mediterranean as *Mare Nostrum* (our sea)—a claim at once geographical and chronological—and of the Italian re-cognition of Corsican and Maltese culture as essentially Italian (see Simeone 1978: 553). The one important difference is that the ancient claim was predicated on the association of epiphanies of a deity with particular place-names, whereas the ecumenical monotheism of Christianity precluded that particular line of argument. On the other hand, the modern culturology of the Fascists drew on a much wider range of cultural traits.

The connection between ideology and scholarship in Mussolini's Italy is abundantly evidenced by the official support given to the ethnological journal *Lares* (Simeone 1978: 549). The unity of Italian culture was still not firmly established at the time; in a very real and widely acknowledged sense, the creation of Italian national character was seen as a consequence rather than as a contributory cause of political unification in the years immediately following that event (Simeone 1978: 545; Moss 1979: 483). The Italians, in other words, wished to forge a cultural unity in the image of the political entity that they had already achieved. Somewhat similar processes were and have since taken place all over Europe (Grillo 1980) and elsewhere, although they are now being resisted by resurgent forms of nationalism, which they in turn contemptuously dismiss as "localism" (see also Nadel-Klein 1992).

The unity of the Italian nation thus envisaged could be reproduced in countless exhibits of popular culture. While it is perhaps true that no ethnographic exhibit is ever free of ideological implications of one sort or another (Buttitta 1971: 161–164), the Fascist regime saw special opportunities in the genre. Artistic creativity and individualism were said not to undermine this essential unity but to characterize the greatness of the popular genius "whence, came forth all the beauty that makes Italy proud of her past. Thus it was ever so, whether it [i.e., Italy] was split between different states, with few communications and limited education, or today, in all the country's compactness and unity, possessing every kind of progress and civilization" (Bona 1940: 476) That unity emerges in lavish exhibits funded by the regime: "For the first time, exhibitions of handicraft are conjoined with those of Popular Arts, thereby creating a synthesis of beauty and life which exquisitely interprets the spirit of this Fascist era" (ibid.).

In the foregoing examples, we see two quite different uses of iconicity for the construction of ideological unity. One demonstrates homogeneity among classes of artifact. The other, more abstract or structural, shows the resemblance created between the organization of an exhibit and the form of the idea it represents. Just as certain nineteenth-century museums are replicas of evolutionism in their layout, so the fascist exhibits of Mussolini's Italy were designed as images of national unity. The earlier understanding of thinkers like D'Azeglio, who saw that the creation of the political entity called Italy preceded that of a true national consciousness and identity, was now inverted: "These motifs which invariably succeed one another through many centuries in every region of Italy do not represent . . . the judgments of local taste, but . . . should be considered as a *sure sign of the ethnic unity which preceded political unity*, as a demonstration of the nation's spiritual unity" (Bertarelli 1938: 31; my emphasis). The ethnic unity in question is cast in the image of its political counterpart, utilizing the evidence of folk iconography. Here, explicitly conjoined, are the two uses of iconicity I have just described.

Defending cultural intimacy: iconicity, rhetoric, and cultural identity

The huge range of possible phenomena treated under the heading of "similarity" (Eco 1976: 192–200) includes, as we have briefly seen, a variety of major categories: language, material artifacts, genetic inheritance, and so on. Were there such a thing as pure iconicity in culture, we should have to refine our definitions and approach the issue in an altogether fresh way. But in practice, as Peirce appears to have recognized (see Sebeok 1979: 113), such purity is rarely a feature of human discourse. The illusion of iconic purity, on the other hand, is a rhetorical device of prime importance in the kinds of ideological formulations we have been considering: because virtually all nationalisms are centrally concerned with purity and pollution, they elevate domestic symbolisms to the level of national essence.

My emphasis throughout this chapter has been on the ways in which the premise of iconicity has been used and on the efficacy of those uses. The ease with which identity and resemblance are confused with each other, moreover, masks the semiotic process itself, and lends itself to the sustenance of self-fulfilling arguments—those based on the symmetry of iconicity—necessary to nationalistic ideologies. The pre-Romantic shift to a view of meaning in which natural signs came to be less and less obviously semiotic phenomena (Foucault 1966: 75–76) prepared the way for investing pronouncements about the rights of nations with the force of natural law.

The ideological debates that emerge are confrontations among divergent truths. Thus, a Greek folklorist may argue that the Bulgarians do not have a national epic of their own but merely copied that of the Greeks (Megas 1946); for some Bulgarians, on the other hand, Macedonia is "a province which *in legendary times* is said to have been Greek" (Slavenkoff 1904: 41; my emphasis)—an idea that seems to be in full spate nearly a century later. These are arguments about territory, couched in terms of origins, and reasoned on the grounds of likeness or dissimilarity. They provide an effective defense of cultural intimacy because, as we shall see again in chapter 5, they naturalize particular interests in order to render disagreement absurd.

The appeal is always to cultural etymology—in other words, to sanctioned, framed iconicity, recast as incontrovertible fact. The iconic reproduction of artifactual forms is foregrounded; into the background, by contrast, recede the logical principles, special pleading, and presuppositions by which that reproduction is invested with ideological significance. It does not necessarily follow that because culture A resembles culture B, those who own territory B must also own territory A. But this presupposition of irredentist discourse is the very rationale of what we might call the appeal to etymology, and its force would be dissipated by critical dissection.

The peculiar cogency of such arguments derive from a structural resemblance, recalling the transformational sets of *La pensée sauvage* (Lévi-Strauss 1962): as original forms are to derivative ones, so culture B is to culture A. The battle over whether Balkan houses are to be considered Greek or not (e.g., Megas 1951) is thus a battle over whether the Greeks themselves are derivative or primary in the wider Balkan context. Cultural artifacts become "good to think" in searching for ways of discriminating between them and us. Once we accept that something actually and absolutely is Greek, Bulgarian, or whatever, we have allowed ourselves to become entrapped by the rhetoric we were trying to analyze. The metaphor, so to speak, has died on us.

The rhetorical uses of iconicity go far beyond nationalism alone. But the paradigm offered by nationalistic folklore illustrates with a wealth of detail how effectively the iconic basis of classification can be employed for rhetorical ends, with or without verbal explication. This rhetorical force derives from a combination of factors: the reversibility of the iconic relationship, the backgrounding of its semiotic makeup, the consequent conflation of identity with similarity, the evidential appeal of sameness, the convergence of popular with scholarly discourse in according respect to the historical implications of etymology. The very heterogeneity of iconicity is what recommends it to the reductionist needs of ideology: it simplifies the awkward, complicated, messy truths about ethnic and other kinds of internal diversity that undergird its bland assertions of homogeneity. For this reason, far from rejecting it as too simplistic an umbrella, we should treat it as a crucial concept in the study of political rhetoric. It is the primary line of defense for the secrets of cultural intimacy.

Chapter Four

The Dangers of Metaphor: From Troubled Waters to Boiling Blood

Of nations and metaphors

Roger Just, in a recent and important paper entitled "The Triumph of the Ethnos" (1989), has suggested that the remarkable achievement of Greek nationalism was to develop a culturally monolithic society in a century and a half, suppressing the once rich ethnic mosaic (see also Andromedas 1976) that had formerly characterized the present-day Greek lands. He expresses surprise at the simplicity of the message as well as the totality of its success: the synthesizing criterion of Greek blood (*elliniko ema*) has been attributed to a motley assortment of social groups and has played its role almost to the exclusion of all other touchstones of identity. If the resounding success of the *ethnos* now looks like a self-evident truth, this was not always so. On the eve of the struggle for independence, it even looked like a rather dubious proposition. But blood is a compelling symbol: indeed, as we know from other societies (e.g., Sobo 1993: 77), the idea of unity based on shared blood works even at those intimate levels where people know perfectly well that, in a literal sense, they are not related at all, but wish to act as though they were.

In this very brief chapter, which introduces several more detailed analyses of issues in nationalism, I start out from the phenomenal success story that Just has so accurately pinpointed. I have argued elsewhere that, in Greece, the logic of nation-state formation harmonized extraordinarily well with the persistence of localist ideologies (Herzfeld 1987: 157). Nation-statism and localism are usually portrayed as mutually hostile, and with good reason; the Basque insurgency in Spain or the continuing agony in Northern Ireland provide instructive illustrations of what happens to state authority when localist sentiment—which may take the form of religious or cultural martyrdom—erupts in violence. For the moment, however, Greece appears extraordinarily homogeneous, no trivial matter in an area notoriously beset by ethnic strife. The successful consolidation of the Greek *ethnos* is indeed a remarkable triumph.

I suspect, in part on the basis of comparisons with neighboring Balkan countries, that the triumph of the *ethnos* among the Greeks may in fact be illusory. In effect, the state is now pushing its luck and may become the victim of its own rhetoric; instead of accepting that a certain degree of political relativity ("segmentation") is probably inevitable, and that the same metaphors of blood relationship that united the country also have powerful roots in the logic of feud, it has refused to see that too confrontational a view of localist sentiment presupposes (and thereby creates) a sense of equivalence and, in consequence, grounds for secessionist sentiment.

It is no longer a question of the Greeks versus the minorities: minorities do not necessarily, at least in a moral sense, conceive of themselves as such, whatever the statistical situation (Ardener 1978). Rather, it is now a struggle between roughly equivalent ethnic entities, in which—because the old relativities no longer obtain—the state cannot tolerate the existence of cultural entities claiming to have ethnic identity separate from that of the dominant majority. It is worth thinking about why that should be so.

One of the enabling conditions for this hardening of positions is, paradoxically, the persistence in nation-statist discourse of the very features of localism that the state most abhors: devotion to family as the primary locus of solidarity, patrilineal ideologies capable of achieving massive violence, solidarity of the blood. In a characteristic exercise in metaphorical expansionism, the state expropriates the language of kinship, treating familistic interests as inimical to the common family of the nation; but this strategy, in a country where family values are still very strongly held (and indeed are recognized as such by the state), can easily backfire when some of the family members, especially those whose membership is in dispute, behave like strangers. It creates the means of dissent against itself. As a striking example, one need search no further than the moment when Palestinian *fedayin*—in an obvious evocation of the *Exodus* story from World War II—sailed a boatload of Palestinian exiles into the waters off Haifa harbor: suddenly the Israeli authorities found themselves internationally cast in the role of their predecessors, the British Mandate authorities.

But the object of these ruminations is not to go over already well-traveled territory. I want, rather, to sketch the probable consequences of the literalization of national identity that characterizes nationalism, with a particular focus on the Greek case. For the Greek success in naturalizing an ethnic identity as nationhood is but one example of the larger effectiveness of nationalism around the world. It is an extreme case for, in part, a linguistic reason. The language of ethnicity is based on a Greek root (*ethnos*), which in Greek also incorporates virtually the entire range of terminology for nationhood and nationalism. This leads to semantic conflations that do not reflect international usage; Greek commentators may in a sense have become the victims of their own linguistic ideology, according to which the historical primacy of Greek makes any discussion of the meaning of Greek-derived terms in other languages a matter for authoritative Greek expertise. And West European and North American commentators are victims of their success in persuading the Greeks of that primacy, since they now find it virtually impossible to engage Greek diplomats or other commentators in the establishment of an internationally transparent terminology.

Anthropology has not been entirely successful in reaching a consensus either (see Eriksen 1993; Li Causi 1995). The tendency to literalize, to seek the essence of a particular kind of identity, is as tempting as it is misguided. In this chapter, I address this literalizing tendency, and suggest that treating national identity as an elaborate metaphor is much more useful as a distancing device. Although those who have a vested interest in maintaining the status quo of the nation-state may not find this approach to their taste, it has the virtue of grounding analysis in empirical research among those most directly affected in everyday life.

Consider, for example, that the entire discourse of familism is, as a self-description of the nation-state, openly and aggressively metaphorical. Official discourse pretends to abhor any language that is not precise, including metaphor, because such language threatens the totalizing semantic control on which every state system must to some extent rely. Literalism, however, sets up the grounds for a particular kind of rhetorical contest. Like generates like; consequently, the impetus toward ethnic self-determination may actually be a byproduct of the nation-statism with which it is so often contrasted. By demanding demographic precision, statist ideologies create the basis for their own subsequent dissection.

Greece offers a particularly good case study precisely because it is, *prima facie*, such an unlikely site of ethnic resurgence. A small country with a population of around ten million, it counts as ethnic Greeks the overwhelming majority of its inhabitants. Successive population exchanges (notably with Bulgaria in 1912 and with Turkey in 1924) have "purified" the landscape. The remaining minority communities are very small, although recent events regarding both the Macedonian and the Turkish communities (to use their terms of self-designation) suggest that demography is not the most significant touchstone. The danger of territorial claims by neighboring nations is often mentioned as a cause for alarm, and it is probably because of this factor that the Turkish and Macedonian minorities attract the most active assimilation programs of the Greek state as well as its deepest suspicion. But other groups, both ethnic and religious, also suffer various forms of discrimination; for example, the Jehovah's Witnesses' refusal to bear arms makes them militarily innocuous but, because it violates indigenous ideas about Greek national pride, exposes them to sometimes severe legal sanctions (see Pollis 1987).

Images of existence: essentialism as metaphor

Tambiah (1989) alerts us to the ways in which nation-states, by building on their underlying metaphors of formation, may provoke relatively disenfranchised groups, notably "minorities," into coalescing into directly analogous entities. While he largely tackles the inadequacies of the nation-state concept to describe the most recent eruptions of violence and thereby moves beyond Anderson's (1983) "imagined communities," I want to go still further and argue that ethnicity itself is not only a highly problematic phenomenon, one that is perhaps only capturable in a state of "emergence" and as "style" (Royce 1982), but also a product, in its extraordinary tendency toward self-reification, of the nation-state's status as a reified model of sociality.

I want to suggest also, using the Greek case as a limiting one (because the minorities, by the Greeks' own argument, are so small), that the implicit patrilinearity of the kinship models thereby invoked is highly compatible with violence. If, therefore, we see today a mild upsurge in ethnic self-determination in Greece, this is largely a consequence, not only of external pressures, but also of the state's own production of ethnicity. Moreover, in Greece the problem is further exacerbated by the fact that ethnicity and nation are conflated in a single term, *ethnos*. This makes the potential for disaster enormous, and indeed quite out of proportion to the strictly demographic scale of the problem. It also makes the Greek case interesting for comparative purposes, as does the fact that Greek reactions to minority attitudes are overdetermined by the discourse of orientalism and Eurocentrism: communists are Slavs and as such not fully European; most other minorities are non-Christian and represent the dangers of the East or, like the Gypsies and Jehovah's Witnesses, defy definition and thus constitute symbolic "pollution" in Douglas's (1966) sense—"matter out of place," the very substance of cultural intimacy.

It is hardly surprising that nationalist ideologies should resort frequently and inventively to metaphor, or, conversely, that they should be hostile to the idea that metaphor is central to their discourse. Pragmatically, at least, these are by no means mutually incompatible positions. In order to make this point clearer, and to delineate something of its significance, I would like to allude briefly to a recent study by G.E.R. Lloyd (1990) of the popular concept of social or cultural "mentality."

Lloyd takes issue with a tradition—largely originated by Lucien Lévy-Bruhl and elaborated by a host of anthropologists, *Annales* historians, sociologists, and psychologists—that characterizes whole cultures in terms of a collective mental disposition, or mentality (*mentalité*). These mentalities are more broadly divided into "prelogical" and "modern" types. Lloyd rejects the whole thesis, largely on the grounds that to be useful mentalities would have to be objectively discrete, whereas the evidence offers no such convenient assurance. I do not have the space to rehearse Lloyd's sophisticated argument in detail here, but wish to retain two aspects of it.

First, Lloyd suggests that the psychologistic reasoning that permits us to divide the world's cultures in so summary a fashion reflects our own prejudices more than it demonstrates observable regularities in non-Western societies in general. This is part of what Kuper (1988) has called the invention of primitive society;

it has also become a common feature of educated nonprofessional talk about the world's cultures. Second, Lloyd suggests that the foundation of such arguments, the idea that primitives use metaphor where their sophisticated contemporaries would use only literal discourse, harkens back to the eristic management of ideas about truth in pre-Classical and Classical Greek courts. Thus, the abstract questions of metaphor and literalness to which Aristotle brough such careful elaboration were grounded in contest—in the agonistic relations that, as ethnographers have repeatedly insisted, are also characteristic of the modern societies of the region (see Peristiany 1965). Lloyd mischievously implies that modern academic debates about literalness exhibit much the same social quality, for reasons clearly accessible in the social history of ideas. The distinction between the literal and the metaphorical thus emerges as grounded, not in universal truth, but in the conditions under which it is given shape; it exists only insofar as it is socially created.

The first of these points, the conceptual poverty of hard-and-fast divisions between logical and prelogical mentalities, is directly relevant to the study of present-day nationalist discourse in Greece and surrounding countries. Greek discussion of differences between the Greek national character and that of the other peoples of the area often turns on the nebulous but evocative concept of *noötropia*, which is a close approximation to *mentalité*. It handily explains away both the strange vagaries of visitors, especially tourists, and the fierce insistence on personal pride and independence on which so many Greeks vocally pride themselves. It is a description of certain stereotypical vices or virtues. As such, it has no analytical value, but it is to be regretted that obvious derivation from scholarly locution has deflected attention away from the enormous currency it enjoys as a term of popular speech. Anthropologists have ignored it, perhaps out of a sense of embarrassment: it purports to describe the very foundations of culture, yet clearly serves instead as a carrier of the kinds of generalizations that most anthropologists would prefer to avoid and regret in the early history of their own discipline.

I would urge instead that we approach it with all due seriousness—ethnographically. That is, we should not treat it as an analytical construct for studying national differences, but as an artifact used in the construction of those differences and as an important link in the relationship between nationalism and scholarship.

Lloyd's second point, about the historical and social origins of Aristotelian literalism, may seem at first blush to be far removed from the scene of modern ethnic and national rivalries. And yet, I suggest, this is not so: for, if the literal-metaphorical distinction indeed emerges as a function of discursive contest rather than of inherently logical properties, as Lloyd suggests, its prominence as both an explicit problematic and an underlying dimension of contests over territory and identity becomes immediately more understandable. Nation-states spend enormous amounts of effort on denying the reality of each other's existence. This is the crux of what Geertz (1973: 240–241), in an early anthropological discussion of nationalist ideology, called "essentialism." It is not merely the attribution of innate characteristics, including a specific national mentality, but the conflation of images with experienced reality.

Benedict Anderson's argument is particularly pertinent here. His work does not specifically address the metaphorical character of nationalist doctrines, but the creation of a suppositious commonality—so often realized in assertions like "I can always tell my compatriots from the way they walk, talk, move, and so on"—is both metonymical (each citizen is a microcosm of the encompassing whole) and metaphorical (each citizen is a version of the national character or mentality). As we have seen in chapter two, this also explains the extraordinarily important role of similarity in forging national solidarities.

An important part of Lloyd's discussion of metaphor hinges on the fact that ultimately it makes little sense to say that something is (or is not) a metaphor. What happens is that the metaphorical basis of the labels we give all entities is pushed into the background. Nationalism is a doctrine of reification. In its usual terms, a nation either exists or does not exist: reality, constituted in these uncompromising terms, generates other, counterposed realities of a similar order (neighboring nations, the enemy, foreign interference); and the symbolic production of a unifying discourse, so often launched with benign goals of collective emancipation, all too rapidly becomes instead a call to arms. Reality has supervened, with disastrous results.

The case of Cyprus is a tragically appropriate illustration of this process; that of Crete before it points up the character of the tragedy. On both islands, over long periods, Greek-speaking Christians and Muslims lived side by side, separated by their respective religions but conjoined in certain ritual practices of local significance and by ties of reciprocity that would be enacted in dramatic public displays on special occasions such as major feast-days. Yet virtually the entire Muslim population of Crete was shipped off to Asia Minor in 1924, while the current hardening of "ethnic" lines between "Greeks" and "Turks" on Cyprus further illustrates the transformation of identities into ethnicity and thence into nationality—a progression that has brought little but disruption and death to the local communities and transmuted local norms of feuding into national "causes" (see Loizos 1988).

Metaphorical usages may also slip easily between very different levels of social inclusiveness. As I have observed elsewhere (Herzfeld 1985a), the Cretan shepherds who adopt aggressive poses of village manhood may also, under appropriate circumstances, work simultaneously on family and national sentiments of solidarity as well. An important aspect of the approach I am advocating here, and in all my work, concerns the parallelisms that subsist among multiple levels of identity. When we study a village community, without intending any claims of typicality we are not *only* studying that community; we are also engaged with several other social entities, overlapping or concentric, clearly or weakly defined, officially recognized or contrary to the social values of the bureaucratic state. In Greece, the state recognizes kinship bilaterally, for example, yet agnatic kinship comes to the fore when the crises of a feuding society supervene, constituting a real challenge to state authority since the official definition of the nation is framed in mutedly agnatic terms.

The parallels among levels of social identification must be studied ethnographically. They do not ordinarily appear in the official pronouncements of the bureaucracy, the political parties, or the national media. They are nonetheless vitally important if we are to understand the perspective of those whose loyalty the state seeks to command.

Let me offer an example (described in detail in Herzfeld 1985a: 9–10). An elderly Cretan ex-shepherd, a former mayor of the village steeped in the heroic legends of resistance against Turks and Germans, recalled the defense of the Arkadi monastery in 1866, when after a ferocious battle some Greek villagers and monks were cornered by the Turks and blew themselves up rather than surrender. Several Glendiots perished in the explosion. The old man characteristically approaches these events from the perspective of his agnatic group, singing of his paternal grandfather and namesake's exploits at Arkadi. The identification is so strong that he is moved to uncontrollable tears. Is he, at that moment, celebrating kin, local, Cretan, or Greek identity? Only a literalist would insist that we should choose only one level of identification, for his performance resonates at all of them. Yet this adumbration of concentric loyalties runs counter to the exclusivism of nation-state ideology. While the old man might wish to identify with the national ideal, his message is always potentially subversive, because it raises the possibility that one of the less inclusive levels of solidarity might eventually prevail and command a more immediate attachment.

In Crete, perhaps, the authorities have little to worry about. Even when such rebelliousness still occurs there, it is usually represented as heroic, typically Greek, and redolent of a love of independence; and the freewheeling sheep-thieves of the hill country cultivate such reappropriations of nationalist discourse with gleeful assiduity. What of the non-Greek speaking people of other areas?

Here the evidence is muddy at best. A major part of the problem is that the principal instrument of research into such matters is the census. Whether or not the occasional doubts about the accuracy and motivation of the census have any foundation in fact, as an instrument it encourages reification. People must either speak one language or two; the census is incapable of registering the evanescent subtleties of code-switching (see Tsitsipis 1983). They must register an official religion; the confusions of local cults, in which the participation of Muslims and Christians together was an occasional feature in the past, has no place here. In short, the census is not only insensitive to the indeterminacies of social and cultural dynamics at the local level, it is almost certainly the catalyst for the very processes of reification that it alone can register accurately. While the Greek census is exactly like any other in this respect, it should be said that inbuilt exclusions such as that of the Macedonian minority may have done more to create that category than any propagandizing from Skopje or Thessaloniki. It may well be that in the census we see more clearly than anywhere else the paradoxical dynamics that permit the state to generate the most serious challenge to its own hegemony. That challenge is a consequence of the mutual dependence of official and popular idioms of identity, a situation that also strongly influences the paradoxical dynamics of cultural intimacy (see chapters 4–5).

It is worth asking ourselves at this juncture what lessons could be learned from recent events in the former East Bloc countries. There, the collapse of centralized Marxist regimes has brought in its train a disturbing intensification of ethnic factionalism. The growing spate of anti-Semitism and persecution of Gypsies and the feuding between Hungary and Romania over Transylvania draft popular prejudices in the service of aggressive new nationalisms (Kligman 1990). What is the cause of such developments, and what light can they shed on the superficially different scene in Greece?

Democracy (or, better, "democratization") is not necessarily equivalent to greater tolerance. On the contrary, as Kapferer (1988) has shown for Australia (see also Bottomley and Lechte 1991), the logic of tolerance, which comes under such names as "multiculturalism" and "cultural diversity," may heighten the sense of otherness and arrogate the egalitarian perquisites of democracy to a majority group. In Australia, the white majority particularly resists the incursion of strangers to its symbolically elevated "mateship" (significantly, an androcentric image). In Greece, the ambiguity of hospitality (Herzfeld 1987b) is an expression of inequality, which only an intimate can level; a stranger must always remain *ipokhreomenos*, under obligation.

Thus, we should not be surprised that the democratization of Bulgaria, Romania, and Yugoslavia should actually have increased ethnic tensions and discrimination against disenfranchised minorities. For one thing, minorities, notably the Jews, have often been accused of siding with the old regimes. Then again, the rhetoric of an exclusive kin group, which (with the exception of Romania) went into abeyance under the internationalist communist regimes, returns now as the basis of a new exclusivism. The language of blood has returned, and with it a greatly increased risk of literal bloodshed: in Bosnia, the pattern of rape, infanticide, and murder recasts the logic of agnatic feuding in terms of a terrible violence, with which it then returns to haunt local communities in the most destructive way as an external force rupturing local affective bonds and leading to irreversible hostility (see Bringa 1995). In vain the Bosnian Muslims tried to emphasize confessional community rather than blood, as Bringa (1995: 32–33) notes; the rhetoric of blood was too widespread in the region, and too easily understood by the cynical Western interests that sustained post-Yugoslav ethnonationalism, to yield its long-established primacy to more peaceful images.

This agnatic logic is also present, in muted form, in Greek nationalist discourse: the "Greek blood" of which Just writes belongs to that idiom. It is worth recalling in this context that Greeks view blood as a thoroughly flexible symbol: the emotionally "boiling blood" of brothers, for example, leads them to embrace each other fervently after long years of absence, but, by the same token, can also lead to hatred and killing when the relationship sours—usually, significantly enough for our purposes, over territorial disputes. In the national arena, the boundary fence separating fields inherited from a common set of parents becomes the international boundary over which nation-states go to war.

The Greek nation appears in early nationalistic discourse under the thin disguise of an agnatic grouping, *to genos* (pronounced *yenos*). This term, an artifact of official discourse with its origins in a romantic reading of Classical Athenian society, may be glossed locally by such terms as *yenia* that also carry agnatic implications in many parts of the country (Herzfeld 1983a, 1985a). Such idioms are also extremely common beyond the national borders of Greece: in the former Yugoslavia, for example, where agnatic kinship is in some areas much more pronounced than even in the most extreme cases in Greece (Hammel 1968; Boehm 1984; cf. Couroucli 1985; Herzfeld 1985a; Alexakis 1980), the language of blood and revenge informs the emergence of national leadership (see Boehm 1984). In Romania, long a contestant against Greek interests for the mantle of Classical presence in the Balkans (see Campbell 1964: 3–6), the Ceauşescu regime adopted a similar rhetoric of patrilinearity (Kligman 1990). It may be that some of these idioms are of Turkish origin (see Delaney 1995), but they also correspond to strongly held local usages. In any event, it is important to remember the common symbolic ground that these countries share—a property also present in more muted guise in Western European countries that consider themselves long shed of such embarrassing hints of prehistory.

Thus, the central concept of blood is not uniquely Greek or even Balkan—indeed, it has a long history in Indo-European and Semitic cultures as a marker of social inclusiveness—but it does appear to play an unusually prominent role in discussions of the perceived threat to Greek cultural and even territorial survival. It is apparent in government pronatalist policies (in the form of official support for families with many children) and in antiassimilationist drives by the Greek authorities in the diaspora. In the diaspora, moreover, it provides an appealing device that seems to transcend the barriers of prejudice against charges of Balkan atavism. A former U.S. Assistant Secretary of Commerce, Andrew Manatos, is reported as saying, "The dilution of Greek blood in the United States is because nearly 90 percent of Greek-Americans are marrying non-Greek-Americans. This marriage pattern is due to the fact that Greek-Americans are becoming less ethnically Greek" (*The Greek-American Herald*, 12 December 1995, 24). This alarm appears in the context of concerns about a weakening of the Greek lobby's support in the face of threats thought to emanate from Ankara and Skopje. It is clear that the symbol of blood translates into familiar terms—as central to modern American kinship ideology as they are in the ancient European world (Linke 1985; Schneider 1968)—the larger fears that Greeks entertain about their collective weakness in the world today.

In the United States and most of Western Europe, the agnatic implications of this ideology are well concealed (but cf. Delaney 1995). In most of the Balkan regions, these more focused meanings still subsist at the level of local-level feuds (the Hatfields and McCoys strike most Americans as belonging to an irrecoverable past). Given their still mundane visibility, their escalation to the level of ethnic conflict can be managed by skilled political actors. This seems to have played a large part in the Bosnian conflagration, and—since feuding relations entail fusion as well as schism—the apparent shift in both Greece and Albania toward at least symbolic expressions of unity in the face of collective threat.

I do not wish to suggest that Greece is about to face a massive increase in ethnic violence. The minorities there are all too small to constitute a real threat in that sense. The problem lies much more in the official perception that hostile foreign governments might use the presence of minorities on Greek soil to advance irredentist goals. The past has shown that such fears are not entirely unfounded and that Greece is probably right not to put much faith in Western support in the event of a major confrontation. Nevertheless, the increasing prominence of minority spokespersons and parties and the continuing vein of nationalist exclusivism in official rhetoric cause politicians and the public alike considerable concern. At the very least, they suggest that the logic of the nation-state provides a model for its own destabilization from within. Spicer's (1992) model of the oppositional development of ethnogenesis has direct relevance to the Balkans. Once launched on the path of confrontation, this process is extremely resistant to restraint.

What are the practical implications of focusing on the metaphorical character of blood in this context? Numerous anthropologists (e.g., Fernandez 1986; Sapir and Crocker 1977) have paid close attention to the uses of metaphor in negotiating identity. If Fernandez is right in seeing metaphor as the predication of a comprehensible sign upon an inchoate subject and to suggest that the subject of the person represents one of the most common targets of this device, the unstable lines that divide outsiders from insiders in the Greek context are a rich field for metaphorical exploration. Greeks recognize in their political discourse a high degree of personification. Political analysts have associated this with a wide range of phenomena, from strong clientelism (Campbell 1964; Kharalambis 1989; Legg 1969) to a very unfamiliar conception of civil rights (Pollis 1987). A constant refrain in media discussions has it that Greeks always treat political events as personally motivated. This does not mean that they necessarily believe that such is the case, but it does suggest that metaphors of solidarity based on affronts to the collective pride will effectively stir up emotional responses. This is clearly the case.

But the idea of metaphor is itself not value free in the Greek setting. Peter Mackridge (1985: 348) draws attention to the way in which public and literary discourse in Greece appears inimical to metaphor. The frequent use of quotation marks around anything that might stray too far from the literal is a common stylistic feature, while newpapers tend to use hackneyed metaphors that are too close to death to do much harm. Such protection of the very idea of referentiality harmonizes accurately with the fears of a nation-state unsure of its claims to unity. The state is the very embodiment of the literal—perhaps nowhere more so than in Greece, where Enlightenment-derived discourse masks a rich array of ambiguities about law, entitlement, and morality (Tsoucalas 1991). In popular discourse, this is supported by ideas about genuine (*ghnisios*) identities and tremendous confusion about categories—such as that of the Jews—for whom identity does not necessarily conflate descent, religion, language, and territory. Thus, to suggest that the *ethnos* is metaphorically constructed shakes the foundations of personal as well as collective ontology.

Under these circumstances one may legitimately ask whether the very term ethnicity might beg more questions than it can possibly answer. Given the Greek origins of the term, many commentators have found it especially slippery semantically in the context of modern Greek cultural politics. Greek public discourse does not admit of the possibility of ambiguity in the definition of the *ethnos*, for which the base model is the Greek nation itself, but it is precisely this semantic invariance that has furnished the most accessible model to other cultural and social entities struggling to find the means of expressing collective identities. In place of a pluralistic vision it offers only the option of generating increasing numbers of mutually hostile "nationalities."

Among European and especially Balkan nation-states, Greece is unusual in the extent to which it is able to make convincing claims to ethnic and cultural homogeneity. It may well be that the dangers Greece faces internally are not as great as the scenario I have just described would suggest. Why do the Greek authorities continue to pound away at this theme, when, that is, by most countries' standards, they have every right to treat it as already successfully managed? Doubtless, as Pollis (1987) has argued, part of the answer lies in anxieties about the unclear definition of rights, a concept that has been absorbed as a piece of rhetorical weaponry without its philosophical underlay. Doubtless, too, the territorial disputes of Greece with neighboring countries lend urgency to the issue: they certainly seem to explain, for example, the denial of Macedonian ethnic identity and the insistence that Thracian Muslims "are not Turks." (The Bulgarian "solution" to its "Turkish problem" has been much less palatable still: it was to force the Turkish minority to leave.)

But I have suggested here that another factor must be taken into account. That is the well-concealed but ever-present lability of Greek political entities. Today's localism could become tomorrow's separatism, and the fact that—while denying that they use metaphor—politicians on every side use metaphors of the embattled person to address issues of cultural boundary creation cannot offer much comfort for the future. Further comparisons with the Balkans and beyond may show a strong correlation between the use of person-based metaphors of the body politic and the tendency to turn a deaf ear on pleas for ethnic self-determination, leading in turn to ever more insistent reaching for referentiality by the disenfranchised populations. In other words, the real danger is internal to the dynamics of Greek politics.

This, then, is the practical issue: a country wishing to avoid a potential ethnic explosion can hardly afford to maintain the confrontational politics that lead to an ever greater hardening of the categories on every side. Nationalistic discourses that seek to suppress internal differentiation, whether at the level of local sociocultural peculiarities or at that of minority calls for self-determination, simply aggravate the problem they are trying to defuse. Hypersensitivity to outside curiosity—to invasions, as it were, of cultural intimacy—breeds ridicule among a country's more powerful international patrons and in the alliances of which the country is a member. This in turn creates a notable lack of sympathy for extravagant calls that may mask very real anxieties, as the Greek experience over Macedonia has painfully demonstrated. The constant harping on Greece's claim to "real" European status, discussed later on in this book (chapter 5), exemplifies another of the less successful defenses of cultural intimacy for political purposes.

Intransigent "ethnonationalism," to use the term developed by Tambiah (1989) as a contrast with more pluralistic idioms of citizenship, provides the model for the battles to which, sooner or later, its own logic is liable to lead.[1] Vico warned of the importance of remembering the embodied and material basis of the metaphors from which even the most abstract terminology and even the most formal idioms of power are derived. Again and again ethnonationalism has proved susceptible to the siren song of referentiality—the call of the literal. As its metaphorical basis—whether as an "imagined community" or more specifically as a brotherhood of agnatic blood—fades from sight, as it becomes essentialized as more and more of a present and unchangeable reality in the people's lives, it can only reproduce itself. The Bosnian experience is not a display of Balkan atavism, as it has become dangerously conventional to assert. It is a lesson in what may happen anywhere when this process, cynically encouraged from outside, is allowed to run its course. Nervousness about internal diversity will not make this problem go away. On the contrary, it is the most threatening element in a situation in which the dangers may not yet be very great. That is the sad irony of many once tranquil nations now drenched in the blood of ethnic strife—and a warning to anthropologists too easily inclined to reify the fluidity of multiple and complex identities into a unified notion of ethnicity.

Chapter Five

Cultural Intimacy and the Meaning of Europe

Essentialism and the Balkans

In the recent brawling over the political mayhem in the Balkans, a dangerous prejudice masquerades as an analytical perspective. It is a prejudice far more deeply and more insidiously entrenched than the atavism that it claims to have identified in Balkan society at large, and that it cites as the pretext for condescension and hegemony. It is the view that pits the allegedly rational democracies of Western Europe against states whose European identity is itself at issue—states that are variously characterized as unstable, kinship based, and small scale. The irony of this perspective is of course that the language in which it is couched is itself that of kinship: that of the stern parent chastising a wayward and fractious brood of children. Unhappily, not only does this paternalistic mode of thought pervade the rhetoric of global and regional *Realpolitik* but it has also become a dominant idiom of analysis. Well may we wonder about the resulting ideological entailment of analysis in its object of study.[1]

It is not my purpose to claim a privileged immunity from such charges for social anthropology; indeed, that discipline has been much criticized for its own embedded colonialism.[2] I do want to suggest, however, that the ethical imperatives behind the discipline's massive self-examination have certainly also raised the stakes in terms of the quality of scholarship, by divorcing it more securely than ever before from the kind of unthinking essentialism that led to talk of "Balkan atavism" and other crude culture-area stereotypes. Indeed, arguments about the mission of anthropology that pit "science" against "morality" partake of the same essentializing and binary discourse in which the panoply of rationalist language serves as the preeminent symbol of late twentieth-century authority, and thus they fail to achieve the detachment they claim as their defining virtue. Moreover, in this discourse "rationality" often serves as a proxy for the equally essentialized West—what the Greeks call "Europe."[3] Thus the vicissitudes of anthropology in Europe give us a particularly illuminating ethnographic perspective on the dynamics of cultural intimacy.

Ironically, this tactic is made possible by turning to one of the most traditional features of anthropological investigation: the conduct of long-term field research in highly localized, usually small communities in which research means above all access to relations of intimacy. The anthropological approach to political life has always been characterized by a focus on the local community. Even when national and international issues are at stake, analysis has always centered on the experiences of people the ethnographer has known under conditions of relative intimacy.[4]

The intensity and personal commitment of this focus have their costs. Anthropological work evokes resentment and, at times, downright hostility in some local intellectuals, who tend to dismiss its concerns as immaterial and (in a quite literal sense) inessential. But these reactions, especially as they are not shared by all local observers, indicate that the research has uncovered something significant—if not, why the fuss? Such reactions are diagnostic: they betray the underlying assumptions and so create the best conditions for an ethnographic examination of elite cosmologies and of the nation-state itself. For while media discourse provides a national-level ethnographic mode analogous to village-level gossip (Herzfeld 1992b), it is the active engagement of anthropology by elite members, sometimes also through the media, that puts the "participant" into the "participant observation" of fieldwork "in" the nation-state. Local anthropologists, who have rightly criticized their foreign colleagues' reluctance to engage with the rate of social and cultural change, especially in the cities, have nevertheless acknowledged that the older studies offer a necessary baseline for evaluating change, which itself may in part be constituted by a cultural rhetoric, even a kind of structural nostalgia, about the confusions of a continually updated "nowadays" (Bakalaki 1993: 57).

Such is the argument for a specifically ethnographic analysis of the nation-state—an analysis that also incorporates, but is not exhausted by, the many more localized studies of villages and towns, and of bureaucratic and other formal institutions. In the sense that a remote village, while not in any analytically useful sense typical of an entire country, may nonetheless serve to draw out some of the latter's more distinctive self-typifications,[5] a single European country may similarly throw the construction of European identity into critical relief.

I shall pursue this analytical strategy with regard to places that have themselves been strikingly marginal to the international power structures, particularly to Greece. In this, I am pushing that strategy as far as I think it will go.[6] The strategy, in effect, makes both the anthropological intervention and the reactions that it elicits a means of gauging what is at stake for nationalistic discourses in the promotion of a particular self-image and its calibration to a particular reading of "Europe." If anthropological interest evokes such intense irritation and anger, there is presumably a reason. What I wish to suggest is that the anthropological demand for intimate access to the body politic violates state monopolies of representation in ways that reveal how those monopolies operate, what they control, and why they matter. This is a classic anthropological move: it examines the stakes that leaders and "high culture" critics may have in what they nevertheless brusquely dismiss to inquisitive outsiders as peripheral or trivial phenomena. As the editors of a recent exploration of beauty pageants point out, gendered and other bodily images of the ideal provide an accessible site for observing the dissonance masked by the smiling faces of national harmony (Cohen, Stoeltje, and Wilk 1996: 6–10), putatively a Western harmony at that. It would be hard to find a better metaphor for cultural intimacy.

A focus on such matters may usefully discommode received ideas about "common sense" or "rationality," a longstanding anthropological concern (see Carrier 1995c; Douglas 1975; Geertz 1983; Herzfeld 1992a; Lloyd 1990; Tambiah 1990). Just as J. L. Austin based his "plea for excuses" (Austin [1956–57] 1971) on the apparent triviality of excuses as breaching unprotected cultural defenses to give major insights into a whole moral universe, so I would argue that it is the very mereness of what anthropologists mostly describe—the "stories" of everyday life—that breaches the sense of a unitary History that nationalist ideologies promote. This, then, is a plea for anecdotes. The point is not to irritate for irritation's sake, but simply to respond to an irritation that already exists in order to discover what it portends. The answer will prove, I think, unexpectedly sympathetic to the predicament of the irritated, although they themselves may well not be terribly reassured.

This is because nationalism, especially in its more hegemonic forms that deny recognition to minority interests, often reproduces still larger power structures. As a result, local elites find themselves between a rock and a hard place: they cannot afford to admit to the international community the existence of internal disunities, yet their refusal to acknowledge such fissures saps their credibility before knowledgeable audiences at home and abroad.

This is especially applicable to the nationalisms of those very countries whose political marginality makes the defense of a particular cultural reading especially crucial for the country's survival. Again, this can be said of no country more dramatically than Greece. So overshadowed by an illustrious past—largely constructed for it by its self-appointed "protectors"—that it must humiliatingly always append the suffix "modern" to its name, Greece nevertheless often finds that these self-same protectors change the rules of the game they have insisted on playing with that country. It is hardly surprising, then, that classicists who wish to import anthropological approaches into their work sometimes now run afoul of a "challenged sense of ethnic and national identity" restive, to say the least, at the prospect of yet more studies of marginal populations (Cartledge 1994: 4).

But that marginality is—and perhaps the embarrassment lies right here—a small-scale model of the predicament of Greece as a country. I want to argue for maintaining (although not to the exclusion of all else) a critical ethnographic watch on the nation's cultural peripheries for the same reason that Greece itself is such an important test case for the significance of "Europe." At both levels, political marginality and the idea of historical centrality are bound tightly together: tradition is the nourishment of national identity, just as Hellas is of Europe.

At the international level, this evokes roughly the same reactions as one finds in official state circles toward the strongly localist orientation of many Greek bureaucrats and politicians. In both cases, the defense of local interests derives in part from the support of powerful patrons, who have every interest in essentializing it as endemic. Internationally, at least, that link is often conveniently ignored: stereotypes provide convenient justifications. Thus, both American policymakers and Greece's European Union partners constantly express deep exasperation at the Greeks' Balkan policy and the Greeks' evocation of a millennia-deep history. One highly placed American commentator unhelpfully declared, "Greece is reminding the world that it too is a Balkan country, the inhabitant of a region where history often induces hysteria" (Talbott 1992). Such gratuitous generalizations must be read in the context of a global moral economy that overdetermined Greece's past at the price of its present independence.

The essentializers—both academic and political (and these are not always discrete groups)—see in such alleged proclivities the evidence they seek of a rift between Western and Balkan ways of doing things (notably Huntington 1993). This idiom, I suggest, is in fact both a diagnostic feature and an integral part of the problem itself. If history is the object of fierce contest, so is objectivity, that supposed product of Western rationality. Consequently, the continual Greek exhortations to foreign visitors to "study history," for example, presuppose that this activity can only have one outcome. Disputed pasts illustrate perfectly my argument that essentialism is a strategy that denies its own existence: no party to such a conflict can ever admit the possibility of multiple answers or of ambiguity. But that is in no sense a peculiarly Balkan problem.

The particular issue of Macedonia is embedded in a long process whereby Greece has been required to plead its value in the modern world on the basis of its selectively reconstructed ancient past; yet what past is *not* selectively reconstructed? The point here is not to approve Greek denials of minority rights, but to situate the problem in the larger context of an international politics of culture, a context in which sensitivity to the violation of cultural intimacy has economic, territorial, and long-term political significance.

Thus, I prefer to read competing national histories as versions, on the scale of international relations, of what Bourdieu, writing of the more modest domain of social life, has called "cultural capital" (Bourdieu 1984). And it is the possibility of applying this instrument of social and symbolic analysis to questions of global *Realpolitik* that particularly alerts us to the possible significance of ethnography—the point at which anthropological analysis connects with everyday experience—for understanding the dynamics of today's fractious Europe. While the Macedonian conflict has preoccupied many regional specialists in the closing years of the twentieth century, as a dramatic contest over cultural as well as economic and territorial resources it typifies a situation in which Western essentializations of a "Balkan mentality" do little more than ensure the self-fulfillment of convenient prophecies. They add insult to injury, perpetuating the rhetoric through which Western interference helped lock the Balkan states into the pattern that the same external forces now mock. It is in this field of political forces that we must read the current predicaments of anthropological research.

This is not only an analysis of Greece. It is a discussion of why a Europe without the fair and full representation of Greek interests will merely lead to ever more repetitions of the political stance that maintains the Greeks' maverick status as a threat to European unity. It is, to illustrate the larger principle with a specific example, about why Greek resentment over the Franco-German attempt to remove Greek from the roster of official European Union languages—the argument was that a reduction to five languages made for greater efficiency—exposes the self-reproducing proclivities of a hegemony in which Greece has become inextricably engaged. It is also an attempt to read from local reactions to anthropological research a more sensitive understanding of the politics of cultural scholarship, not as an incestuous field of backstabbing relevant only to the players and perhaps a few talented novelists, but as an integral part of the larger international dynamic. This chapter is about the politics of mereness. Should Greece be considered merely Balkan? Are the concerns of anthropology merely anecdotal and marginal to national realities? I intend to show that such questions reveal the contours of a vast field of political play.

This chapter should thereby also help to sharpen the definition of cultural intimacy, which, for immediate purposes, can be understood as the sharing of known and recognizable traits that not only define insiderhood but are also felt to be disapproved by powerful outsiders. The term's hints of domesticity are especially apposite in the context of nationalism, which is commonly characterized by a projection of kinship metaphors onto the larger scale of the nation—in other words, the metonymic extension of the face-to-face *Gemeinschaft* that constitutes the ethnographer's traditional arena of operation.[7] It is a familiar dilemma: to return for a moment to the self-presentation of flight attendants, trainees are trained to accept "home" as "an idea without an immediate referent" as they move from one base city to another (Hochschild 1983: 100). The stretching of domesticity is routinized in actual experience.

This projection of kinship is what most of all gives the lie to attempts to represent the modern centralized polity as radically different from such acephalous and supposedly kinship-based societies as the Nuer.[8] More remarkably still in the context of that Eurocentric perspective, patrilineality—although analytically a separate issue from segmentation—plays an important role in images common to most forms of European nationalism, usually in the rhetoric of blood, as discussed in the previous chapter.

In Evans-Pritchard's description of the Nuer, it becomes apparent that while agnatic kinship substantially sets the organization of social relations at the more intimate levels, it becomes more and more tenuous as the scale of social connections expands. Thus, the patrilines represented by the largest groups are, in a literal sense, largely fictitious. The same is no less true, I suggest, of the "fatherland" idiom that Delaney (1995) has skillfully identified as a pervasive feature of secularist Turkish nationalism, which shares with its Western European antecedents deep historical and ideological roots in the Abrahamic religions. In this regard the avowedly secular or Western nation-state is grounded in the metonymic stretching, to extend Anderson's useful portrayal, of the agnatic imagination.

Hence cultural intimacy. It is no accident that the pat Greek phrase for the defense of that intimacy, often heard as a reason for not discussing admitted weaknesses of the nationalist argument before a foreign audience, should be: *ta en iko mi en dhimo* (matters of the house [Classical Greek *oikos*] [should] not [be exposed] in the public sphere). The Classical *oikos* was apparently a productive household unit embedded in the patrilineally organized *genos*—the latter, a term often used in modern times and specifically in contexts of Romantic Greek nationalism to mean the whole Greek people conceptualized, Nuer-like, as a huge descent group. The *dhimos* (deme), the unit of social organization that underwent its own metonymic stretching to give us the term "democracy," is no place for washing the family's dirty linen—as we might express the same sentiment, using an idiom perhaps no less grounded in common European notions of the sanctity of the body and the male role in defending its privacy.[9]

It is in this context that I interpret Greek attempts to regulate the national image abroad. International spats over national images are in no sense new (see Jervis 1970: 7), nor are they uniquely Greek. They do seem to arise with striking predictability, however, over a very specific genre of disputes: those which concern a sexualized sense of national dignity. The Saudi response to British media portrayals of the execution of a royal princess and her commoner lover in 1977 illustrates this principle dramatically. The Saudi government insisted that the whole affair was an internal matter (Sassoon 1974: 36–37)—an appeal to the metaphor of domestic inviolability that reached its apogee in Greece under the military regimes of 1967–74. For the Saudi authorities the principle of privacy was thus violated twice over: first, by the sexual irruption by a commoner into the royal patriline, and, second, by the ocular penetration of a national veil of decorum by the media of a categorically uncircumcised and therefore polluting West.[10]

It is at this point that I would expect a Greek nationalist to object, not without sympathy for Saudi resentment: "We are not Muslims, and our sexual codes are the very reverse of such oriental barbarities." In so doing, however, the hypothetical nationalist—bearer of a powerful strain of post-Ottoman hostility to Islam that has already overdetermined Greek responses to the Bosnian conflict—would in fact be reproducing the Saudi stance of defending the national honor. The one key difference, to which we shall return briefly below, lies in the Greek's peculiar predicament of having to appeal to a Western orientalism (in Said's [1978] sense), but with the ironic twist that Greece itself has been represented in precisely this orientalist sense among the very powers before which it feels compelled to strike this attitude of European superiority. Clearly, orientalism is more relative and negotiable than appears to be the case in Said's textualist, and decontextualizing, perspective; and it is this property that has led me to generate a more agent-oriented view of it (Herzfeld 1991a: 16)—hence "practical orientalism."

Practical orientalism is the translation of hegemonic ideology into everyday practice so that it infiltrates the habitual spaces of ordinary experience. It is here that we can no longer afford to do without anecdotalism. For unless we can appreciate how the discourse of cultural difference enters the encompassing realm of everyday sociality and sensual habit—how it colors the visual, flavors the olfactory, and tempers the emotional—we shall never know why people are moved to follow the extraordinarily uncompelling, abstract principles of national and transnational identity. From choices between bargaining and market formalism to decisions about dress, language, and food, the people of this land situated, as they are tirelessly reminded, on the crossroads between East and West viscerally experience the pragmatic complementarities of cultural dualism. In Greece, at least, Kipling was formidably wrong: the twain—East and West—meet all the time. The Greeks struggle to keep them apart, but their difficulties in this regard are, as we shall see, overdetermined.

The Greeks have certainly had their troubles with orientalizing media representations. Perhaps the two best-known films about Greek life in the West are *Never on Sunday* and *Zorba the Greek*. Both encountered storms of opposition domestically, in large measure because of the central position they gave to themes of sexuality and revenge; these were seen as demeaning to the Greek image abroad. In particular, the scene of the widow's death by stoning in *Zorba the Greek*—note how the film title "nationalizes" the personal narrative of Nikos Kazantzakis's *Life and Social World of Alexis Zorbas*—gave enormous offense. This must be read in the context of the fact that an older tolerance for so-called honor crimes has for a long time gradually been giving way to a reluctant perception that such tolerance ill suits a civilized society (see Safilios-Rothschild 1969).

In the same way, although at the more restricted level of a locality defending its interests before a national (rather than an international) tribunal, the television serialization of Lilika Nakou's semi-autobiographical novella, *Madame Do-Re-Mi*, prompted a parliamentary demand for an official inquiry. This work ends with the humiliation of a cosmopolitan, out-of-town teacher who, struggling to understand the ferocious parochialism of a genteelly decaying provincial Cretan town, has inadvertently led her presumably virginal charges into the red-light quarter. While much of the indignation ostensibly focused on the apparent lack of hospitality displayed by the townspeople to the teacher-heroine, it is clear that the deepest source of anger lay in the exposure of sexual irregularity (and, contrarily if understandably, in the suggestion that the townspeople held backward, rural ideas about such things). Both sexuality and hospitality, in any case, are matters of a domestic pride projected onto larger social and cultural identities. In this context, it is important to recall that orientalist discourses feminize the populations they purport to describe. The anger emanated particularly from the morally as well as politically conservative town elite; leftists, more accustomed to challenging official images, were generally much happier with both the book and the film.

Less spectacularly, and without the sexual element discussed here, another purported media offense deserves brief mention. This was the decision of the state television agency to contract the British journalist David Holden to make a film about Crete. The response was a parliamentary uproar. Opposition politicians particularly demanded to know by what logic or evil design the state had entrusted the creation of a nationally significant document to "the present-day Fallmerayer"—an allusion to the nineteenth-century Tyrolean pamphleteer and ardent Pan-Germanist whose denial of the ancient heritage of the modern Greeks, intended to strike a blow against Russia by strengthening Turkey, earned him the Greeks' still unabated hatred. Holden had written a decidedly tactless book about Greece and its people under the colonels, *Greece Without Columns* (Holden 1972), in which he gratuitously derided the Greeks' seeming obsession with the ancient past and suggested that there were endemic social and moral reasons for which the country had been saddled with its detestable dictatorship. He was thus representative of the supercilious Western European discourse about Greece, and it may have been the political implications of his book rather than his specific denial of the Greeks' ancient heritage that earned him the sobriquet of "Fallmerayer."

The Greeks' unease does not only concern the vexed status of ethnic minorities, which officialy do not exist.[11] It also concerns the enormous diversity of the country's regional culture. In the past, that diversity could be treated as the multiple refraction of a transcendent homogeneity: all Greek folklores were versions of an original ancient culture, to which the leaders of a national renaissance would lead them back in triumph. But the Classical past, its hold weakened in the educational sytem as well as through an increasingly diverse intellectual reappraisal of the received historiographic wisdom, no longer exerts the unifying force on the present that it once—at least for public consumption—was able to command. In this context, an excessive focus on regional cultures might seem to encourage political anxiety while it also undercuts the universalist claims of a modernizing elite.

To exemplify the questions thus raised, I now turn to a recent study by a distinguished Greek scholar of the relevance of Greek legal history for understanding Greece's complex relations with the several encompassing administrative regimes that comprise institutional Europe (Kozyris 1993). In several key respects, his study is the antithesis of this chapter. It can also be usefully contrasted, as I shall briefly show below, with the critical work of the political scientist, Adamantia Pollis. The fact that both are Greek scholars working in the United States gives particular force to the contrast between their respective positions: both are necessarily familiar with the human rights discourse in current American and international politics; both have had to take positions with regard to Greek institutional practices within the larger framework of the European Union; and both are aware of the perduring admiration of Classical culture that continues to flavor the rhetoric, but not much else, of the Western powers' ambivalent relations with the Greek state. Finally, both are, I believe, genuinely concerned to see Greece take a more secure and honored place within European and international contexts. That their assessments differ so radically reveals a great deal about Greece as well as much about the significance of cultural intimacy in the redrawing of European identity.

Kozyris's goal is to show that Greek legal history exhibits a long and by now irreversible accommodation to the European ideal. In one important respect, despite his concern to demonstrate the modernity of Greece, his position continues the romantic philhellenism of the nineteenth century, for he argues that Greek law demonstrates the European character of Greece, while conversely the global history of law demonstrates the Hellenic character of Europe. This argument reproduces the key argument of nineteenth-century folklore; this is an important point to bear in mind when we see that his major complaint against anthropology is its seeming obsession with the local practices that formed the major preoccupation of nationalist folklore studies. Kozyris's views are representative (I assume he would not disagree) of a significant population, for which I am therefore using his argument as an ethnographic illustration: it is accessible in printed form and thus can more easily be discussed in a scholarly or intellectual forum than the daily conversations it typifies, and he can hardly dismiss it as marginal or irrelevant without fatally weakening his case.[12]

Kozyris explicitly bases his argument on the claim that Greek law has a Classical lineage. He conflates the latter with the "Roman-Byzantine" legal tradition that nineteenth-century Greek historiography had very explicitly rejected as foreign to the true Greek spirit.[13] While there is no doubt some rather shadowy substance to his claims of conceptual continuity, its most striking feature for my present purpose is its direct refutation of the exclusion, so explicitly argued by Huntington (1993), of Orthodoxy from the European tradition. Kozyris thus again follows the romantic-philhellenic path, this time in his attempt to reconcile an "oriental" Byzantium with a "European" Hellas. This in turn leads him to insist on an institutional, top-down reading of Greek legal history and specifically to dismiss village-level ethnography as irrelevant to the country's European destiny.

Kozyris proceeds with the implicit but unmistakable tools of a rationalistic epistemology that reproduces the most literal reading of Weber. This is a reading that sees Greek law as escaping the local constraints of culture and achieving transcendence—the claim that has been made for Classical Greek philosophy (see Humphreys 1978) and that thus declares its Enlightenment and neo-Classical ancestry as clearly as if it had spelled it out. This is a radically different view from that which sees Greek law as shaped by divergences among European traditions (e.g., Pollis 1992) and by the more pluralistic and fractured view of Europe that calls for new attention to local and minority identities.

Kozyris's approach essentializes both Greece and Europe. Like other writers of more obviously partisan intent (e.g., Zahariadis 1994; cf. Karakasidou 1994), Kozyris overlooks the cultural basis of rationality itself, and its entailment in the construction of identity. Thus, in circular fashion, he insists on the appropriateness of national-character generalizations to support these essentialisms, thereby ignoring the historically demonstrable linkage between national (and even minority or ethnic-group) mobilization and mass numbers (see Urla 1993 on the Basque case, for example). Consistently with his position, he dismisses the evidence of ethnographic reporting as irrelevant to the main issues, and my own (1985c) attempt to bring it into productive dialogue with legal scholarship as "collage."

Because Kozyris is a careful, conscientious scholar, his article offers something of a test case for my present argument. Unlike some recent journalistic attacks on the work of anthropologists (see below), his discussion is a measured critique buttressed by a solid review of sources. I mention all this not only out of respect for his standards but also in order not to trivialize what follows. A critique of his paper is at some level no less anecdotal than the most traditional ethnographic reportage, as I have already intimated. I can already imagine readers sympathetic to my argument wondering why I bother to respond to Kozyris's very different mode of reasoning at all. Here, however, I wish to invoke the principle of parity. If we are to make a reasoned defense of ethnography, we must be willing to treat a learned analysis as no less diagnostic of its author's world view (cosmology or ideology) than are villagers' gossip and daily practices of theirs. This perspective shows no disrespect for good scholarship; but it does entail deep respect for ordinary people, scholars included.

For a project conceived in these terms, Kozyris's study offers rich pickings. Central to his argument is that Greek absorption into the European Union legislative structure does not represent so much the successful incorporation of Greece by Europe as it does the return of the European tradition to its rightful home: "It is generally agreed that the foundations of Western legal culture rest upon the humanistic spirit and the basic values articulated by the Ancient Greek philosophers and statesmen. . . . It should also be noted that the very idea of a federation of states was not merely conceived but played a major role in the structuring of relations among the Ancient Greek cities" (Kozyris 1993: 31–32).

Thus, Kozyris suggests that the incorporation of Greece into the European Union fulfills the destiny of both. Without the least hint of irony, he goes on to claim—using as his source the *Encyclopedia Britannica*—that the Delian League exemplifies the European federal tradition at source. Perhaps so; but in that case one might wonder why the example of heavy-handed and domineering Periclean Athens, so resented by its junior partners in the League, does not offend the anti-imperialist sensibilities of the present-day Greek legal establishment as much as the linguistic and cultural imperialism of the Franco-German power clique.

Adamantia Pollis provides another view, expressed in these pithy terms: "An integrated Europe cannot absorb an integral Greek state" (Pollis 1992: 191). In fairness to Kozyris, it must be admitted that Pollis's argument speaks to a rather different set of issues. Nevertheless, a brief inspection will show that one issue is of concern to both: the relationship between Greek legal culture and the historical basis of Greek identity in general. Pollis wants to show that the official denial of minority identities and the unfair treatment of certain religious groups are incompatible with current European Union integrationist goals and that they spring from a confluence of legal positivism (see also Pollis 1987) with local Greek values, a combination that runs counter to the dominant legal culture of most other European states. Her perspective challenges the conceptual ethnic cleansing that produces the sort of historiography espoused by more conservative scholars from the great nineteenth-century nationalist historian Paparrhegopoulos to Kozyris.

It is clear that what lies at the heart of this legal argument is a fundamental disagreement about culture. For Pollis, a pluralistic understanding of citizenship permits, indeed demands, the recognition of minority concerns and has nothing to do with questions of European identity or essence. In her argument, European membership is an administrative category rather than a congenital condition. For Kozyris, by contrast, what is European is also Greek, and this is a question of inalienable cultural heritage.

Although Kozyris does not argue his case in the earlier language of blood—an idiom for the perpetuation of which earlier schools of anthropology must certainly shoulder their share of blame—his position does reproduce what I have called the "ecumenical ethnocentrism" (Herzfeld 1982a: 49) of those same nineteenth-century writers whose occasionally embarrassing effusions he dismisses as irrelevant or marginal. Yet I think we should be understanding of such arguments. In a world where the Classical heritage seemed to many Greek leaders to be the sole source of international legitimation, and which they in turn controlled as a "scarce resource" (Appadurai 1981; cf. Sotiropoulos 1977), such arguments furnish a means of symbolically inverting—Ardener's (1975: 25) "englobing"—the authority of the dominant and the oppressive. Indeed, it would be hard to find a more literal illustration of englobing in this sense than the idea that Europe is but a variant of Greece—a neat inversion of the post-Enlightenment expropriation of Hellas from the Greeks of modern times.

Lest anyone doubt the salience of the englobing model for understanding the Greek political and cultural response to the power of the European Union, let us return to the dispute over the future of Greek as an official European Union language. Minister of Culture Thanos Mikroutsikos's response would not have seemed out of place in a politician of far more conservative bent: "The Greek language, along with Latin, constitutes the mother tongue of Europe, and presently, both the international scientific terminology and the 'dialect' used by technocrats in the European Union and its organs have their origin in the Greek language. In other words, Mr. Lamassoure [the French Minister for European Affairs] must consult the Great French dictionaries and encyclopedia Universalis before proceeding to the implementation of his views" (*Greek Star*, 5 January, 1995, 1). One might argue that Greece's interests would today, when foreign diplomats can no longer be counted on to know the ancient language, be better served by simply condemning the Franco-German initiative as mere international bullying, incompatible with the partnership ethos of European Union ideology, just as one might argue that territorial definitions of the entire Union are more appropriate to Greece's needs than are the endless arguments about ethnic history and nomenclature that the Macedonian dispute, in particular, has raised to fever pitch. At a more brutal but perhaps a more insistent level, the use of Greek rhetorical style has worked in circular fashion to confirm the other European Union partners' dim view of Greek rationality (McDonald 1996: 58).

Kozyris's argument demands a respectful reading for another reason, and this is the candor with which he recognizes the relationship between claims of heritage and the issue of (cultural) sovereignty. Near the end of his article, he observes: "Many [Greeks] feel that if the Greek state is to become modern it must not only reject the backwardness imposed for over four centuries by the Ottomans but must also rejoin the West by catching up with the progress made there. This is particularly true in the legal field. It becomes more palatable if we recognize that the Continental legal systems derive from the Ancient Greek conception of justice and that they continue, in a sense, the Roman-Byzantine tradition" (Kozyris 1993: 34). I quote this remarkable passage at length—it goes on without a trace of irony to cite an earlier piece by Pollis in support of its position—to show how easily popular stereotypes may pervade scholarly discourse: the appeal to four centuries of Turkish misrule is a good example of the collective avoidance of responsibility (*efthinofovia*) that Kozyris so derides elsewhere in his article, and that I have traced to precisely the kinds of inheritance practice that he considers irrelevant to a serious understanding of Greek modernity (Herzfeld 1992a: 134–139). Still more to the point, I want to emphasize the specifically political implications of what he is saying. For it is clear, at least in this passage, that he is acknowledging the extent to which Greeks still look to more powerful countries for approbation; and this is the source of their deep preoccupation with issues of cultural intimacy.

But this "syndrome" (to borrow the term he applies to what he views as negative cultural traits [Kozyris 1993: 45, n. 27]), while itself a recognition of political marginality at the international level, also leads him to deride the marginal concerns of anthropologists: "The Europeanization of Greek law has also been accelerated by the gradual modernization of the Greek economy. . . . This has reduced the importance of traditional law. For instance, even in property law . . . , regulations about the ownership of trees and about animal theft, fascinating to anthropologists, grow pale in significance when contrasted to rules that set zoning or building standards, regulate condominization, or control the content and marketing of milk products."

Since these two anthropological "fascinations" happen to be among the topics with which my research has been particularly concerned, let me respond from a basis of direct experience. If it is true that animal-theft is so unimportant—I have already dealt indirectly with the trees in my comments on the sources of *efthinofovia*—one would still like to know why so much parliamentary time and police effort has been deployed against it. I have already mentioned the wider ramifications of animal-theft in the form of still persistent clientelism. Here I would simply point out that the recent history of conservative politics in Greece has been extensively marked by such issues, yet it is precisely the more conservative political forces that have expressed the greatest sense of cultural embarrassment over the continuing presence of animal-theft on Crete. (Let us also recall that these same forces expressed the most determined criticism of the televised *Madame Do-Re-Mi* in the national Parliament.) It becomes increasingly clear that belittling anthropological interest in these questions is closely linked to the defense of a very specific version of cultural intimacy, one derived from Western hegemony and its local representation in Greece. The issue is not about what does or does not happen in Greece but what it is seemly to discuss in an internationally public space: *ta en iko mi en dhimo*. It might thus be asked (and indeed often is asked with some perplexity) why anthropologists persist in discussing such matters.

This is a book about cultural intimacy, and it is not the place for an extended analysis of Greece's party-political culture.[14] But it might nevertheless be useful to inspect the correlation between such dismissals of local customs and minority concerns—in other words, the voices of the relatively disenfranchised in Greece—and a conservative ideology that would extend older hegemonies

by subjecting Greece to the cultural hegemony of "Europe."
Kozyris (1993: 43, n. 14) emphasizes the significance of "systematic economic, political, and legal analysis." I agree. But I
would argue that such analyses must also be directed at those
who wield power, not only at those who are subject to it.

Were tact all that was at stake, the irritation that this question
usually indicates would be an eminently reasonable position. But
tact is not the whole story; hegemony is the larger part of it.
Here, in fact, some readers may find my position surprisingly
sympathetic to the dilemmas of those whom I have apparently
been criticizing up to this juncture. For what I propose to ask is
why—by whose fiat—certain cultural traits must be seen as negative. Whose narrative of progress is called into being by the very
mention of Europe? Kozyris sternly admonishes the Greeks to
develop greater respect for the law. There are certainly many
others who would echo the same sentiments. They would regard
all that agonistic jostling as "un-European," and, from this angle, it would indeed be tactless for those pesky anthropologists to
point out that, by the evidence of these same critics' own complaints, it is hardly "un-Greek."

But tact, I repeat, is not the issue. At stake is the politics of
marginality, a politics of which, in international relations, Greece
itself is a clear victim. Surely it is offensive that—virtually alone
among nations—Greece appears to require the prefix "modern"
in order to remind others of its existence, or that its language is
so unimportant today that larger powers within the European
Union can unilaterally propose to do without it. (Admittedly the
move failed—but for how long?) By the same token, however, it
would hardly be logical to endorse the argument that outsiders
should stop fussing about the rights of the tiny number of people
who could be considered ethnic minorities (which officially do
not exist—the position Pollis criticizes). That is the very argument that we have seen advanced on the international stage at
the expense of Greece. Moreover, respect for minority rights and
the recognition of local idiosyncrasy are integral to the official
doctrine of the "new Europe." Perhaps, then, the insistence on
the European identity of Greece is less of a persuasive argument
on the international stage than it is the continuation of an ideological position idiosyncratic to Greece.

In fact, I suggest, the concern with Classical roots and European identity, the anxiety that Greeks sometimes ruefully acknowledge as *proghonopliksia* (obsession with ancestors), is the

symptom of a deeply wounding sense of social, cultural, economic, and political dependency. If one commentator on a recent dispute (Konstantinos Hadjidimitriou, *Ethnikos Kyrix,* quoted in 1 March 1994) rather plaintively wondered why foreign commentators seem disenchanted with romantic philhellenism, for example, I suspect that such hurt and puzzlement arise from the perception of precisely that dependency. Apparently the same Western intellectual establishment has duplicitously moved the goalposts and changed the rules of play. Romanticism has given way to deconstruction, and those whom romanticism had once "constructed" as true Hellenes now feel, in every sense, undone.

This is apparent, for example, in some of the conservative attacks on Martin Bernal in both the scholarly literature and the popular media. In Bernal's (1987) controversial critique of the racist underpinnings of Romantic German philology, the critics apparently resent the fact that he discerns not only African but also Semitic elements in ancient Greek culture—as in fact did the ancient Greeks. Their modern successors are outraged, but their umbrage may also be a sign of the fear that their one claim on the respect of the world is about to be dismissed by the very people who originally awarded it to them. The issue is not whether Bernal is right, but why a supposedly scholarly issue should raise such public passions.[15]

To understand the full implications of Bernal's insights into the significance of nineteenth-century Aryanism, we should remember that its pernicious development as Nazism in our own century is but one, if indeed the most terrible, of its consequences. Greek national autonomy is one of its less obvious victims. The nineteenth-century European disregard for the Greeks' own views of their origins (Bernal 1987) finds an ironic echo in both the marginalization of modern Greece to its glorious past and in Greek national leaders' steadfast disregard for the ideas of local populations about their origins and identities (see Karakasidou 1993; Schein 1975; Wace and Thompson 1913).

At one level these arguments replay the debate between Fallmerayer and his philhellenic and Greek critics. Like Fallmerayer, present-day detractors of Greece find much scope for easy, cheap shots, such as making fun of so-called Greek hysteria over such matters as the name of Macedonia. Like Fallmerayer, too, they are at best ingenuous in arguing that the Greeks have simply got their history wrong. Such statements are dangerous nonsense and are a significant part of the problem they are supposed to clarify. Like the equally insensitive refusals to countenance the return of the Elgin Marbles to Greece, they overlook the fact that the Western powers were responsible for defining these things as central to present-day Greek identity in the first place, just as German legal positivism and German Aryanist philology have, in the face of such obtuseness, served as conceptual fuel for new forms of intolerance and racism in a country that has long claimed to be free of such things.

Like Fallmerayer's critics, however, the defenders of Greece's present-day cultural reputation often fall into the trap of treating the hostile doctrine—then the denial of continuity with the ancient past, today the directly related denial of the Greeks' Europeanness and modernity—as though it posed an ontologically meaningful question. Their mistake was, and is, to take on the belittling talk on its own terms. But was this an innocent mistake? It is no coincidence that those who most passionately defend the Greekness of Macedonia are often the same people who sneer at local Greek-speakers as not "pure-blooded Greeks." It is not a far cry from such opportunist arguments to the coexistence of readings of animal-theft—or, to take another example, the Cretan and Cypriot dialects—as at once "Homeric" and "Turkish."[16]

Is it possible for Greece to escape this tangle of mutually complicit hegemonies? Defensive responses to the cultural ideologies of European hegemony—which in their less obviously risible forms concern such matters as the name of Macedonia or the use of Greek as an official European Union language—can induce affectations of comic despair among Greece's self-appointed friends. But contempt and condescension only perpetuate the problem. A great deal hinges on establishing a different kind of relationship between Greece and the other member-states of the European Union. It affects all of them equally.[17]

Breaking out of such patterns of condescension and resentment, as I have suggested, is the real test of European identity. The question should not be posed, as it so often is today in Greece and throughout the European Union, as one of whether there is a transcendent European unity, and how far a Balkan state like Greece can partake of it. Arguments about whether Greeks are European conform to both the legal positivism of the state bureaucracy and the taxonomic habits of ordinary people; and the dangers they pose are rendered largely invisible, and therefore all the more insidious, by an entirely unrealistic assessment that most other Europeans think in much the same terms. The sort of essentialism that these conceptual habits represent locks all the European polities, the Greek included (but not to a greater degree than the others), into an inflexible grid that paradoxically subverts the goal of achieving meaningfully inclusive European identity. And it resuscitates the error of Fallmerayer, which his opponents in Greece and elsewhere merely perpetutated, of both essentializing cultural identities and, more narrowly, of assuming that only a Greece yoked absolutely and indivisibly to its ancient past could possess the dignity of an independent nation-state. The Greek elite's reproduction of this ideology of disdain for their own culture fits the sternest Gramscian model of hegemony.

At stake is a redefinition of the cultural intimacy that currently preoccupies many Greeks. What does the sense of urgency about being European convey? If the answer is to suppress both minority and local idiosyncrasies in the name of a positivized and Eurocentric representation of national character, the new Europe will turn out to have a very old face. It is not a comforting thought.

The test of European identity will thus truly be played out on the margins to which powerful European players continue to confine Greece. Will the collusion of international with local elite domination give way to international respect for what Greece is today, rather than for what Greece was in the past? The answer seems directly tied to the extent to which the Greek authorities will be able and willing to develop a corresponding respect for disenfranschised voices at home. These are not issues for Greece alone. Unless both processes occur, the new Europe will have failed on its very borders to achieve that sense of definition that has already eluded it for so long. What happens in Greece does indeed have consequences for the meaning of Europe. It may not be the meaning that Greece has been taught to seek. It is, I suggest, of much greater importance still.

Chapter Six

Structural Nostalgia:
Time and the Oath in the
Mountain Villages of Crete

Introduction: reciprocity as nostalgia and practice

The static image of an unspoiled and irrecoverable past often plays an important part in present actions. It legitimizes deeds of the moment by investing them with the moral authority of eternal truth and by representing the vagaries of circumstance as realizations of a larger universe of system and balance. I use the phrase "structural nostalgia" to mean this collective representation of an Edenic order—a time before time—in which the balanced perfection of social relations has not yet suffered the decay that affects everything human. Structural nostalgia characterizes the discourse of both the official state and its most lawless citizens. In fact the idea of a time when state intervention was unnecessary for the conduct of a decent social life provides these two parties with the common ground of their continuing mutual engagement. For the state the model legitimizes its intervention as an act of restoring a formerly perfect social order. For the lawless, the model offers evidence of a condition of moral corruption that makes engagement with the state an acceptable, pragmatic accommodation; for people who define themselves in opposition to formal authority it is obedience, not lawlessness, that requires justification.

In the modern United States this argument plays out around the idea of the "Founding Fathers' intentions," enshrined, according to conservatives, in the notion of states' rights and minimal external regulation. But it is also conjured into a different sort of presence by violent factions such as the so-called militias, which seek to restore a pristine condition of unfettered self-regulation, often buttressed by ideas of racial or ethnic purification. While attention has largely centered on the major division between liberals and conservatives, it will be especially interesting to see how these tensions work themselves out among those who agree on the conservative theory of strict constitutionalism but not on the appropriate way to put it into practice. The United States, a country where the "right to bear arms" is still an article of faith for many, witnesses arguments about whether this right encourages alienation and criminality or might reverse the drift away from self-sufficiency, arguments that would sound extremely strange in any liberal European democracy. The militias' antistatist ideology rests on images of rugged individualism, frontier justice, and the feud of the very patrilineal Hatfields and McCoys. The United States is a society where—feminism and dietary concerns notwithstanding—a significant part of the population continues to applaud notions of masculine fellowship: the ideology of the "regular guy" discussed in chapter 7, buttressed by a symbolism of meat eating, hard drinking, and the reciprocity of morally acceptable violence. Australian "mateship" offers a similar case (Kapferer 1988). In both countries nationalism, racism, and masculinist lawlessness are mutually entailed in ways that suggest close parallels with the emergent liberations of the various Muslim *fedayin* movements and the relatively recent history of national emergence in the Balkans.

This suggests an instructive irony: as self-styled Westerners discursively seek to distance themselves from the "atavistic" Balkan and Muslim worlds, usually by decrying a supposed lack of rationality in those populations, they find themselves imitating precisely the same paradoxical strategy of simultaneously exoticizing their own past and pointing to it as the source of their national character. In the account of Cretan animal-theft that follows, therefore, we must be careful, even if only for analytical reasons, not to fall into the same trap. Indeed, the advantage of focusing thus on a supposedly marginal population is precisely that it throws into question the ideological assumptions of those who, as we saw in the last chapter, insist on such groups' marginality in the first place. The mutual engagement of lawless shepherds and legalistic state officialdom is the consequence of a logic that is not opposed to what we now call modernity, but socially and historically lies at its very base. We can best hope to tease out that mutual entailment by focusing on the symbolism that the state and its outlaws share.

Two features are crucial to the definition of structural nostalgia. One is its replicability in every succeeding generation. Each youth cohort groans at its parents' evocation of a time when everything was better: people were more generous and uncomplicated, kindness was more disinterested, women were chaster and more aware of their familial obligations (Herzfeld 1983b), and men were more directly implicated in the reciprocities of hospitality. Each cohort in turn reproduces the same yearning a few years or decades later. A rhetoric of change and decay may thus actually be quite static. It seems likely, for example, that in Greece the dowry has "always" been viewed as an urban or foreign importation of recent date, and that people have found it convenient to blame their sense of moral discomfort with the idea of "paying the groom" (not to speak of the financial hardship involved) on vaguely defined, external forces. Similar laments about moral decay seem to march unchanged across the generations in many countries. Their static quality provides moral cover for some very adroit and not at all static maneuvering over access to the resources that the bureaucratic state makes available to even its most disaffected and marginal citizens.

The second feature concerns the object of this rhetorical longing. That object takes the form of a damaged reciprocity: the virtue that has allegedly decayed always entails some measure of mutuality, a mutuality that has been, perhaps irreversibly, ruptured by the self-interest of modern times. Whether that virtue is generosity, love, respect, or simply transactional honesty, it has lost its pristine perfection and may be in danger of disappearing altogether. That the mutuality in question may not have been one of equal terms is obscured by the rhetoric of nostalgia: the relationship between nobles and commoners or parents and children at a time when "people knew their place" is represented as ideally one in which those at the lower end of a hierarchical relationship were compensated by the total security it offered. Alternatively, democratic or egalitarian ideals, as Kapferer (1988) has argued for Australia, may actually exclude groups on the basis of their ancestry. Such fictions obscure the inequalities on which they rest by recreating the idealized fellowship—the "mateship" of Australian white males, for example—of a mythological past in which both blood and motives were pure.

The idea of a once-perfect reciprocity has permeated social thought, where it is mapped onto various moral perceptions of the world. Not surprisingly, Marcel Mauss, theorist *extraordinaire* of reciprocity, bears especially close inspection in this regard; Carrier (1995b, 1995c) has noted how Mauss's evolutionist lament for the precommercial order of exchange fits an exoticizing strain. But there are many other examples of the same phenomenon; after all, early sociological theory emerged at a time when many of the European nationalisms we know today had reached their apogee. Thus, Engels's primitive communism and Maine's precontractual primitive society both reproduce this feature. Among later models, Gluckman's (1955) "peace in the feud" idealizes reciprocal violence. This model also reappears as a form of "indigenous functionalism" in at least some of the feuding societies studied by anthropologists; among these are the villages in Crete I shall discuss at length in this chapter.

Nor did these ideas disappear at mid-century. Constantine Doxiadis (1968: 5), the Greek urbanologist, wrote of the loss of "social cohesion" as well as aesthetic pleasure that came with the expansion of scale and complexity in modern times. His views projected the antithesis of structural nostalgia into the future; he proposed a return to the human scale of planning that would in turn disinfect social life of the pollution of twentieth-century chaos. It was in every respect a nostalgic solution, and it was predicated on an image of earlier social life grounded in reciprocities of respect and affect.

In a strikingly similar vein—and as further evidence of the sometimes disturbing convergence of nationalism and social thought—the ideologies of nationalism posit a prestatist era before the corruption of foreign dominion brought social discord and cultural confusion in its wake. Like Doxiades's ekistics, too, these ideologies promise a bright future in which harmony will accompany the ultimate national resurrection; in Greece, the religious overtones are explicitly recognized. And indeed the religious traditions of Christianity on which important aspects of European and other nationalisms were modeled included images of a lost communicative perfection—Babel, the wreck of mutual understanding—as well as of an Eden into which human sin imported the imperfection that we know as temporality.

Nostalgia for an originary perfection is common to much nationalist historiography, as it is to religious narrative. Both explain the compromising of purity—the very core of cultural intimacy—in terms of the corrosion of time. One might also argue that modern structuralism is guilty of the same idealization of pure and timeless form, corrupted by processes of transformation and overlays of conscious thought. But in rightly rejecting the timeless perfections of structuralism, some anthropologists (e.g., Bourdieu 1977; see Ortner 1984) have been too inclined to overlook how ordinary social actors in many societies, including their own, use similar models.[1] People generally ignore human agency when it suits them to do so. Thus, the failure of orthodox structuralism is not merely that it posits the existence of timeless structures in a social vacuum (Bourdieu 1977: 82), but also that it overlooks the ways in which social actors invent, refashion, and exploit such structures as moral alibis for their contingent actions. Giddens (1984) has made this process central to his theory of "structuration," but he, unlike Bourdieu, has been unwilling to argue the case through detailed ethnography. In this chapter, following the "militant middle ground" position argued in the introduction, I propose to recover some of these strategic uses of perfect and timeless form in an ethnographic context.

Let me offer a small preview by way of illustration. A Cretan shepherd, suspecting that a rival has stolen his animals, hales the suspect before a miraculous icon at the dead of night and makes him attest his innocence on oath. Only the intervention of the saint can guarantee the good faith that once bound all shepherds together. When it interrupts the pattern of raid and counterraid, ideally a contest between moral equals, the oath momentarily appears to reconstitute the fractured perfection of reciprocity. In today's fallen condition, the denial that one is playing a game is part of the game itself. Structural nostalgia thus gives a spiritual basis to a literally temporal advantage.

It also disguises the strategic manipulation of present time; and here it becomes particularly relevant to the study of nationalism. Bourdieu (1977: 4–7) argues that such manipulation is central to the accumulation of symbolic capital. An animal-thief's victim, for example, does not retaliate at once, because the tension that delay can create increases the force of the eventual riposte. When a boy began raiding an older and quite powerful shepherd because the latter had not thought to offer him a cigarette, he did so in such gradual increments that, when the truth finally came out, the combination of self-restraint and cunning gave him a status made all the greater by his youth (Herzfeld 1985a: 171–173). Time, whether in the form of age differences or as the imbalance created by an unavenged slight, brings inequality. The struggle for personal dignity is an attempt to redress the balance, to achieve temporal equivalence, and thus also to recreate from one's own perspective some small part of the just and perfect order beyond time. This structural parity, however, can only be achieved from a particular agent's point of view. The evocation of structural nostalgia is a moral ploy. It is as much a strategy as the trickery that it is usual to condemn in one's foes.

Similarly, nation-states fight against those they accuse of having corrupted their moral, cultural, and demographic purity. Like villagers bemoaning a former state in which all lived in perfect amity—*aghapimeni*, as the Greeks say, evoking the New Testament notion of divinely inspired love (*agapē*)—national governments accuse each other of disrupting a natural order of mutual respect. But there is another way in which the state is sometimes obliged to address structural nostalgia, as we shall see in this chapter, and that is the yearning for a time of perfect social balance when the encompassing state's own legal and disciplinary intervention was not necessary. Because almost any state ideology requires a narrative of progressive decay from which the bureaucratic state will now rescue the nation, the authorities sometimes find themselves entrapped in the logical consequence of their intervention: they are an intrusive presence at the local level, representatives of a virtually foreign and therefore evil force, themselves a symptom rather than a cure of the national ailment. Whereas Cretan shepherds complain that the authorities have interfered with the very quality that most clearly proves their transcendent Greekness—their love of freedom from official restraint of any sort—the structural nostalgia of the state classifies as criminals these men who see themselves as the embodiment of national heroism.

Fig. 1: Map of Crete

Structural nostalgia in and against church and state

Such disputes make it clear that structural nostalgia is indeed a strategic resource, shared by these irreverent shepherds with the state and with the religious community of which they, and it, are part. There are in fact rather obvious historical reasons for this. In very schematic summary, these include both the active involvement of the lower clergy in the local-level spread of nationalism and its ultimate triumph, and the extent to which the heroic image of the Greek who fought for independence against Turkish oppression abounds with images of pastoral masculinism taken from social contexts appreciably like those obtaining in the Cretan mountains today. One of the priests I found in Glendi when I first did fieldwork there had been a shepherd, and therefore inevitably an animal-thief, before entering the church; Cretan monasteries used to contain many ex-thieves. In the state context, a disproportionate number of police officers has long been recruited in the Cretan pastoralist villages.

This shared history reproduces a theme of the struggle for national independence that, as I have already noted in the introductory chapter, confronts the bureaucratic state with a specific dilemma: how to discipline the very forces that were necessary to its own emergence, but that now threaten its newfound authority? That dilemma is probably typical of most postliberation nationalisms. In the discourse of structural nostalgia, we shall see one area in which the parties to this tension could find apparent common ground, each interpreting the signs of that commonality in ways that suited its respective needs, and neither really appreciating the extent to which they differed—a striking illustration of the semiotic illusion of iconicity.

In the cycle of Cretan animal-theft, there is one particular device that can arrest the seemingly endless temporal flow of feud,[2] and thereby restore a sense of balance. This is the oath of innocence, sworn between rivals in a usually remote and deserted chapel. By recalling actors to a sense of moral duty and mutual respect, it brings structural nostalgia to the service of mutual trust in a society where otherwise irreversible suspicion would prevail. For the suspension of that endemic distrust means suppressing the slights that have accumulated through time, and doing it in a way that allows the actors to regain their pride intact. In effect, actors use religious means to restore a nominally ideal state of peace. To the extent that this works, it represents a vin-

115

dication of the moral order. Conversely, when it fails, it confirms the flawed condition of all humanity (Campbell 1964: 354; Herzfeld 1987a: 28–32, 46). These are the cosmological aspects. In practical terms, its success gives the actors a breathing space, while its failure can be used by each side to claim moral advantage over the other. Cosmology is not incompatible with even those aspects of social practice that appear to violate it.

In the absence of centralized institutions, or when the ability of the latter to intervene is circumscribed, actors look for a more abstract source of moral authority to justify halting hostilities. Indeed, the encroachment of centralized institutions on local self-management, a process that has certainly happened in Crete, may weaken the values that sustained peacemaking as much as violence. This weakening occurs in part because courts and their officers deliberately remove the ultimate responsibility from the immediate actors, and because the actors have little faith in the bureaucrats' ability to conjure up divine wrath in their support.[3] Structural nostalgia here takes the form of longing for a time when trust did not require the intervention unattainable in the bureaucracy-ridden present; it becomes the enabling condition for tricks, lapses, and excuses, but also for attempts to restore harmony even provisionally. Indeed, all such attempts must in the nature of things be provisional. While total trust is socially impossible, its temporary evocation may be strategically useful and socially desirable. Its breakdown can be blamed on the bureaucratic state, or on the even vaguer force of modern chaos: in this secular theodicy the sheep-thieves, ekisticians, and generations of social theorists find themselves in strange agreement with the most authoritarian of government agents. Actors maintain their local social standing not only by defying each other but also, perhaps especially, by standing up to these looming larger entities. Their moral entitlement to structural nostalgia lies in their defiance of an official order with which they share that fundamental premise.

Modern highland western and central Crete has a long-standing tradition of reciprocal animal-theft embedded in a morality of vengeance and reciprocal hospitality. The Cretan highlanders take great pride in their resistance to bureaucratic officers and express contempt for the equally bureaucratic functionaries of the church. Their ethical rhetoric despoils the official discourse of clerks and priests by a variety of discursive bricolage; it turns that discourse against its originators, using moral arguments (including the approval of Christ as the victim of bureaucracy and the patron of cunning shepherds) to support the illegal and ecclesiastically disapproved practice of reciprocal animal-theft.

By exploring the continually renegotiated reconciliation between the structures of religious orthodoxy and the practices entailed in reciprocal theft, I wish to suggest ways of moving beyond the conventional dualities of theology and folk religion, as Charles Stewart (1989, 1991) has recommended, or religiosity and instrumentality, or indeed structure and practice. I suggest that some versions of structure are best seen as practice, or more specifically as rhetorical devices that social actors use to good effect. In this framework, the use of religious paraphernalia in the resolution of theft-related disputes belongs to actors' strategic explorations of the tension between ideal order and daily experience. I will demonstrate this tension with a discussion of what the shepherds told me about specific confrontations. Their accounts illustrate the ways in which Cretan shepherds themselves interpret and negotiate the paradoxes of a contested moral universe.

Swearing innocence: supernatural sanctions

By "stealing to befriend," Cretan shepherds actively seek the admiration of potential allies through a series of reciprocal livestock raids that ideally culminate in ties of spiritual kinship between the principals.[4] Severely repressed by the dictator Metaxas (1936–40) and the military junta of 1967–74, animal-theft, which traditionally flourished during times of war and foreign occupation, also tends to burgeon in more democratic times, as politicians offer patronage (and especially protection from the law) to tough, powerful shepherds who control large agnatic voting blocks. The least effective thieves have generally found themselves excluded very rapidly from the game and have usually switched to agriculture—a despised occupation that bars them from further attempts at raiding, since they no long own livestock for their victims to steal in reprisal. A more recent pattern of commercial, nonreciprocal raiding today allows the older shepherds, as they complain about the decline of thieves' morality (sometimes even at police-sponsored meetings), to forget that their own raiding was not always reciprocal and that they, too, did not readily spare the weak. The view of the past that they now counterpose to the selfish, brutal present bears the classic marks of structural nostalgia: social balance, reciprocity, moral parity, observance of self-enforcing rules.

The ideal Cretan animal-thief, when challenged, admits to his deeds. Being heroic (*andras*, a man) means taking full responsibility for one's own actions, and thus to be reckoned with (*ipoloyisimos*). Reciprocal hostility between nonkin looks forward to the possibility of conversion into the positive reciprocities of alliance, whether through spiritual kinship or through other ties. Conversely, raids on kin, spiritual kin, or covillagers evoke charges of "pollution" (*oghoursouza*[5]) that recall the parallel of incest. A suspect may refuse to admit to a particular deed, especially on those comparatively rare occasions when he finds himself confronted by the victim himself rather than by the latter's emissary.[6] The victim may at that point demand that the suspect "take an oath," usually in a remote church in the dead of night and on pain of supernatural sanctions for perjury. These sanctions are often violent and are credited with impressively selective accuracy. The villagers of Keramia tell of two sheep-thieves, one of whom refused to swear a false oath and lived to be ninety, while the other, who "was afraid" of his accuser (rather than of God), took a false oath, and died immediately thereafter.

The usual form of the oath intimates the terrors of divine punishment: "As my hand moves away from [the icon of] the saint, thus may my soul separate from my body if I am at fault to you" (or "if I know anything"). This suggests a theological metaphor: the hand, signifying the reliance of the human upon the divine, simultaneously affirms the dependence of the corporal upon the spiritual. A man whose word proves worthless is a mere husk, a body without socially recognized spirituality. It is through the hand that a man realizes that spirituality. A handshake reestablishes normal relations after either an oath or a full confession of guilt. Thus formally initiated, contact thereafter grows visibly more protracted and elaborate—one often sees shepherds fondling each other's arms or backs—as men become more at ease with each other. The hand is both symbol and instrument of male incorporation in the most literal sense.

Sometimes, if these staunchly anticlerical shepherds do not want to enter a church at all, they make the sign of the cross on a stone and use that instead of an icon; then the oath begins, "As this cross stand stands out [from the stone] . . ." (Herzfeld 1985a: 204). Both oaths may also reinforce the terror of perjury by adding: "and [may my soul] not go to God but to the devils, if I know anything about what you ask me." Sometimes, the oath specifies the sanctions the perjurer may expect to incur (e.g., "may I not live out the year if . . ."; the secular equivalent, heard in response to police interrogation, may be: "Even if I should be shot, I am not to blame for the animals"). The form "I am at fault to you" (*sou fteo*), moreover, recasts the social dimension as a relationship of accountability between two particular individuals; this form of reciprocity, damaged but now undergoing repair, reproduces the general premise of ultimate social interdependence in an immediate context of competitive male behavior and values. Shepherds may also add the formal court promise to tell the truth and nothing but the truth.

Some saints seem more commonly invoked, although none has an exclusive status. At one village (Miriokefala), shepherds used to promise the *Panayia* (Virgin Mary) a quarter of a stolen animal if they were successful on a raid. The equestrian St. George—prototype of the idealized youth (*pallikari*) among the shepherds (Campbell 1964: 272; Machin 1983)—is the patron saint of three of the major churches where oaths are taken by suspected thieves (Diskouri, Dramia, and Selinaris). In one mainly agricultural village near the south coast, I was told that the locals prefer the remoter church of St. John the Divine to the church of St. George, which is located right inside the village: distance and secrecy, as we shall see, are practical virtues. Other churches where the ritual is often conducted are dedicated to the Holy Cross, to St. Fanourios, and to St. Nicholas.

But the key distinctions appear to lie less between specific saints than between the local refractions—in Evans-Pritchard's (1956: 196) sense—of a particular saint's grace (*khari*).[7] To a skeptic from Glendi who insisted that there was only one St. George, an ex-shepherd replied, "One [St. George] is a miracle-worker, the next a sinner!" While such segmentary refraction of holy figures may be doctrinally unacceptable, it appears prominently in daily acts of veneration as well as in blasphemous utterances (Herzfeld 1987a: 166) and gives concrete expression to both conflict and alliance. It also foregrounds one of the bases of cultural intimacy: if even "a" St. George can be a sinner—a member of that social (rather than hagiological) fellowship of Christians—members of the community have a fine exemplar for actions that they would nevertheless prefer never to reveal to outsiders, especially the intrusive agents of state and church. Indeed, the local priests' refusal to hear confession from the shepherds underscores their insider status; as covillagers deeply enmeshed in the nexus of raiding-related activities, they already know what sinners these men are and do not wish to get involved in ecclesiastical or bureaucratic sanctions against them. These local priests are, again, directly analogous to the local clergy who took up arms with the *kleftouria* (the world of guerrilla thieves) against Turkish oppression against the wishes of the higher church authorities.

A shepherd who seeks to repair or create an alliance must invoke saintly grace at a level where it will be socially inclusive enough to incorporate both his own and his adversary's loyalties. Geographical distance and the icon's reputation for miracles together decide the choice of church. This is the pattern whereby, throughout Greece, a local shrine may eventually become the focus of even national sentiment (Dubisch 1988: 122; 1995: 173).

Distance lends enchantment

Geographical distance reflects both the need for secrecy and the view that more remote locations may be more effective sources of supernatural reinforcement against perjury. Oath taking occurs by preference at night, and only rarely in central village churches. Even though the suspect almost always protests his innocence, the very fact that he has been called to account in this way may affect his reputation. Some villagers say that using a church that one might enter every day undermines the solemnity, and therefore the efficacy, of the ritual; one man jested that the saint of one's own church would know too much already. (Perhaps he was thinking of the village priest, who avoids hearing shepherds' confessions for precisely that reason [Herzfeld 1985a: 242].) Moreover, the sight of two shepherds—in general a cynically anticlerical group of men—heading determinedly for a church door admits of only one likely explanation: "What else would they go to a church for?" At the mountain monastery of St. George at Diskouri, near Glendi, so deep was the perceived need for discretion, and so familiar was the late abbot with all the local shepherds (whose deliberations he could often hear clearly from his cell), that the principals would often send a third party to get the church key from the abbot in order to avoid recognition—or, at least, the admission of recognition, given that genuine concealment is virtually impossible (and that even secrecy is performed in a rather dramatic way, thereby justifying people's assumption that in fact nothing *can* be kept secret). Secrecy operates in favor of the chapels of comparatively remote monasteries, as against more accessible village churches. The monks' presence also intensifies the sense of sanctity; the monks themselves, many of whom come from shepherding families and are not as prone as village priests to betray the secrets of the confessional, understand the need for discretion. At least in theory, however, any church may serve. There may also be good practical reasons for seizing the first available opportunity. The use of a simple stone for oath taking, which removes the action from priestly prying altogether, also gives the suspect little time to recant or to summon kin who might discourage him from taking the oath at all.

The distance shepherds are prepared to go for the ritual is an index of the gravity of the particular theft and the intensity of feeling it has provoked. Thus, the evocation of religious sentiment simultaneously appeals to practicality: faced with an arduous journey, and with the outcome all the more certainly against him, a guilty party is more likely to confess right away. On the other hand, there is clearly not much point in taking a suspect far from home unless continuing suspicion threatens a wider network of social relationships, especially within the village community. When the principals are from different villages, the oath is often the last available recourse.

There is one general exception to the preference for distance and remoteness. Some monastery shepherds, although enjoying the status of monks themselves, seem not to have been above the occasional minor raid in the past and might often be called upon to take an oath of innocence. They were particularly careful not to commit perjury, probably because they were more constrained than ordinary shepherds to show respect for saintly retribution; moreover, they could be forced to swear on the icon of their own monastery, where specific perjuries would compound the sacrilege against the offender's original monastic vows. These shepherd-monks (*kouradhokonomi*) could not indulge in large-scale countertheft without becoming an embarrassment to the church. They did have recourse to other means of creating social ties, particularly as dispensers of monastic hospitality, as kin to many ordinary shepherds, and through the creation of spiritual kinship ties with others. They also had no need of perjury, as their occasional thefts could only have been intended as warnings rather than as a means of initiating large-scale cycles of reciprocal theft.

Supernatural sanctions and social relations

The most commonly attributed supernatural consequences of perjury include injury to a limb, sudden paralysis making it impossible to leave (or enter) the church, loss of sight or of an eye, and the destruction of one's family. Commenting on a case involving this last sanction, a skeptic insisted that it was not the action of "the saint" (actually the Holy Cross): "It just so happened that he got wounded! And the whole district became terrified that whoever 'ate' monastery animals would suffer injury—and especially if he took a false oath and didn't own up." That was supposedly the end of raids against the monastery: thus, even if one accepts the skeptic's interpretation, social effects flow from the attribution of supernatural sanctions. The consequences of perjury, observed one villager, are inexorable, "even if you have God as your father"—a phrase that once again domesticates the divine, bringing it down to the level of social intimacy.

The icons with the greatest reputation for miracle working, punitive or not, mostly belong to independent monasteries rather than to local chapels. Monastery churches, being on their own territory, are neutral in relation to intervillage disputes; they also provide a neutral context for resolving strife between covillagers or kin (cf. Brown 1971: 83–94). The Glendiots' preferred locations for oath-taking rituals are the Diskouri chapel, which is close to their own village, and the roadside chapel of St. George at Selinaris near Agios Nikolaos. The first of these is relatively accessible, but stands in its own land and controls the water supply to Glendi and two other villages. The sanctions that this St. George produces can appear more embarrassing than punitive. A perjurer is said to find the saint's icon leaning away from his hand as he swears. This may be a play on the oath itself ("as my hand moves away . . .") and specifically omits evocation of death (the separation of soul from body). The rejection of the hand embodies and enacts the saint's rejection of the perjurer's soul, much as an affronted shepherd may decline his opponent's handshake, which is proffered precisely in order to test the relationship. But the saint does not subsequently appear in person to exact his revenge. In the 1930s, local thieves would go to Diskouri at the command of the police to swear never to steal again. They soon discovered that the saint did not punish them when they broke this solemn oath, apparently because bureaucratic duress invalidated it. The state has rarely resorted to this method

of prevention since that time. The geographically much more distant St. George of Selinaris, by contrast, is credited with ferocious reprisals against perjurers: one "goes in and trembles."
Also, if one passes by without stopping to pray in the church, a
fatal accident is likely to follow swiftly. For this reason, it is an
appropriate locale for the resolution of particularly serious conflicts; when, for example, a former mayor of Glendi was accused
of writing libelous letters about some of the women in the village
in order to discredit his political foes, he affirmed his innocence
on oath at Selinaris, and the accusations rapidly died away.

By emphasizing physical distance from their home villages, the
principals avoid the fragmentation of daily social life and revert
instead to a total spiritual fact with its social analogue in their
encompassing Christianity.[8] Religious faith (*pisti*) brooks no
questioning: "believe and do not investigate (*pisteve ke min
erevna*)." The shepherds realize this same principle socially,
through the trustworthiness (*embistosini*) that makes any further
doubting of motives socially unacceptable and morally indefen-
sible. *Embistosini* encompasses the duality of religious and social
values. When an accuser says of a local church, "I don't have *embistosini* in the Panayia, let's go to Diskouri," he does not spurn
the Virgin Mary as a hagiographical entity, but rather expresses
his faith in oaths sworn at a place already credited with miraculous powers.

A case of what was characterized as betrayal illustrates the
conceptual articulation of oath-taking with social relations. A
thief was arrested; the victim was locally suspected of having
reported him to the authorities, an act that could have led to a
full-scale cycle of vengeance killings. At the first trial, in the pre-
fecture capital of Rethemnos, the thief was convicted and sen-
tenced. He appealed, and the case was heard in more distant
Khania. Note that, as with the oath-taking ritual, geographical
span increases with the seriousness of the situation. Mutual
friends of the thief and his victim meanwhile increased pressure
on the victim to withdraw his testimony. Fear of this pressure allegedly became fiercer than fear of perjury, and, at the appeals
trial, the accuser retracted the charges, saying that the thief's repeated protestations of innocence led him to propose a trial by
oath at Selinaris, and that the accused's ready acquiescence must
be taken as proof of his innocence. "For I believe that he did not
'eat' them from me.[9] And I made a mistake. And I ask the court's
forgiveness." Distance lent authority to holy shrine and appeals

court alike, and the case for the prosecution was dismissed. Although the accused had in fact committed the theft, no judge would challenge even the reported voice of that higher and more distant judge, the miracle-working icon. Selinaris is the "Supreme Court" (*Arios Paghos*).[10]

Physical distance and the terrors it evokes, human and divine, do not necessarily mean that shepherds believe each other in such situations. Their actions appear to be dictated mainly by social concerns. The question of belief, both in the validity of the oath taken and in the supernatural sanctions that supposedly befall perjurers, is in any case beyond analysis, although its representation as part of the strategic play is not.[11] Others' motives are ultimately both impenetrable, as villagers themselves insist (see also du Boulay 1974: 84), and automatically suspect. The practice of resolution by oath permits a face-saving avoidance of further conflict in the name of higher truths, but this implies precisely the opposite of ingenuous trust: it furnishes a ritualized means of letting a rival escape further retribution without necessarily changing one's mind about his guilt. The invitation to take the oath comes invested with a guarantee that the matter will end there. The very sanctity of the process is what protects the lie that it may—and, in the general estimation, often does—conceal.

Reluctant accusers: risks of the oath

The oath-taking ritual is called *ksekatharisi* (clearing up), a term directly reminiscent of the so-called clean oath (*katharos orkos*) of the innocent man, of being clean in the sense of being innocent and therefore willing to take the oath, and of having been cleansed/cleared (*ksekatharismenos*) of suspicion (by taking the oath) or of the ongoing burden of guilt (by owning up). This set of terms, clearly opposed to pollution, and especially to being soiled (*magharismenos*) by perjury, conflates the establishment of truth with the restoration of social relations. For today, in contrast to the idealized past, perjury is far from rare: "now," it is said "we have become polluted." If a man agrees to take the oath, however, he has ritually constituted his own innocence and can no longer be challenged without offense to his person and to the social body.

Since lying is commonly expected of animal-thieves, their victims, thieves themselves, place little confidence in their oaths. Reciprocally, the suspect may put his accuser off with an excuse, procrastinate, or even refuse point-blank. Once he has agreed to take the oath, however, he has accepted full responsibility before the saint and before God. Despite the terrifying stories of supernatural punishment, perjury is precisely what many people expect of the guilty. Contrary to Austin's ([1962] 1975: 42–43, 154) account of judicial decisions, in which the verdict socially constitutes innocence or guilt and may be challenged if it is unconvincing, oath-taking establishes a conventional truce in which further investigation is henceforward proscribed: "I [the victim] am obliged, I must never mention it again." At the end of the ritual, an accuser may say to the suspect, *"Khalali sou"* ("I don't begrudge you it"), an expression that surrenders all rights to the stolen animal or object. This is hardly a reassurance that he really accepts the suspect's innocence. A former monk remarked that once a shepherd has sworn his innocence, "he is considered 'cleansed'—not completely, of course, but, well . . ." Such temporizing speaks for itself. In the wicked present world, the very expression "to take an oath" (*na paris orko*) can and commonly does mean "to perjure yourself." Wickedness is the rule, not the exception.

Except as a last resort, the oath is thus a bad risk for the shepherd whose animals have disappeared. For the perjurer, moreover, there are numerous ways of squaring deceit with conscience. To say that one has not "eaten" another's sheep, for example, is ambiguous (see note 9). One Milopotamos shepherd asserted on oath that he had not ingested the stolen animals; and he had not done so in a literal sense. His accuser, however, understood him to be wholly uninvolved in the theft, which was also not true. Such niceties avoid any necessity for actual perjury. Even if the truth comes out, the victim may not exact revenge. Mere evidence cannot gainsay an oath's holy authority, and it is both blasphemous and a heinous solecism to suggest that it might.

The shepherds' reluctance to place suspects on oath also stems from the theological implication of the challenger in the perjurer's sin. This is explicit: "you take on responsibility" (*pernis efthini*, a phrase that captures the reciprocity entailed by the perjurer's "taking" an oath); the accuser is to blame for having forced the suspect to such a pass. Harming any being, however evil, imposes a burden of sin. Even those who exorcise demons or banish the evil eye must shoulder that burden. If the suspect is in fact innocent, the accuser carries a more direct sin (*amartia*) and is significantly more guilty (*enokhos*) himself, both socially and theologically, for he has dared to think ill of his innocent fellow-shepherd.

The responsibility that attaches to unfounded charges is dramatically symbolized in a tale about a man mistakenly accused of arson. Forced against his will to take an oath at the reputedly miraculous church of St. Nicholas at Keramia, he called on the saint to exercise poetic justice: "If I'm not at fault to you, he [the saint] will show the miracle on your head." This literally came to pass: within three months, his accuser died of a cerebral haemorrhage. Once again, theological exegesis parallels social exigency. A guilty person, when pressed to take the oath, usually prefers to return the animals because, as a former policeman explained in unwitting evocation of Mauss's (1968: 160) concept of the spiritual bond (*lien d'âmes*), "these people have close ties among themselves."

Suspicion, like animal-theft itself, is reciprocal, and a challenger may not refuse to take an oath in its turn. This is the social corollary of the theological reciprocity just noted, according to which those who accuse wrongly—even if through error rather than malice—may be punished by the saints or their own consciences. (It is worth noting that intention, in this society where people claim not to be able to read each other's minds even while they try to do so, has little to do with blame; a man who accidentally causes the death of another easily becomes the socially agreed target of revenge by the deceased's agnates.) In the ritual of the oath of innocence, the accuser has committed himself to a reciprocal agreement, the intention of which is to restore goodwill. He therefore cannot escape the implications of reciprocity in the administration of the oath. The accused may, for example, demand that his accuser swear in return that the missing animals are actually missing. Then again, if the accuser has himself started a cycle of theft against the accused, it would be logical for him to assume that this latest theft was in revenge. In that case, the roles are reversed and the current suspect demands that his challenger swear innocence in turn. Reciprocity is thematic: if the suspect is charged with some other offense, such as having reported the accuser to the police, the countercharge should be analogous.

Above all, a challenger may not openly doubt the oath once it has been taken. To do so is not only a denial of common humanity (being *anthropos*), the nexus that explains the need for trust in the first place; it is also "unmanly." This makes sense in terms of the commonly held view that manliness is a matter of courage and self-control. It takes strong nerves not to keep checking on a potential enemy. Among the toughest shepherds, forbearance can be a sign of strength. Eternal faith (*pisti*) in the divine order provides the prototype for the necessarily more transient condition (cf. Hart 1988: 187) of being persuaded (*pistemenos*)[12] that restores social harmony.

The practical risks of using the oath are considerable. It is clear that the rhetoric of trust does not preclude trickery. On the contrary, it nurtures deception. At the same time, shepherds recognize that they are participants in a common social environment, and this imposes limits on their willingness to condemn one another to permanent social exclusion. It may be more useful to prevent a rival from committing perjury because the latter is a strong and powerful shepherd with good connections, or because the victim is more interested in keeping the raiding cycle alive. An example will illustrate these limits.

A pair of shepherds, having agreed with a thief to give up all claims on a stolen animal in exchange for the return of the bell,[13] and having consummated the agreement by establishing a relationship of spiritual kinship, then sneaked off to the thief's partner and tricked him—unbeknownst to the first thief—into agreeing to take an oath of innocence. At the last moment, however, the older accuser and a kinsman who had hidden himself in the priest's sanctum came forward with the bell. The thief had no choice but to confess. In this way, they stopped him from committing perjury—although this was expressed as a practical and social concern that the suspect should not implicate himself by becoming branded a perjurer—and at the same time scared him into giving them an animal to replace the stolen one after all. Behind this crafty trick lies not only practical advantage but also a concern to avoid both spiritual pollution and political stupidity by implicating in perjury a rival who might someday become a useful ally. Its special brilliance lies in exacting compensation without actually committing the solecism of asking for it.

Shepherds are thus careful to avoid knowingly letting their rivals commit perjury and are thus reluctant to use the oath. One South Cretan shepherd adamantly refuses ever to do so. He argues that it would be wrong to risk luring another shepherd into the sin of perjury over anything so trivial as a stolen goat. The only time he did use the device was when he was serving as a member of one of the state-supported local shepherds' committees set up in the post-junta 1970s to combat animal-theft. In this case, he was not acting solely on his own behalf. Admittedly, any form of cooperation with the authorities carried overtones of "betrayal" (*prodhosia*). By helping to narrow the field of suspects, however, he could plausibly claim to be protecting the interests of the community as a whole, while his use of a dramatically traditionalist device protected him from charges of betraying the culprit. Like the casting of lots in inheritance, it removed responsibility from the agent to an impersonal, cosmological authority, and the accused thief made an independent decision to confess rather than risk divine wrath or eventual exposure as an antisocial perjurer.

A shepherd must always remember that if his use of the oath causes a rival to lie, he himself may lose social worth. He may not challenge a declaration of innocence made under oath. Thus, he has cut himself off from any right to retaliate. If it should later emerge that the suspect was in fact the thief, the challenger—who has allowed himself to be cheated out of his just vengeance—may be as humiliated as much as the perjurer. At that point, his only reasonably sure means of regaining some degree of respect is through dramatic vengeance such as the destruction of the perjurer's entire flock, an action that would probably be privately applauded by the latter's home community as well, less privately, as by the avenger's.

The oath brings accuser and suspect face-to-face and carries an attendant risk of violence, rather than permitting the indirect negotiation through third parties that is the normative and preferred mode of operation. Even when shepherds are able to claim more or less plausibly that they have stolen by mistake—that is, from their own allies or kin—and decide to make amends, they prefer to leave the animals in a neutral place where their owners will find them, rather than taking them back in person and risking a violent confrontation. One's closest friend can be suspect until proved innocent, and shepherds openly doubt that allies would avoid raiding them if they could get away with it. It is the rhetoric of error that usually allows allies to gloss over a botched attempt by one side on the other's flocks. The only alternative is extreme moral outrage and its attendant mayhem.

A successful administration of the oath should, by contrast, defuse violence. Guilty parties generally prefer to approach the brink of taking the oath instead of either confessing or refusing outright. The gradual yielding that this permits improves the chances of a peaceful resolution. If a suspect refuses to submit to the test of the oath, he provokes doubts, not only about his innocence but also, what may be more important in the long run, about his manhood. In so doing, he forfeits the respect on which worthwhile alliances are based.

Only if the challenger has acted inappropriately may the suspect legitimately decline. Then, the demonstrated immorality (*dropi*) of the challenger may work to the suspect's advantage. The latter may then want the former to go on suspecting him erroneously, without being able to arrive at a satisfactory resolution of his uncertainty. Conversely, when a challenger looks like a potentially worthy ally, owning up, even falsely, may seem to offer more advantages than taking an oath of innocence. False confessions, however, constitute as spurious a claim to manhood as perjury. It is best to tell the truth, for then the moral burden of response falls on the challenger.

The practical principles of the oath of innocence are internally consistent. A shepherd will only administer the oath to a rival whose personal courage he has some expectation of respecting. A cowardly rival is of no interest. First of all, he will be of no use as a future ally. Then again, if he is afraid of telling the truth, his perjury works to the discredit of both parties, as it may raise embarrassing questions about the accuser's judgment as much as it does about the culprit's social worth. Finally, perjury has no obvious effects as long as it remains undiscovered. A shepherd who suspects that his rival has taken a false oath can do nothing about it without, once again, raising awkward questions about his own initial judgment. Since he has accepted the rival as a virtual equal, the latter's perjury would imply that he has exercised poor judgment and that, in so doing, he has participated in a truly appalling sin.

From the Word of God to the word of honor

Nonetheless, narratives about actual cases of perjury are far from infrequent. To understand the apparent paradox, we must first abandon the assumption that the values entailed in reciprocal animal-theft are necessarily at odds with Christian morality. For the shepherds, the theological and the social belong to different but closely interwoven orders of truth. The social order represents a refraction of the divine through the divisive complexities of everyday experience. Social life is riddled with secrecy and de-

129

ception, so that apparent revelations may be disproved by subsequent evidence. Social life lacks the revealed quality of eternal truth; knowledge is contingent upon the flow of time.

People understand the workings of the divine order through its particular appearances in daily experience. Thus divine retribution for perjury parallels the logic of vengeance against those who violate the canons of reciprocal theft. Similarly, the idea that a man who exacts a false oath from another carries an equal share of the burden of sin parallels the social humiliation he suffers when his gullibility becomes a matter of public derision. Shepherds also see perjury as analogous to the betrayal of covillagers to the authorities, and, what is especially significant for their manhood and for my larger argument about the sources and images of cultural intimacy, to the rape of women from one's own village. All these acts are violations of boundaries (*oria*), and as such are also, as we have already seen, forms of symbolic pollution (*oghoursouza*). Sin, whether theological or social, violates the boundary between those one can treat categorically as one's own and others: "Whatever the 'job' is, whether it's called 'theft' or '*atimia*,'[14] when it's in your own neighborhood it isn't right and you shouldn't do it." Rape in the home community, for example, like animal-theft and violence, is socially concentric with incest but at a more inclusive level and allows the rapist no defenders.[15]

Thus, a "clean oath" springs from faith in the Word of God. Concomitantly, "cleaning up" the social relationship requires faith in one's opponent's word. The social both reflects and refracts the theological, so that to accuse a man of lying under oath is at one and the same time to say that he has been a poor specimen of manhood and to denounce him as a sinner and as lacking *theofovia*, fear of God. This implies not only that he has perpetuated the injury to the victim (who might have little claim on other shepherds' sympathy in any case), but also that he is beyond the human pale itself: these anticlerical shepherds unconsciously echo Durkheim as precisely as they do Mauss.

Lack of the fear of God characterizes animals in contrast to humans, Turks in contrast to Greeks. By initiating the procedure of the oath, the victim challenges the suspect's probity but still does so in a manner that admits of recovery through the "manly" act of proud admission. By then accusing the suspect of perjury, however, a victim would turn a single act of the socially accepted practice of animal-theft into a collective, irremediable, and categorical condition of, simultaneously, sin and solecism. This intolerable insult can only be countered with homicide—precisely the extreme of violence that the oath is ideally meant to preclude. Perjury, because it is known to happen, can be a convincing charge. It identifies an individual's depravity with the modern condition that makes such depravity possible to begin with, the condition that occasions structural nostalgia. But the charge mars a culprit's reputation for personal strength. It fits a social framework in which men compete over the very possession of manhood and in which few can expect to maintain their reputations intact for a whole lifetime.

The oath provides a sanctioned means of defusing tension. In my introductory remarks to this chapter, I showed how the gradual increments of raiding by the offended boy achieved a more effective result than a single massive raid would have done. Another young Glendiot avenged himself for long-past raids on his father's flock by stealing the culprit's lead ram—and thus the symbol of his own masculinity—as well as several ewes. When challenged, he agreed to swear on the icon of St. George in the village church. He confessed to one theft, then another, then yet another, all the time working his way up to the most serious confession of all: the theft of the ram. Through his strategic timing of the discussion, the Glendiot gradually lured the other into a state of admiration for his candor—a situation, moreover, in which he could then accuse him directly and with impunity of having ruined his father. His adversary had long assumed that his own theft had gone undetected and had hoped to neutralize the Glendiot by making him either swear or confess. He now had to accept reinterpretation of the Glendiot's theft of the ram—which would have been considered a disgusting act under ordinary circumstances[16]—as a just reciprocation.

The immediate circumstances favored resolution. Because the entire exchange took place late at night and in secrecy, there was no external pressure to continue the feud, and the game ended in a tie. Only the priest, having been asked for the key to the church by the thoroughly profane Glendiot, must have suspected something (and was in fact free to ask what was happening because he was a member of the same patrigroup as the young man). In the contest over manhood, such delicate arrangements reduce the risk of actual bloodshed: "We made a compromise then. He didn't even ask for money; that is, [he had a right to do so because] the animals that I had 'eaten' were more, I'd 'eaten' more of his animals than he had [of mine]." This forbearance meant that resolution was possible: "And we shook hands there and then, and we never, that is, 'bothered' each other again." Villagers say that the absence of pressure from third parties, or from the principals' agnates, contributes significantly to the lessening of tension. Audiences can be dangerous in a society where public performance makes and breaks manly reputations. Secrecy allows much more play to constructive negotiation. It is the guarantee of true intimacy, which is the space in which mutual hostility may give way to affectionate complicity. As such, it is the perfect model for the cultural intimacy of the nation-state, in which sheep-thieves and politicians make cozy deals that the former affect to despise and that the latter deny before the critical eyes of the outside world.

In this instance, in the privacy of a night-time encounter, the principals could quietly work out an interpretation of events that allowed them to evade the dangerous logic of insult. The accused both showed his manhood through confession and justified his actions on moral grounds. By thus claiming a moral balance with his accuser, he established the right conditions for a truce. Asymmetrical relations, by contrast, are a denial of the lesser partner's masculinity. Indeed, this logic also governs the occasional use of the oath between people of different genders. At the church of St. Nicholas in Keramia, men sometimes come from other areas to put their wives' fidelity to the test of the oath. A woman will not delay confession to the last minute as a thief might, and she may not put her husband on oath. Male infidelity does not usually carry the same sanctions as female (e.g., du Boulay 1974: 124). Initiating the procedure of the oath is a mark of superiority. Between shepherds, contestants in an unstable struggle, such inequality may sometimes be reversed; between spouses, whose inequality is divinely ordained, never.[17]

Oaths as social refractions of the Word

The oath invests social relations with theological force. Like ties of spiritual kinship, whose instrumentality in the social and political world reflects rather than contradicts human relations with the saints, it is cosmological in a literal sense. The *kosmos*, literally the world, but also people (as in the French *tout le monde*), is what comments, gossips, backbites, and quarrels, but it is also the stage on which the thieves' actions acquire meaning and force. Relations of mutual trust convert all the negative aspects into positive ones. When an innocent suspect agrees to take an oath, "the hatred goes away" as a result: "If I am determined not to believe him, we won't go to the church at all!"

The oath detemporalizes a touchy situation: by treating the suspect's word as a ritually validated truth, it recasts it in the terms of eternity; it neutralizes past disputes in favor of present and future harmony. It begins in confrontation, and the danger of violent breakdown increases right up to the last minute. Usually, however, a thief only just stops short of the oath itself, when he may legitimately subordinate his fear of another shepherd to the fear of God.

Bourdieu (1977: 7) writes of two different ways of managing time: manipulating the tempo of the action to increase tension, and "strategies intended simply to neutralize the action of time and ensure the continuity of interpersonal relations." These are not, however, mutually exclusive idioms. Here, the manipulation of tempo aims at achieving the sense of detemporalized continuity, of what we might well call eternal friendship. Strategies that express hostility through temporally marked and creatively deformed acts[18] achieve, in the logic of Cretan reciprocity, a timeless love (*aghapi*)—the social harmony that is both the correct relationship with God and the former condition of society (cf. Stewart 1991: 91; du Boulay 1974: 249).[19] The ideal end product of oath-taking is usually described in this kind of language, which is also the language of structural nostalgia. In short, the oath returns the participants to that edenic state of pure reciprocity when trust made a shepherd's word sufficient.

Perjury is an affront to that love and to its accompanying sense of value (*timi*, often translated as honor).[20] It is a denial of the possibility of trust. Conversely, the informal word of honor (*loghos timis*) is the earthly refraction of the divinely ordained Logos. Indeed, shepherds regard the word of honor as the purest contractual form; it requires the least external regulation and is thus conceptually closest to God's Word. It is embedded directly in the social relationship, without saintly or legal mediation, and this is symbolized by the handclasp, which, in the oath, is replaced by the laying of the hand on the icon. In the postlapsarian world the oath breaks down: "I don't believe in you, in your words." Note the plural, "words": plurality is associated with evil in popular Greek cosmology (Stewart 1985b:60) and—as in the blasphemous refraction of divine images—expresses social discord. ("Words" are also that most disruptive of social phe-

time

133

nomena, gossip [see du Boulay 1974: 206].) It has therefore become necessary to appeal to a saintly guarantor, not just a generic St. George or Panayia but a localized refraction credited with perhaps terrible and certainly miraculous powers. The shift from a handshake to the placing of the hand on the icon, signifying saintly mediation, literally embodies the decline of direct and universal trust. It marks a shift from ecumenical harmony to a segmentary perception of mutual dependence, and to a world in which mediators—priests, monks, and bureaucrats—have become a regrettable necessity. A shepherd boasted that no rival had ever managed to get him inside a church, that his word had always sufficed: antiecclesiastical sentiment here ironically converges with closeness to God, just as lawlessness invokes the same principles of structural nostalgia as those whereby the state justifies its enforcement of law. The placing of a hand on the Bible in court represents a further and final decline in the embodiment of trust: the physical images of saints, themselves a more exigent and localized replacement for the handy stone or for the word of honor, now yield to the ultimate specificity of abstract print and the paraphernalia of the extrinsic bureaucratic state apparatus. Among shepherds who despise all kinds of "penpushers," even the Holy Writ seems a poor substitute for the direct and pervasive Word of God.

Cynicism and the state

The common claim that shepherds formerly took oaths much more seriously is an extension of these same ideas. Perjurers resemble those who steal flock animals for purely financial gain: both undercut established idioms of reciprocity. Indeed, one of the commonest forms of perjury today—the recanting of sworn testimony in court—most often serves commercial thieves. Villagers may criticize perjury of this type, but they attribute it to the fallibility of the legal system and to their own reluctance to betray the perjuries of specific individuals. One illiterate old man, asked by a judge whether he know what perjury was, is said to have replied, "You get your deserts [that way] *(to dava sou čerdhizis)*!"

To the thieves, oaths sworn in court are less sacrosanct than those sworn on the basis of mutual trust *(pisti)*. In the words of a notorious Glendiot animal-thief: "In a law court, to get someone else off [a charge], they say, it [i.e., perjury] is not important. . . . In a church, you shouldn't do it. In church, you're afraid to."

134

The court represents the hostile bureaucratic state, and saving a fellow shepherd from jail is morally good: villagers identify religious priorities with social rather than legal morality. Even in lowland villages, supposedly more inclined to legality, men prefer to take an oath in church rather than go to court. It is clear that the ideal world of reciprocal theft is closer to God's order than are the legal institutions of the state.

Nostalgia for the past equates morality with respect for the Word: "in the old days, the word of honor was enough." Even the use of icons to reinforce a simple word of honor implies relative distrust. In Glendi, a small boy once swore on a stone that he would not betray the older girl who had put him up to stealing a pig, but, when put on his word of honor, could no longer pretend ignorance; such was the hierarchy of obligations internalized by a boy of seven or eight: "I preferred to break the oath [rather than the word of honor]; and I still cannot break my word." The smaller the degree of formality, the closer men come to God's intentions. To Cretan animal-thieves, the bureaucratic nation-state, like the official church, represents the intrusion of moral corruption into society.

Personal pasts reproduce the general nostalgia. One former shepherd maintained that in his youth he had never put anyone on oath, as the culprits were always proud and ready to confess. The ferocity of his reprisals insured him against the insult of others' lies, while his value as a potential ally made others actually want him to learn of their daring. But practical advantage, as we have seen, has theological and moral parallels that both explain and reinforce it. The purest word of honor was that which did not even need to be specified aloud. It was closer than any modern formula to the ineffable Word. In court, at the other extreme, legalism—the bureaucrat's insistence on establishing facts by writing them down—absolved him of any moral requirement to tell the truth at all. Defense counsel who try to make shepherds swear falsely in court can hardly increase these supposedly lawless highlanders' respect for judicial process, any more than do the politicians who solicit their patronage by intervening in that process on behalf of convicted thieves.

The oath, although less pure than the word of honor, may nevertheless serve to restore the link with God. In official contexts, however, people falsely "take the oath" in court on the Gospel without fear of supernatural consequences. In court the Book, which for the state represents the unity of Deity and the Greek

Orthodox people, does not have the punitive force of local refractions of particular saints. These saints are entailed in an unending contest between local solidarities, whose unity lies in their common recognition that the social world is in fact an irrevocably divided one. (Note again that this paradox is the fundamental condition of cultural intimacy.) To surrender to the blandly homogeneous bureaucracy is thus to deny the contestatory fellowship of being human. It is necessary to lie in order to protect socially recognized truths (see also Gilsenan 1976: 208–10). In the modern bureaucratic world, blasphemous falsehood becomes the only defense left to the divine ordering of human life.

A word at the end: the ends of words

Asad's (1987) argument that Catholic monastic discipline redirected rather than repressed human emotion also holds generally true for Orthodox monasticism. The monks are *of*, if not fully *in*, the same world as the shepherds, whose calling provides a powerful metaphor for the role of Christ and of the church;[21] that much is clear from their entailment in pastoral practice in both senses (as in the role of the *kouradhokonomi*). In monastic life, however, discipline triumphs over strategy, an encompassing institutional unity over individual will. The shepherds' use of ecclesiastical paraphernalia reverses all these things. The shepherds define their moral purity in opposition to institutionalized values, and engage in reciprocal relations with each other rather than with centralized authority. Their pragmatic morality thus refracts the Divine Word, Logos, through the divisions of social life. This atomized perspective results in a multiplicity of more or less reliable words (*loyi*)[22] of honor. "In the Beginning was the Word." Today there are merely words, serving endless ends.

But Eden is always only just out of sight. Such structural nostalgia, however, has considerable social importance. What Giddens (1984: 25–29) calls the "duality of structure"—the reciprocal interplay of structure and agency, here represented by the idealized Word and pragmatic "words"—means that the formal ideology we recognize as structure is that very stuff that "socialized agents" (Bourdieu and Lamaison 1985: 94) mine for strategic resources. Questions of trust, which is a distinctly orderly notion, arise in situations of continuing uncertainty (Gambetta 1988a: 218). They turn on a questionable but necessary capacity for predicting and anticipating the actions of others and thus represent attempts to control present time. The continual suspicion that marks everyday experience is corrosive, and there are moments when it is easier for all concerned to reach a truce based on mutual respect. In such situations the actors join forces to reclaim the eternal verities. They strive for a temporary suspension of temporality.

Thus, in rejecting a simplistic opposition between Orthodox ecclesiastical values and those of the Cretan animal-thieves (and with it the view that the thieves treat the church without any regard for theological considerations), we are instead able to translate the "dialectic" between doctrinal and local concepts of Orthodoxy (Stewart 1985b: 40)[23] into the more general dialectic between structure and strategy. Simplistic oppositions between local and official religion, or between instrumentality and spirituality, miss this dimension of a shared and contested universe of ideological discourse. In analyzing the practice and ideology of oath-taking among animal-thieves, we have been able to see that the thieves' perspective challenges and reverses the ecclesiastical monopoly of ritual, but that it does so in a way that relocates ritual practice in real time. It provides a symbolic means for creating conditions under which mutual trust, theoretically impossible in the wicked, real world, can be restored. The pragmatic corollary of this symbolic construction is that shepherds can thereby limit the effectiveness of excuses based on notions of original sin and human baseness. That "we are human (*anthropi*)" is a common justification for wrongdoing; but "common humanity (*anthropia*)" is its very antithesis, being founded on the acceptance of some degree of moral responsibility for the effects of one's actions on others.

Strategy thus converts structural nostalgia into practice. It translates the aboriginal Word into a Babel of pragmatic "words of honor" that stand for conflicting interests and motives. Trust works when reciprocal interest makes it work. This is the practical theodicy of self-acknowledged sinners. The interplay of values between the pastoral church and these frankly anticlerical pastoralists is central to the cosmology—and to the imperfect *kosmos*—that they share, and so defines the boundaries of their social and cultural intimacy.

They also share those boundaries with the secular state. In this they share a close resemblance with Spanish Anarchists, who shared an ideology of strict chastity with the repressive Francoist regime that tried to destroy them (Mintz 1982: 91–99). Indeed, if the authorities have recently been more successful at making inroads into the villagers' resistance to their intrusions, it is because the very Maussian view that modern, commercial animal-theft represents a corruption of the original reciprocities rings true with both the villagers and the authorities. When money enters in, all notions of tradition and custom—key elements in the nationalistic folklore on which the nation-state based so much of its official historiography—are compromised. For many decades now, the villagers and the police have been negotiating their way toward this common point. This is not to deny that older forms of raiding were extremely unequal in their effects, as a number of commentators on my earlier work in Glendi have indeed noted (e.g., Damer 1986), but to suggest that the practice of disguising such inequalities with a rhetoric of pristine tradition became steadily less convincing as the commercial and political dimensions became more direct and obvious. Ethnographic parallels suggest that it may always have been fragile (see Hill 1992:274). Rather as (in Mauss's scheme) the revealing of direct interest undermines the quality of the gift, so too the banality of commercial wealth has left the animal-thieves looking less and less like the revolutionaries whose mantle they have for so long claimed from national history. As a result, they have begun to occupy a different space in the structural nostalgia of the state, as the end-product of a process of progressive corruption by the forces of international crime and capitalism. But the pervasive evidence of a moral space shared by the state and its outlaws helps us to understand the persistence of intimacy as a key theme in official discourse and bureaucratic strategies. The state does not exist except through those who staff its offices. They know whereof they speak—none better than those parliamentarians who, having risen to power partly through their patronage of animal-thieves and other miscreants, disguise that embarrassing intimacy behind ringing denunciations of precisely the practices that their vote-seeking methods have perpetuated so effectively. Small wonder, then, as we saw in the last chapter, that anthropological interest in these matters should discommode the elite's modernist claims to a place in "Europe."

Chapter Seven

Social Poetics in Theory and Practice: Regular Guys and Irregular Practices

Rhetoric and the constitution of social relations

The core of social poetics is to treat essentialism as a social strategy. This deliberately reverses the goal of most essentializing, which is to turn happenstance into the permanent and the inevitable. In this chapter, I shall be concerned with the application of ideas that have emerged from the study of rhetoric. I do not limit that domain to the verbal, but follow a convention already widely accepted in art history and related fields whereby any symbolic system used as an instrument of persuasion—or, as we might now say, used for performative effect—can be examined under this heading. Moreover, the "null hypothesis" of social poetics describes a situation in which a person's actions are so ordinary, so commonplace, that they escape attention altogether. This comment has an altogether poetic purpose: to underscore the ease with which we assume that anything labeled poetic must be highly dramatic, aesthetically unusual, and probably immodest. In fact, I suggest, the real test of any model of social analysis is whether it can be used to understand the mundane in social life, for the noticeably ordinary features of social interaction only register when their very ordinariness seems extraordinary. Otherwise, we do not even think of people as particularly ordinary.

Much of the language associated with this approach carries unfortunate associations. Some brush-clearing is therefore in order. The term rhetoric, in particular, conjures up a host of misunderstandings—precisely those that, as we have seen, have given metaphor a bad name. Its use implies that there is a clear demarcation between the rhetorical and the real: figurative devices are in some ontological sense less real than literal language. Yet we can see immediately that this is misleading, especially from the perspective of social context. The notion of literality is a truth claim; it is made in order to persuade. It is itself rhetorical.

As such, it has much in common with the notion of iconicity. Just as iconicity seeks to background the fact that it is a signifying relationship, so too literality is a claim to represent—indeed, to be—the unmediated truth. We have already seen how iconicity serves the interests of nationalism by rendering its contingent claims as eternal realities by removing them from the domain of social practice to that of cultural essence. Literality is an equally central feature of religious dogmas, the various so-called fundamentalisms. Indeed, we can say that iconicity is a special case of literality: to reverse a popular phrase, things *are* what they seem to be.

The success of literalizing strategies is all around us, resulting in a devaluation of the very phenomenon that makes it possible: rhetoric. I have already noted Lloyd's (1990) argument that the denigration of metaphor was itself a rhetorical device with its origins in the social practices of the Athenian law courts, and that its further reification as a particular type of mentality serves the ideological goal of separating the irrationality of exotic peoples and times from the rationality of the West. While anthropologists have also done much to unpack this ideological baggage,[1] Lloyd's contribution is especially valuable in that it situates the genesis of this habit of thought in the context of a historically and culturally specific social practice—that is, in an important sense, ethnographically.

Calling another's performance rhetoric is a denial of its truthfulness. As such, it carries a strongly pejorative moral tone—further evidence of its strategic character (and its capacity to essentialize an implicit reality) if we still need to be convinced. In ordinary usage, the term implies pretension, bombast, even deliberate dishonesty. As a result, the social sciences have generally treated rhetoric as epiphenomenal to a real world to which it blocks access.[2] Yet the consequent refusal to take rhetoric seriously is symptomatic of precisely what rhetoric does best: it backgrounds its own rhetoricity. Thus, all claims that social science should be free of rhetoric, that it should make modesty its watchword, may be as rhetorical and immodest as anything they oppose. They suffer from the ultimate epistemological self-deception, the illusion of pure, direct, unmediated knowledge.

But the social sciences simply offer a special illustration of a larger principle, the role of rhetoric in everyday social action. A social poetics treats all social interaction, not only as employing rhetoric, but also as rhetorical in its own right. That verbal rhetoric plays an important part in channeling and shaping social relations has long been recognized and discussed (see especially Bauman 1977, 1986, 1987; Bauman and Briggs 1990). But I want to argue something more radical: that the entirety of social interaction—not just the linguistic and quasi-linguistic aspects—is rhetorical. This move allows us to use the insights already generated by speech-act theory in order to trace the actual operation of social agency in the creation of social relations.

In this chapter, I propose to sketch the necessary presuppositions for a rhetorical account of social relations in general, and to follow that account with a brief discussion of how this approach can be used to examine even those kinds of social relationships that—in the conventional sense of rhetoric—might appear to lack it altogether. The point of this latter move is twofold: first, to demonstrate the comprehensiveness of rhetoric as opposed to some arrangement separating it from social reality; and second, to argue against a similar division internal to social relations themselves, between rhetorical and nonrhetorical actions. For unless we can apply the approach to the whole range of social practices, including the academic and the institutional, it will not be very useful.

Such an account, which belongs to what Bourdieu (1977) has called a "theory of [social] practice,"[3] explores the relationships among cultural form, performance, and the creative deformation of structures and normative patterns. It should illuminate in specific, descriptive ways how emergent social structure can be creatively modeled and explored through the daily interactions of sentient human beings. In so doing, we jettison the epiphenomenal view that rhetoric is necessarily secondary to social organization. Instead, we treat social organization *as* rhetoric (although it is certainly much else as well). This helps us to get from the agnatic kinship of villages and sublineages to nation-states and large segmentary political systems and to break down the equally false distinction between the "reality" of local-level kinship and the "simulated" character of its larger realizations,

141

treating these differences of scale as differences of degree rather than of kind.

These issues are not usefully approached through some new subfield of "the anthropology of rhetoric." First, that label still carries heavily verbocentric assumptions. Second, rhetoric is not an inert, cultural phenomenon, but the source of social continuity and change in all areas of social life. Third, and consequently, it is important not to separate rhetoric from the material world to which, as a causative agent, it belongs. A rhetorical perspective on social life can plausibly be claimed as more attentive to the traditional concerns of materialists with causation than are approaches that insist on (literalistically) separating physical objects and economic relations from expressive forms.

Thus, I prefer the term "social poetics." The very name poetics conjures up an automatic series of misunderstandings. These, I suggest, can somewhat mischievously be turned to analytic advantage. A reviewer for the *New York Times Review of Books*, noting a sudden vogue for the term poetics in the titles of works in the social sciences (including my own *The Poetics of Manhood*), was moved to observe that, while this development was no doubt well and good in its own way, social life was full of nastiness as well, so that we should not insist on its "poetry" to the exclusion of all else:

> The passion for poetics sounds like a welcoming of feelings, especially irrational ones—something therapists have taught us to desire. . . . We want analytic books about our lives to be romantic, sensitive, soulful. We would like to live with poet's license.
>
> While there's no harm in this, we do have to be careful. As Roland Barthes said, it is not enough to misname things in order to poeticize them. (Broyard 1986: 15)

Indeed not. But Broyard did just that, by confusing the technical category of poetics with a romantic version of poetry—the best-known realization of poetic principles, perhaps, but by no means the only one.

Such condescending reactions, moreover, cultivate and exploit the popular version of positivism. Poetics, a term derived from the Greek verb for action (*poieō*), is an analytic approach to the uses of rhetorical form. It is not a compellingly romantic term at all, nor is its usefulness restricted to language (and even there it is not confined to verse). But the ease with which a distinguished literary critic fell (or jumped) into the semantic trap of confusing poetics with poetry serves an extremely useful purpose: it works iconically, to suggest the evasiveness of the phenomenon itself. For what I am describing has an extraordinary capacity to recede into the background of consciousness. Skilled social performers are not necessarily dramatic or even particularly impressive; on the contrary, some of the most effective performances are among the least palpable. The evocation of a grand model—consider Turner's (1974) Becket and Hidalgo—works best when it is not too obvious, except, of course, in cultures where dramatic self-presentation is normatively inflected with an unambiguously high moral tone.

Let me first, however, address the relationship between social poetics and language. Some writers whose position is close to my own have argued that the term poetics creates too much confusion (Brenneis 1987: 248, n. 3; cf. Bauman 1986: 1, n. 1; 1987: 9) and call for greater clarity. They specifically worry that terms like poetics are possibly wrongheaded because they imply the primacy of language (the language analogy). But this caution, however justifiable (the problem is with the terminology rather than the concept), springs its own traps. For example, even while exemplarily calling for the reintegration of poetic with social theory, Bauman (1986: 2, 7) reserves the former term for the purely linguistic manifestations of rhetoric. This has the real advantage of highlighting parallelisms (in Jakobson's sense [see Waugh 1980]) within verbal texts, but, by the same token, it risks obscuring the external parallelisms between narrative and social structuration. This undercuts the integrative power of such models.

Furthermore, the available terminological alternatives to poetics are hardly less problematic than poetics itself. Among these, the most promising are aesthetics and semiotics. An aesthetics of social life is certainly not far removed from the poetic model I have proposed here (see Brenneis 1987); historically, Russian formalist and Prague School concepts of aesthetic defamiliarization directly anticipate Jakobson's poetic function. The difficulty is that the term aesthetics hardly escapes the romantic misrepresentation that has plagued poetics, while its etymological focus on sensual experience (*aisthēsis*) rather than on the relationship between form and action (*poiein*) pushes the social context of action into the background. And semiotics, which is often treated independently of social context altogether, similarly lacks the orientation to action that is etymologically conveyed by poetics.

The rejection of language-derived models and the excessive privileging of language as an autonomous domain of social action and experience are but two sides of the same glittering but counterfeit coin. These exhibit, if on a less grand scale, exactly the ironic equivalence that subsists between scientism and the more extreme appeals to an infinite regression of argument. Here, then, is another argument for the "militant middle ground," a stance enjoining vigilance lest language either be made the measure of all symbolic things or banished on charges of verbocentrism; other charges disregard the centrality of language in social life much as the blanket condemnation of essentialism ignores the strategic necessity of essentialism to any concept of agency. (Indeed, the presence of agency only becomes apparent through the essentializing practices that give it form.)

The ironic convergence of hostility to language and the tendency to place it on a remote pedestal has historically been a peculiarly Eurocentric phenomenon and can be traced to the power of the printed word (see also, with varying degrees of historical usefulness, Aarsleff 1975; Anderson 1983; Goody 1977; Harris 1980; Ong 1982). It has progressively and repeatedly frozen poetics into a stiflingly linguistic formality and has represented its implicit orientation to action as a synchronic study of literary structure. Its separation from language is one refraction of the more general repression of the social character of language. Scholars have been highly successful at seeing the biases that "scriptism" introduces into the study of oral art (e.g., Bauman 1977). We must not now, however, fall into the other half of our ironic conjuncture of positivism and relativism, by losing sight of the common grounds of meaning in language and in other forms of action—a point more fully recognized in informal, indigenous conceptualizations of meaning (e.g., Herzfeld 1981, 1985a; Rosaldo 1982) than in academic discourse, which tends to reject these formulations as though they could not be considered fully theoretical at all.

Thus, the fear of language analogies exposes us to the same logical and ironic difficulty as the secondary role accorded to language in most social science: a separation of language from action that speech act theory proposes to reverse. Dropping poetics as the organizing metaphor for a social approach to cultural form would only reinforce that separation. Indeed, Austin's perception of the role of etymology in social life ([1956–57] 1971: 99–100)—a rare acknowledgment of the importance of linguistic

form in social interaction—should now be applied to anthropological practice. Poetics means action, and restoring that etymological awareness would also more effectively integrate the study
of language into an understanding of the role of rhetoric in shaping and even creating social relations.[4]

Language-based models or language-derived models?

For reasons that have emerged in the foregoing discussion, it is
important to clarify the distinction between language-based and
language-derived models of nonlinguistic modes of expression.
Language-based models treat linguistic form as fundamental,
and their components (e.g., "grammars" of architecture or music) as literally identical to the corresponding aspects of language;
language-derived models examine the uses of language and of
other semiotic systems in terms of possible commonalities of ideological context and practical action. Language-derived models
are more acceptable because they do not predetermine the structural characteristics that different semiotic modes employ.

Models of this kind were often regionally used to study language use. They do not necessarily determine our understanding
of the other semiotic phenomena to which we apply them. They
do not provide a "language analogy," but an "analogy with language use"—in other words, a model that focuses on the interplay
of structure, action, and form rather than on form alone. It would
be useful, therefore, to outline some of the possibilities of extend-
ing language-in-use models to other semiotic domains. This approach does not produce language-based models; it generates
semiotic models from a heuristic use of linguistic illustrations, a
very different kind of proposition. Art historians would have no
trouble at all with such an extension of rhetoric into nonverbal
and even quite static areas of cultural production. Thus, for example, Gombrich (1979) has documented etymologies in the
rhetoric of Renaissance and later architectural ornament.

Other language-derived models can be introduced with the
same logic. Drummond (1980a), for example, has emphasized
that a flexible version of sociolinguistic creolization models can
explain more general cultural processes (see also Hannerz 1987).
Rather than hypostatizing cultures as having the fixed boundaries
of nation-states—a habit that demonstrably derives from the entailment of cultural scholarship in nation-state ideologies (see also
Handler 1985b)—we can instead treat them as processes of for-

mal flux embedded in patterns of political contest and inequality. In a conceptually related move, but in the sphere of political action, Pels (1996) has productively suggested the language-derived model of "pidginization" to describe the extraordinary symbiosis—in part through mutual incomprehension—that underlay the British colonial administrative method known as "indirect rule," pointing out that the British were so confined by a narrowly scriptist understanding of the meaning of language that they never realized how creatively the local leaders were able to "deform" the formal properties of colonial chieftainship. Finally, as we have already seen, the model of diglossia can be expanded semiotically to include vast areas of cultural tension between, in essence, collective self-display and self-knowledge. Conceived within an action-oriented rather than a referential theory of meaning, a distinction that corresponds to the one I have proposed here between language-derived and language-based models, it acquires the flexibility to describe irony and other potential subversions of normative culture and so breaks down the barriers to cultural intimacy.

What these models describe is a negotiation of identity through the deployment, deformation, and transformation of form. It is what Boon (1982) has dubbed the "exaggeration of culture." Such studies as Bogatyrev's (1971) work on Moravian folk costume identified the role of cultural form in signaling social identity but did not focus either on people's active capacity to constitute social relations or on the capacity of conventional form for mutation with effects in the observable, material world. Similarly, Stacy (1977), following Shklovsky, recognizes the potential of the concept of defamiliarization for discussing collective social styles but does not by extension analyze the constitutive power of individual agents' defamiliarizing tactics.

These difficulties also revert to a possible weakness of Austin's ([1962] 1975) view of language-as-action, in which the constitutive properties of language still presuppose a prefabricated cultural reality: the judge who declares a person guilty produces a wholly felicitous performative utterance because this is the predictable privilege of every member of the acknowledged class of judges. A poetic account of social relations must not merely explain individual prowess (which is a meaningless, romantic notion on its own, closely related to the conflation of *poetry* with *poetics* as a view of individualized genius), but should also, and simultaneously, contribute, to an account of cultural change at the level of collective representations.

146

Let me now sketch by example some of the advantages to be gained by an extension of the Jakobsonian view of poeticity beyond the purely linguistic. Jakobson's poetic function is "the set (*Einstellung*) toward the message as such" (1960: 356). In verse, to take the most obvious example, it is the extraordinariness and diagrammatic properties of the verbal form that constitute the basis of "feel." As a result, the content, through its conversion to a more explicitly connotative mode, becomes enriched as well.

In social life, such devices have led to a considerable emphasis on the more ritualized aspects of interaction, most notably in the works of Erving Goffman. But the emphasis on "frames" and the heavy use of dramaturgical metaphors entail a risk of reification, leading eventually to the separation of the present fluidity of interactional poetics into analytically separable performative and everyday aspects. By reuniting these dimensions in the framework of a single poetics of social interaction, we may hope to capture in this area what Jakobson realized for language: that the ordinary and the set-apart are features of a continuum, and that they are what they are in large measure because they focus attention on their being what they are—in other words, because a social actor has so engineered their "set toward the message."

On the ordinary, the ornery, and the merely regular

This is perhaps clearest in a mental operation that we in fact perform all the time and that represents an unreflexive theoretical perception embedded in everyday speech and action. Take, for example, terms like "regular guy" and "ornery bastard" in modern American slang, and reflect on what the respective etymologies of these designations imply. A "regular guy" is remarkable because he is so unremarkable as to deserve comment. Language is revealing here: in theory he might be a very ordinary sailor or professor, for example, but unless his actions highlight the eccentricities associated with these professions his ordinariness involves no creative deformation. As a "regular guy," on the other hand, he shows mastery of the rules of good fellowship; he is reliable and friendly to the point where he actually stands out—but not to the point of appearing to show off. He negotiates a balance between the dull and the silly so carefully crafted that it is neither: he masters the rules, not they him.

The "ornery bastard," similarly, is not literally a bastard; and if he were truly "ordinary" people would find nothing noteworthy in his daily actions. The metaphor places him at the margins of social acceptability. Such metaphors are a rich source of insight into the processes of symbolic boundary creation, since they play on the outer edges of what appear to be a society's constitutive rules (cf. Douglas, 1975: 90–114, 249–318). This applies with particular aptness to the "ornery bastard," since the latter, like the "regular guy," is acknowledged as an emblematic stereotype, a genuinely American product, as can be seen from the frequency with which he figures in Westerns and spy thrillers. His orneriness is indeed a form of ordinariness. It is, in fact, so ordinary that it excites comment. Here, historical processes have embedded into the language a clear use of distortion (slang) in order to underscore the extraordinariness, as it were, of this type of ordinariness. Such usages all fit a larger group of tropes, in which the metaphoricity of an utterance is foregrounded by making an obviously specious or exaggerated claim for its literalness: "this car is a real lemon," "we were literally boiling with fury," and so on. A British slang version of this practice—the use of the word right, as in "He's a right fool"—turns literalness into social normativity in a very direct, blunt fashion.

Note that much of this discourse concerns male sociality. This does not mean that there can be no equivalent poetics of female action; on the contrary, separating the two, as I have done (Herzfeld 1986, 1991b), can analytically expose the ideology of differentiation that such usages reveal. It may be easier to identify a "poetics of manhood" in cultures where men enjoy greater freedom of verbal expression in public spaces; but neither speech nor silence is a prerogative of either gender, and gendered concepts of articulateness may provide enormous play for the uses of irony and other mocking devices. Whether such devices empower the weak is another question—being reduced to using them may itself foreground weakness—but we should at least recognize these attempts at dismantling the structures of power from within. An appreciation of the political resource that I have been calling cultural intimacy in this book is not an insignificant gain.

Ethnographic comparisons

When we turn from English-speaking societies to modern Greece, not all the structuring principles of social interaction are entirely different; but they are often differently used. The aggressive Greek male stance is characterized by a mode of conventionalized difference. It is precisely because the interactions of Greek male villagers are so highly routinized that a man who demonstrates a greater degree of flair may gain a correspondingly greater degree of acceptance or admiration. But the risks are high. He can easily become ridiculous; in practice much depends on his preexisting relationships with his covillagers. If these are cordial, his performance has a better chance of succeeding. But a good performance may also increase that cordiality.

In the Rhodian village where I did fieldwork in the early 1970s, a community largely marked by what for Greece is an unusual degree of outward reserve and sobriety, one man is known for the flamboyance of his gestures. This is not the place to offer a detailed analysis of his physical movements, although, arguably, the ethnographic account would be incomplete without such a representation (see Farnell 1994a, 1994b).[5] On one occasion, he entered his favorite coffeehouse, executing little dance steps and playing to the hilt the full range of conventions that required him to look straight at all the customers already seated there. His greeting was boisterous, his self-presentation strangely contrasted with the quiet mien of the others. Yet they accepted him, and did so despite the fact that his humble origins might have led them to expect a still stiffer code of self-restraint than they imposed upon themselves.

The man was a successful entrepreneur. As he had explained to me in painstaking detail, he was probably the only farmer in the village who had taken full advantage of government policies regarding afforestation and the redistribution of land; and, when the government offered loans for the improvement of agricultural properties, he was the only inhabitant to make an effort to get some of the money, which he used to develop his irrigation system.

In his eccentric dance routine, he was, I suggest, daring fate: he was performing his right to be included in the company of his peers. This, moreover, was a performance both in the theatrical sense of a demonstration of skill and in Austin's ([1962] 1975) sense of an action that becomes constitutive of its social environment. His dance steps and boisterous greeting were based on the confident knowledge that, when it came to comparing degrees of industriousness (a paramount virtue in this particular community), he could hold his own with the best. Indeed, other villagers were uncharacteristically flattering about his hard work. His manner thus did not so much challenge the village order as hint that he was morally in a position to bend the rules. He was demonstrating a social competence that went beyond the reproduction of mere conventions to the expression of his individual distinctiveness within the larger setting.

His hard work would not alone have sufficed to gain him such warm acceptance in the community. Another man, the owner of the coffeehouse, was cordially disliked by most other villagers precisely because he *had* succeeded (or so it was said) in amassing large amounts of money by siphoning busloads off the tourist route for lunch in the highly scenic village. But this man was well placed by kinship and land ownership at the very core of the community. He clearly felt no need to seek recognition—indeed, he was something of a recluse—and so he never achieved the popularity of the man with the dancing feet.

I do not wish to suggest that the difference between them can be explained solely in terms of their respective public performances. It is clear that other dynamics were at work, including a strong perception that the coffeeshop proprietor was earning the cash that men like the dancer—who had started out with far greater economic disadvantages—were spending in his establishment. In a village where any hint of nonreciprocity invited censure, this contrast was surely constitutive of the relative social esteem in which these two men were held. But what the dancer tested with his delicate eccentricity was the willingness of the others to include him in their exclusive company. Each time he succeeded, he made it harder for them to reverse their attitude. And he succeeded, I suggest, because his routine reminded them that he was unafraid.

His action is the converse of the "regular guy" phenomenon: instead of foregrounding an abnormal normalcy, it emphasizes an individuation that conforms, in its internal articulation, to social conventions. It is also, in another sense, the converse of the Simmel's ([1908] 1971) image of the stranger, the outsider who claims a measure of insiderhood and thereby becomes a potential threat. The villager overcame his slightly dubious social origins to the point where he could (and did) pontificate about social morality, the importance of hard work, and the rights and privileges of the true Pefkiot. His self-presentation modeled that achievement. By almost ironically prolonging his stare around the room as he entered, for example, he foregrounded the message of social normativeness at the expense of another interpretation: that he was perhaps just a little odd. Just as he was not quite an insider, but (since he had lived in the village most of his adult life and was in fact of village extraction) was not clearly an outsider either, so too his behavior was not quite normative but yet was sufficiently close to the norm to command acceptance. A poetic analysis of social interaction allows for the recognition of precisely this sense of approximation and ambiguity in a way that more positivistic analytical modes suppress.

Such a view of social interaction is, moreover, entirely consistent with an action-oriented approach to human semiosis. Jonathan Cohen (1975) has succinctly urged the extension of an essentially Austinian perspective on language use to nonlinguistic codes as well. In the case of the Pefkiot entering the coffeehouse, for example, we can see enacted an appropriately poetic (or diagrammatic) shaping of the actor's social relationships. To understand this more fully, let us turn briefly to the social values that are in play in the scene in question.

The ethnographic literature on Greece contains extensive discussions of the concept of *filotimo* (see especially Campbell 1964; du Boulay 1974; Friedl 1962; Herzfeld 1980b). The common semantic base of the widely varied realizations of this concept of social worth seems to be a sense that the possessor of *filotimo* behaves in accordance with the expectations of his community. Thus, a pauper's *filotimo* does not entail the same lavish outlay of generosity that a wealthier individual's would. There are also differences linked to sex, age, and degree of closeness of the relationships involved; and the pattern also seems to vary considerably among regions and even between more or less neighboring villages. The Pefkiot whose behavior we have been examining is an intrusive member of an almost totally endogamous community; he was an adopted child, and as such a member of a category that Pefkiots associate in cautionary tales with betrayal of parents (e.g., that of the foster son who volunteered to hang his stepfather when no other volunteer could be found); and he was initially poor. His strenuous (and often ingenious) efforts to overcome his poverty, however, presaged a certain flair in his management of self. His ability to appear mildly eccentric, yet to do it in a way that simultaneously recalled socially acceptable behavior by deforming it to an inoffensive but still noticeable degree, reproduced that same flair. In other words, his actions iconically modeled his social standing, by presenting a virtual diagram of his relationship with others: a man strongly attached to the center of village society in spite of circumstances that would have marginalized a less effective player. Through their blending of the creative with the conventional, his actions played on the iconicity that defined community membership and so— again utilizing the principle of iconicity—also graphically reproduced the tension between a position of social strength and a history of personal marginality.

In search of embedded regularities

Presumably the comparative perspective suggested by the two sets of examples that I have briefly outlined here could be developed on an empirical basis. The two ethnographic settings invert each other: the Greek example demonstrates the conventionality of the highly individual (indicating how hackneyed the image of the individualistic "Mediterranean peasant" has become), while the American example shows how the overtly conventional (or "regular") actually works well only when it becomes eccentrically different. In both cases social actors test the possibilities and limitations of an encompassing iconicity—"national character"—but in instructively different ways.

The contrast between the two systems lies at the level of social values; the structural principle involved is the same in both cases. In Greek society, although not to a uniform degree, self-regard is viewed as an appropriate attitude in males; in the English-speaking countries, by contrast, a measure of reticence is usually preferred. The structural principle, however, seems not to change. In both cases, an intensification of everyday attitudes sets the individual performer apart. A particularly striking example of this is the custom, found in many cultures, whereby noted performers deny their own ability to sing or tell tales (see Bauman 1977: 21–22); pretensions of false modesty are far from uncommon in the performing arts world of today. What such devices do—just as Greeks do when they say, "Not that I want to praise myself, but . . ."—is to "reduce" an artistic performance to the level of the commonplace, since the artist, like Simmel's ([1908] 1971: 146) stranger, is both an insider and an outsider. Those who are good at self-presentation are artists precisely because they are able to deploy the necessary ambiguity of social interactions for the enhancement of their own goals.

For the stereotypes of the "regular guy" and the "ornery bastard" not only to exist, but to furnish negotiable models for the conduct of social relations, presupposes an embedded concept of normativity. Paradoxically, however, such normativity is not re-alized—given immediacy—except through some kind of defor-mation. At such moments, not only is the identity of the particular actor heightened, but the very principles whereby the actor can deform the normative model become the arena of in-quiry into what the embedded theory of meaning is. Moreover, these male models only subsist in the implied presence of a con-trast with female equivalents. In a culture where the ideal-typical images of the two genders are contrasted, as in Greece (and as in the United States and Britain to a greater extent than is some-times admitted), that contrast is itself a resource for the contin-gent contrasts that same-sex individuals dramatize among themselves. A man's mockery of female speech, a woman's ironic imitation of a man's narrative of derring-do—these devices, which presuppose a shared vocabulary of norms, must be pre-sented as performances in order to perform their task. Thus, a woman who unthinkingly bursts into a Greek coffeehouse and berates the men assembled there in a manner unbefitting her ideal-typical role is mocked as a "female-male woman" and her pretensions made ridiculous by an ironic declaration of "war" (Herzfeld 1985a: 71). But another woman who laughingly tells the story of a pig-theft—in which a *woman*, speaking in a *high*-pitched and *rapid* vocal style, recounts a the theft of a *non*-flock animal in broad *daylight*—inverts every rule of male contest in deed and word and contributes to the growing erosion of male pride because she makes it clear that she does not really care very much about the outcome; she has not laid her defenses bare (Herzfeld 1991b: 86–88).

Another reason for the apparent predominance of male models in both American and Greek social poetics lies in what, using an-other Jakobsonian term, we might call the "unmarked" character of male dominance in both societies (on this term see Waugh 1980: 74). That men define what it means to be human (*anthropi* in the Greek context), and even to be *decently* human (again *anthropi* in Greek), has until recently been such an everyday inequality as to be virtually invisible. The notion of the commonplace rests on self-evidence, which is in turn culturally and socially defined. But skilled actors, female and male alike, can deform that self-evidence for their own purposes, whether they succeed in incrementally al-tering the larger structure of values or not.

In other words, self-evidence is made, not given. It does not rest on the existence of "self-evident truths," but on the presentation of contingent circumstances as self-evident truths. In this sense, literality is itself a trope, an ironic trope for the conditionality of all social experience. The rhetoric of self-evidence thus contains the means of its own decomposition; through ironic plays on the vocabulary—gestural as well as verbal—of ordinariness, it allows actors to explore the cultural rules through which they can reconstitute regularity in each situation as it arises. The "regular guy" is rarely so very regular: more often, his regularity consists in actively disobeying the laws of the larger society, such as the nation-state, within which his peer group is embedded. But what is irregular for the encompassing, regulative entity becomes instead a positively valued eccentricity—a regular irregularity—for the members of the encompassed group, thereby uniting it in a new, maverick iconicity.

The poetics of the commonplace is thus ultimately an exploration of how members of the social group fashion and refashion their imagined iconicity. Regularities, which seem to be embedded, are subject to negotiation. But this is not free play: the deformation of norms requires a skilled appreciation of what others consider the norms to be. And there are limits to invention as well as traps for those who cannot back up their eccentricities. Had the Rhodian "dancer" been a poor man, his actions would have seemed merely pathetic: a social poetics, while recognizing rhetoric (in the broadest sense) as constitutive of some aspects of power, must also account for those more grossly material dimensions in which it is both embedded and a constitutive factor. While a performance of calm confidence can bring a shaky financier back to solvency, stretching the performance over too long a period or showing a poor grasp of its limits can be disastrous, as every financial scandal seems to show.

I have focused on relatively obvious examples. But there are many instances where the operation of poetic principles is much less accessible. As a male ethnographer in Greece, for example, I experienced relatively substantial difficulty in detecting what I later decided were ironic usages in the self-presentation of women. Yet such unobtrusive performances are surely no less constitutive of what an observer construes as the prevailing social order than are the flamboyant acts of the strong and confident. This is the challenge for social poetics, not only in the obvious domain of gender but also as we turn to the political changes now taking place in the world. How do these local-level performances incrementally affect changes in political orientation? Why do voters sometimes applaud the nationalistic drumbeats emanating from the capital but sometimes deride them? And when and why do they decide to follow them? Clearly some of their motives are grounded in immediate economic self-interest. But we have also seen that the symbolic capital of claims on the distinctions of "European" identity exercises a material attraction all its own at the national level, even while individual actors negotiate the content of that identity.

This is why a social poetics, properly construed, must address the actions of the whole range of society. Because of my training and early inclinations, I developed some of these ideas in the context of rather orthodox ethnographic settings. Now that ethnography has extended its reach across the symbolic boundary between elites and others to incorporate the politics of the academy and the arts, a comprehensive model of social poetics offers a more flexible approach to the mutual engagement of all kinds of actors—to heed Bakalaki's (1993) timely call—and a recognition of the involvement of all these actors in exploring the possibilities of models formerly thought to be confined to one or another sector of the population. The least literate of Greeks, for example, may have recourse to notions of "European" sophistication far in excess of what the residual exoticism of anthropology has been able to register (see especially Bakalaki 1994).[6] This in turn engenders some creative new uses of notions of tradition. In the next chapter, I briefly sketch one example of the latter—mindful, however, that rapid education will make the tactics of the main character no less transparent to his erstwhile audience than it will be to the present reader of this book.

Chapter Eight

The Practice of Stereotypes

Stereotypes in action

Anthropologists, as we have seen, sometimes stand accused of rendering caricatures of cultural and social reality. Certainly, such accounts as Banfield's (1958) notorious "amoral familism" or Foster's "image of limited good" (1965) generalize far beyond any acceptable level, while Fabian (1983) has pointed out that the American national character studies of the cold-war period are redolent with ideological special pleading. The criticisms hurt precisely because anthropologists generally see their discipline as committed to working against any form of cultural and racial prejudice. This makes it hard for them to see the prejudices that their own work inadvertently conveys—prejudices, moreover, that it often shares with nationalistic ideologies. Indeed, one courageously irreverent study of Gypsies' misadventures in the British social bureaucracy (Okely 1994) reveals embarrassing affinities between official and anthropological thinking. On the whole, however, anthropologists have been reluctant to play this dangerous game with the reputation of their own profession.

Yet they can hardly avoid it, given the accusations—some of which I have documented in this book—that spring from the ironic convergence between nationalist self-stereotypes and the kinds of cultural representation that have especially interested the discipline. It is not necessary to endorse stereotypes in order to study them with a measure of pained self-recognition; and do-

156

ing so may be a better assurance of good faith than all the antiracist declarations in the world. Indeed, this tactic offers the possibility of understanding the social life of stereotypes from within—a cultural intimacy of anthropology, as it were.

This is not, perhaps, a major departure. At some level, much anthropology consists in the analysis of prejudice, other people's as well as our own. To a very large extent, this is what studies of ethnicity and nationalism are all about, and parallels can be identified at the interstices of class, gender, and professional forms of conflict. The act of stereotyping is by definition reductive, and, as such, it always marks the absence of some presumably desirable property in its object. It is therefore a discursive weapon of power. It does something, and something very insidious: it actively deprives the "other" of a certain property, and the perpetrator pleads moral innocence on the grounds that the property in question is symbolic rather than material, that the act of stereotyping is "merely" a manner of speech, and that "words can never hurt you." But this is the self-justification of the gossip, and it is interesting to note that Greek peasants and urban laborers seem to have a more practical, and more performative, view of the matter: "A [wicked] tongue has no bones, [yet] it breaks bones" (see also Hirschon 1989: 176–179).

The categorical systems of local communities absorb (or are forced to swallow) increasingly regimented typifications of "others," emanating from above and authorized as the weapons of a locally reproduced form of power. When we reach the point where those "others" excuse their actions to visitors in these terms—"we're warm-blooded Mediterranean types, what else can we do?"—hegemony appears to have done its work too well. The resistance that irony makes possible does not really empower the weak. It may help them to "englobe" (Ardener 1975) their oppressors, but, as many feminists (e.g., Ferguson 1984; Fletcher 1980; Showalter 1986) have pointed out, it offers more moral satisfaction than change in the material conditions to which the powerful have accorded value. Indeed, subversion carries its own risks. As Handelman (1990) has shown, the very possibility of making up contrary rules can result in the production of "fun"—and its instant marginalization. For it is the powerful who determine the "rules of the game" (see Appadurai 1981).

The use of stereotypes does not do much of an immediate nature for those who are stereotyped, except in this ironic sense (as

Chock [1987] and Norman [1994] have noted). Because stereotypes do serve the interests of power, however, they carry the possibility of subversion and sometimes are used to achieve it; more often totalitarian regimes, as in Nazi Germany, use them to incite the majority population into becoming an instrument of the state repression of minority groups. In this sense stereotypes do represent a cruel way of "doing things with words" (Austin [1962] 1975), and they have material consequences. I would only add that it is not just words that are at stake. White middle-class individuals who take studious care not to seem to be avoiding physical contact with black (or poor, or disabled) people may be responding to exaggerated performances of "otherness" by the latter, or to exaggerated stereotyping in their own minds.

Poetics and practice

This position is the basis of a politically committed, critical social poetics—a poetics that can provide the link between the wordy texts of propaganda and the subtly nonverbal creative acts that constitute the interactive signals of a Goffmanesque world (see especially Goffman 1959). In the analysis of modern conditions, it makes little sense to ignore the "practical consciousness" (Giddens 1984) that social actors bring to what were once, perhaps, much less reflexively apprehended realizations of social and cultural difference.

In Greece we see a country that has internalized the stereotypes of both Europe and the Orient; the Greeks certainly use both. And use is the issue. In their practical orientalism we find the best evidence of the reproductive menace of hegemony. It may also, as I shall suggest, provide the weak with a protective wall of practical discourse, in which the deformation and exaggeration of accepted convention becomes a testing-ground—an event-as-model, in Handelman's (1990) terms—for possibly revolutionary, or at least comforting, ideas. Whether, in this resocialized Jakobsonian poetics, a poetics of "otherness" that is neither primarily linguistic nor carefully apolitical, is to be treated as a strategy of oppression or a tactic (de Certeau 1984) of resistance, it clearly can "do something." It is this intersection between everyday experience and the structures of power that impinge upon it that constitutes the ground of social poetics. Hegemonic texts without a visible subject and social actors in tribal or peasant isolates are equally meaningless in today's world. The space in which they meet constitutes the nexus of political action, and the visible matter upon which the work of empowerment/disenfranchisement is performed typically consists of stereotypes.

A bureaucrat reminisces

An elderly, retired tax official in the town of Rethemnos, a man whose origins lay in the legendary mountain fastnesses of Sfakia in the southwest part of Crete, took enormous pride in these origins and never lost any opportunity to boast of the manliness of Sfakian men, relate the historical origins—as he saw them—of Sfakian customs and people, and denigrate the local members of other political alignments (he himself was an active supporter of the then-ruling socialist party, PASOK) as lacking in these traits of manliness.

Seán Damer (1988) has documented the creation of the Sfakian "legend," although again I would prefer to use the term stereotype. He argues that an increasingly marginalized economic backwater came to rely ever more desperately on a rhetoric of male pride that became, for all practical purposes, ever emptier. There is much merit in his argument. It suggests that the sort of male posturing that characterizes the mountain areas of Crete has become a commodity, perhaps useful to Greek nationalists and to the tourist industry on Crete, and certainly expressive of a situation in which these people do not control the framework of their economic destinies and indeed are themselves commoditized.

There is another side to the picture, however, and that is the role of male self-presentation in the constitution of local power. A man's standing depends in large measure on the kinds of patronage of which he is able to boast, and this has long been one of the major channels through which outside interests have come to dominate the local economy and political life. This process has been framed in an increasingly self-conscious traditionalism. Indeed, it is quite clear that the specificity of "tradition" grows in relation to the alienation of the local actor from the local social framework. It is thus not merely epiphenomenal. To view it as such is to become complicit with the state's devaluation of marginal communities—obvious parallels include dismissive treatments of African Americans as "musical" or state discourses that elevate the "peasant" or the "good wife" to an honored but isolating pedestal (see Herzfeld 1986; Rogers 1987). These are devices of marginalization: they relegate their subjects as ancestral or protoypical, closer to nature, and constrained from speaking with their own voices. To the extent that the Hobsbawm-Ranger (1983) view of tradition as an elite fake has merit, it lies not in the denial of grassroots ideological alternatives (anticipated in Hobsbawm 1959: 23), but in the suggestion that elites encourage the construction of stereotypes. The corollary, however, largely overlooked by Hobsbawm and Ranger, is that official stereotyping—whether of the national self or of some despised "other"—offers a basis for both contesting and reproducing power relations at the local level.

The retired tax official, a professed socialist, espoused a view of the Sfakians according to which they were the descendants of the ancient Dorians. This not only gave his own ancestry a local pedigree of insuperable antiquity but also legitimized the Sfakians' lawlessness as part of the internally contradictory foundation myth of the Greek state. The people of Mount Ida (including the people I had studied) were, he claimed, of Minoan descent. They were, so to speak, the older inhabitants. Note here that the premise of greater age does not necessarily confer greater authority. By the time of our discussions, Sfakians had faded from the political scene and were no longer heavily implicated in animal-theft, whereas the regionally more dominant people of Mount Ida were both politically powerful and active in raiding. The representation of the Mount Ida population as Minoans acknowledges their historical primacy but curiously undercuts their manhood: the Minoans are thought to have been relatively effeminate in relation to the warlike Dorians, whose mark is still allegedly identifiable in the Cretan (especially Sfakian) dialect. Thus, this Sfakian representative of the state used a gender-based idiom to criticize, implicitly, the current locus of local power. Of Iraklio, the most powerful economic center, he said, "They're all hybrids (*mighadhes*)"—a clear devaluation of the city, consistent with the rhetoric of the shepherds but also a significant claim on both the nationalists' purism and a larger Eurocentric anti-urban ideology of long standing (see, e.g., Mosse 1985: 46).

Now one might argue that this was all quite irrelevant to real politics. In fact, however, this man was actively engaged in trying to discredit one of the conservative (New Democracy) candidates in the upcoming municipal elections, and we should see his elaborations of history and his evocation of stereotypes as part of a larger game, one in which several other male actors played in similar ways. He was setting himself up as a member of a culture that, while marginalized, was also viewed as the repository of modern Cretan, especially male Cretan, values. It was thus important to remind people that he was himself a Sfakian, and that he also understood and knew those supposedly older *Ur*-Cretans who still did lawless things like stealing sheep but didn't do them as well as his own "Dorians."

His attacks on the New Democracy candidate were all phrased in terms of masculinity: "He has no patriline." "He's a member of the *kakosiri* [those of bad rank or *sira*, a self-consciously 'picturesque' disparagement of small, weak patrigroups]." "He has no manliness." Greek political rhetoric works by claiming for the future what one hopes will in fact happen, so he kept insisting that the candidate would surely fail. What was more, he argued, the candidate's own natural constituency, the true conservatives, would support other candidates because this one was actually a deserter from the Left and would therefore never be one of them. This, too, was phrased in the rhetoric of patrilineal identity. In short, my informant was clearly trying to coopt his enemy and the electorate in a rhetoric that would allow him to devalue the conservative candidate's legitimacy and make it morally offensive for anyone to vote for him.

The tactic appears to have succeeded. The candidate did receive some votes—largely, my informant had sourly predicted, because, as a small but centrally located tradesman, he could cow his considerable band of creditors into supporting him as the price of continued forbearance on his part. In this way, the candidate's trump card also played into the rhetoric, willy-nilly: shopkeepers, so the argument ran, are not real men. But it also won out over the more obviously material imperative of debt obligations. The tax official used the stereotypes to discourage people from voting for the opposing party: the men, in particular, became progressively afraid of being ridiculed for their failure to uphold the historic masculinism of Crete, itself cleverly allied here to a localist reading of nationalistic historiography.

We should also note that this entire tactic was based on a rhetoric ostensibly opposed to the actor's political party's policies. The socialists had condemned patronage and influence peddling, and indeed had made considerable progress toward securing the support of the small patrigroups in the animal-raiding villages by attacking the system of protectionism by which the larger patrigroups allegedly exchanged bloc votes for protection from police surveillance; yet here was a passionately self-proclaimed socialist invoking the most characteristic language of the opposition's preferred mode of patronage.

His tactic was nevertheless effective. It identified his place of origin with a tradition marginalized on the larger, national scene but locally given high moral value, and at the same time it identified this tradition with a political party that had ideologically rejected everything it stood for. He was then able to use this symbolic formation to attack the candidate of the other party in terms that his neighbors, and fellow voters, could clearly follow and appreciate. His tactics displayed a sort of "practical romanticism," very much like the "practical orientalism" whereby Rethemnos shopkeepers encourage foreign tourists to bargain and so lure them into paying outrageous prices. It is an approach to social relations whereby the actor adopts the stereotypes of a dominant discourse and deploys them in the pursuit of personal interests.

It is hard to know whether this Machiavellian meddling was intentionally ironic. I was not directly privy to the political bargaining that went on and relied on the account of the main actor for my information. It is thus possible that I was being presented with an even more aggressive use of the stereotype than would have occurred among fellow townspeople: I was being told what a splendid Cretan my informant was. Manipulative uses of self-stereotypes are far from uncommon in Crete, where the overwhelming offer of hospitality can be inescapable. Every attempt to counter hospitality is met with a normative refusal: you are on Crete, Cretans don't allow visitors to treat them, that's just against the custom.

Stereotypes and resistance

Such uses of stereotypes can play on multiple ironies (see also Chock 1987). Commentators have often noted that people in subordinate positions will exaggerate the expectations of their actions that stereotypes engender. Tugging the forelock or salaaming in apparently bashful obeisance is an unanswerable tactic, the performative dimension of Hegel's insight into the master's dependence on the slave (Hegel 1977: 522; see Scott 1985: 288–289). Much less clear is the question of how those involved in such socially ambiguous encounters determine how far exaggeration and understatement can go.

It is not only the obviously subordinate who find themselves using such devices. Bureaucrats, for example, often invoke some nameless system in order to justify their more capricious actions; de Certeau's (1984) discussion of the *perruque* in France exemplifies the other side of this process. Bureaucrats are never autonomous actors but reproduce the power relations to which they are themselves subject, sometimes humiliatingly so, in their dealings with clients. It is not necessary here to appeal to some psychological notion of catharsis or compensation; bureaucrats engage in contests over very small stakes of status and advantage with their colleagues and deploy the symbolic capital provided by obligingly dependent clients to that end. At the same time, clients must be made complicit, and it is here that the stereotypical "system" allows bureaucrats to hide behind a stereotype of the faceless self that otherwise embodies all that is most odious about the administrative class.

Resistance, like power, is diffuse and hard to define. Those who appeal to stereotypes of the powerful, however, do have access to one important locus of stereotype production: the media. To take a relatively straightforward example, newspaper accounts of bureaucratic inflation and irresponsibility—a theme much favored by Greek journalists precisely, I suggest, because it is so recognizable—offer endless stories in which, through multiple but predictable permutations, the same elements appear over and over: the refusal of the bureaucrat to be accountable in any degree, the condescension of bureaucratic language and the almost institutionalized inequality in the use of "pronouns of power and solidarity" (Brown and Gilman 1960) between bureaucrat and client, the arbitrariness of the bureaucrats' actions.

This arbitrariness is the crux of the matter. In it are conflated the arbitrary—that is, capricious—use of power with the dissociation of the utterance from material reality. A client protests that the bureaucrat is being ridiculously petty; the bureaucrat laughs. The bureaucrat's pettiness is its own goal: it is an objectified effigy, as it were, of that arbitrary power—*l'arbitraire du signe politique*, laid bare. It is caricature that admits its own absurdity and uses it as a weapon, a performative utterance that—like the mediums, economists, meteorologists, and other prognosticating wizards of contemporary society—flaunts its failure to produce clear answers as the unanswerable evidence of its political clout: it is, after all, still in power. Against this use of the bureaucratic stereotype, there is no effective resistance. The stereotype is itself the locus of resistance by the bureaucrat, against both the hordes of importunate clients and the cliques of exigent superiors.

Stereotypes and the modern condition

Why study stereotypes? They constitute, I have suggested, a significant proportion of the categories traditionally studied by anthropologists. As the discipline shifts its focus from categories to practices, stereotypes remain central to the task. Ethnic jokes, racial slurs, tactile avoidance of "others" (or the avoidance of seeming to avoid them), assumptions about where to go for good food or music, extraordinary precautions to protect one's money or one's chastity—all these are stereotype-based actions to which their subjects will respond in a variety of tactically informed and ethnographically interesting ways.

In the present age, with its educated consciousness of cultural and other collective sensibilities, the resilience of stereotypes seems to call for more of an explanation than would have been the case in the self-confidently evolutionist academy and frankly racist elite society of the previous century. The surprise is not that stereotypes have come under critical scrutiny, but that they are still alive and well. In an intermediate stage of anthropological thinking, stereotypes were either dismissed as mere prejudice and therefore as antithetical to the disciplinary ethic, or as excessively ordinary because they were part of our own world. Yet to deprive "others" of the capacity for stereotyping, to refuse to recognize such on-the-ground essentializing strategies as in some sense a privilege of all human groups, is a condescending reversion to the otherness of the noble savage.

Afterword: Toward a
Militant Middle Ground?

In presenting these reflections on a common set of themes, I have tried to get some critical purchase on the nation-state by showing that its apparent fixities are the products of the very things they deny: *action*, *agency*, and *use*. In recognizing that essentialism and agency are two sides of the same coin, as are state and people, I have aimed at a "militant middle ground" between these obstinate polarities for anthropology. That middle ground similarly collapses the supposed opposites of epistemology: empiricism and speculation, infinite regression and the most crass forms of scientism, the rejection of language as peripheral and its excessive adulation as the defining code for all human ways of making meaning.

Polarities are a convenience. They are useful for sorting out issues. But, like all classificatory devices, they can also become a substitute for thinking: they get essentialized, turned into fact. They become part of a moral universe that disregards its own moral character: the science-morality debate is a good illustration of this, especially as it leads in turn to an equally pernicious binarism, that of ethical prescription about the appropriate degree of political involvement by anthropologists in moral issues that concern the societies they study.

The tone of such debates is deeply embedded in the history of cultural relativism and the ambiguities that it has engendered. By the middle of the twentieth century the nascent concern with anthropological field ethics led to a strongly hands-off attitude that conflated respect for local culture with avoidance of any direct political engagement. This stance also entailed prescriptive remedies—often in the form of strong recommendations to avoid substantive engagement with "internal" politics—for the kinds of moral problems that ethnographers repeatedly encountered in the field. To the extent that anthropology did have an active moral mission, as opposed to a passive code of ethics, it was one of applying at home the lessons learned abroad. By the process that literary analysts know as "defamiliarization," the same process by which in a social poetics we recognize cultural forms through creatively distorted renditions and unexpected analogies, for example, scholars like Margaret Mead sought to shock their home societies into recognizing themselves in the mirror of Samoa or New Guinea. But the corollary of this early form of reflexivity, as also of European functionalism with its insistence on tightly sealed and homeostatic social entities, was the pose of lofty detachment that I have just mentioned: a standing injunction never to interfere in the cultures of one's hosts or in any way to criticize their normative activities.

While the motive behind this position was benign, it had two unintended consequences that were markedly less so. First, its implications today generally strike us in retrospect as condescending: it expresses the tutelary power to safeguard the culture of exotic peoples because "they" are presumed to be incapable of doing so. It also suggests a powerful impulse toward structural nostalgia in the form of preserving—as in fact ethnological museums attempted to do—the perfection of societies supposedly still untouched by the corrosive forces of modernity: money, the debasement of pure and disinterested reciprocity, all the evils through which the *Gesellschaft* has destroyed the *Gemeinschaft*. If the citizens of countries where anthropologists have cast a long shadow feel diminished as "natives," might this well-intended hands-off stance not be a significant part of the problem?

But there is a corollary to that complaint. Once we agree to dissolve the demeaning category of "natives," and with it the argument for an intellectual protectorate not unlike the political varieties created by colonialism, we have in effect made space for anthropologists to become cultural critics. They may well then raise such issues as gender equality or minority rights. On minority questions they must negotiate between competing essentialisms because, as we have seen, the essentialism of the nation-state may provoke massive outbreaks of essentializing in response. Alternatively, some groups may reject both the idea of the unitary nation-state and the minority status it gives them by default. In either case the defense of rebuffing foreign criticism as "intervention in our internal affairs"—or, more fashionably, "cultural imperialism"—identifies the majority (or otherwise stronger) population's perspective as that of "the nation."

True, anthropologists may hesitate before publishing findings that might bring minority survival tactics to the authorities' attention, for publication can sometimes bring disastrous consequences ranging from petty harassment to genocide. In this sense exposing the privileged cultural and social intimacies of small or disenfranchised groups may not be a kindly act. But the worst consequences can be avoided if such reporting is coupled with an equally penetrating critique of the nation-state. For the second negative consequence of avoiding political engagement with the nation-states we study is that it allows our desire not to embarrass a geopolitically weaker country to overwhelm our concern for the disadvantaged within. What is more, if we take seriously our hosts' wish to be treated as moral equals, as indeed we should, such avoidance of criticism is not only condescending but inconsistent as well. We should be equally free to argue with the abuse of power at whatever level we encounter it.

In the places where we do our work, moreover, there are often intellectually vivacious individuals who are able and willing to make the official, majority case to us. With such people it is surely insulting to refuse engagement. We expect them to speak openly to us about their views; why should we hide our own? Obviously considerations of tact are not trivial; and, no less obviously, our ability to discomfit our local friends is often greatly exaggerated—indeed, the shoe more commonly fits the other foot! It is not that we know better, as the cynical use of human-rights discourses for geopolitical purposes sometimes implies. But when it is apparent that we are already privy to the cultural intimacy of our hosts, it is hypocritical to pretend otherwise or to ignore the consequences of that knowledge. Besides, disagreement is not with a country but with specific people; all Greeks do *not* think alike, for example, and, for all their talk about "mentality" (*noötropia*), they would be deeply and justifiably affronted by any claim that they did.

Whether and where we publish our insights is sometimes a difficult matter. It is here above all that anthropologists must be willing to accept direct, personal responsibility—often after carefully consulting other interested parties—for their actions. That is the price they pay for the privilege of access, and they should not complain if their hosts criticize them in turn. They are engaged willy-nilly in cultural and political criticism and the choices are theirs to make. If they are willing to accept these responsibilities, they have a ready-made answer to the all-too-common charge of "meddling in our internal affairs." For there no longer are any purely internal affairs—if indeed there ever were.

In this connection it may be helpful to remember that the Greek junta of 1967–74 was especially adept at using this rhetoric. It coupled vociferous complaints about foreign interference in the nation's internal politics with an equally strident denunciation of all citizens who dared to appeal for foreign help in their struggle against dictatorship as "non-Greeks." Indeed, the colonels unceremoniously stripped these activists of their Greek citizenship, whereupon some—notably the late actress (and subsequently Minister of Culture) Melina Mercouri—trapped them in the essentializing logic of this action by demanding how a handful of colonels could deny them their birthright (Mercouri 1971). But note that the terms of this conflict set a dangerous path for the future. Even now many relatively liberal citizens are reluctant to replace the argument of blood with that of a more pluralistic, cultural definition of citizenship. In fairness, it must certainly be added that other European nations, notably Germany (Soysal 1994), have not entirely abandoned the model of natural nationhood either. And that only compounds the problem, since it undercuts the incentives for change.

The usefulness of the blood metaphor lies largely in the defense of cultural intimacy. If one is not born to the nation, so the argument goes, one cannot possibly understand the national culture, and one may be in danger of attributing to it various traits that are in reality foreign in every sense. The Greek colonels, for example, backed their resentment of outside meddling "in the internal affairs of the country" with cultural warfare against a remarkable range of forms of collective self-exposure: supposedly Turkish-sounding music with politically subversive lyrics, minority languages, men's beards and women's miniskirts (expressive bodily metonyms of disorder and moral embarrassment, respectively), and even the obscene passages in the plays of the fifth-century B.C. Attic comic writer Aristophanes. As the guardians of the national birthright who had arrogated to themselves the right to decide who was Greek, they tried to protect the dignity of Greece's status as the very source of Europe. The attempt ultimately failed because the colonels' cultural incompetence drew derision instead of respect, both at home and abroad. Nevertheless, it is important to remember that their talents had a popular base; the idiom still occasionally appears even in more democratic times, as when, at the height of the Macedonnian crisis, the journalist Takis Michas faced trial for describing the Macedonian hero-king, Alexander the Great, as "the slaughterer of the peoples."

And yet "the things of the house" cannot always be kept out of the public or international space—out of the *plaza*, to turn to a Latin American version of this idiom. It can also be counterproductive: secretiveness breeds suspicion far in excess of what is actually concealed and may make an entire country the laughingstock of the international community. (One can argue that this is proof of the power imbalance, as indeed it is, but that does not allay the practical effects of so much secrecy.) Moreover, "the things of the house" are an integral part of the national identity for the insiders themselves. Not only do they know how unrealistic official representations of national culture often are but, as I have argued in these essays, it is paradoxically the insubordinate values and practices that make patriotism attractive from day to day. The house guards intimate secrets that are themselves the basis for family solidarity and that, from within, do not necessarily appear in a negative light at all. Large numbers of Greeks claim Slavic, Koutsovlach, or Albanian ancestry, acknowledge the Turkish derivation of much of the culture they know and love, chuckle over tales of splendid dishonesty among their nearest and dearest, and—even while shaking their heads over the wild stories of certain animal-thieves—evoke precisely the same national stereotype of defiant independence as they fiddle their tax returns. Tax evasion as a basis for national solidarity? Oddly enough, I suspect that "regular guys" the world over would admit, under conditions of intimacy, that this was so. And the defense of the realm typically falls to those same regular guys.

Even official rhetoric appeals to a nostalgic model of corrupted structural perfection, the same model by which the animal-thieves justify both their recourse to oaths and their continuing defiance of the corrupt state itself, in order to justify its intervention in everyday life. When Kozyris says that Greeks must develop greater respect for the law he participates in the same logic, in this case framed as a return to archetypical European virtues. Speaking as an insider who recognizes a national proclivity for disobedience, he thereby concedes that ideal-typical character of supposedly marginal activities, of which animal-theft is an extreme (but for that very reason effective) illustration.

In short, proclivities for lawlessness and other forms of misconduct are part of the friable basis of patriotism—a virtue in which the animal-thieves, not coincidentally, are second to none. Patriotism, despite the usual caricatures of nationalism, often gives cultural criticism ample play. But that play takes place among insiders, and anthropologists' privileged status is especially ambiguous at that point. And while it should not surprise us that "the things of the house should not be discussed in the public sphere," national cultural secrecy is surely a lost cause from the start. Even before *Zorba*, tourism had already "opened" Greece to the world—and "opening," whether of the body personal or of the body politic (see Hirschon 1978), is what transnational communication is all about.

As part of their defense of cultural intimacy some Greeks would argue that they are not unique in respect of any of its supposedly negative features: other people have the same troubles, commit the same sins. The ironic flip side of that argument is exceptionalism, the claim that no one can possibly understand the culture because it *is* unique. But indeed these defenders of the inner spaces are right when they say that other countries display the same responses, including a similar mixture of exceptionalism and resentment at being singled out for critique. If at times the Greeks' defense of cultural intimacy seems extreme, this is again helpful as a clear illustration. It serves to highlight what may elsewhere be more diffuse even though it is no less present, and it finely illustrates the geopolitical forces that provoke that kind of defense. It thus helps us to situate the poetics of cultural identity in relation to the pressures of global politics. It also constitutes an important response to those who would argue that social poetics belongs to some hermetically bounded zone of "symbolic anthropology"—to an intellectual Ruritania that no more reflects the intended epistemology of the approach than the idea of a perfect cultural and demographic isolate corresponds to the actual experience of life in a nation-state society. Hence the importance of a militant middle ground: militant because it is forever threatened by our desire for closure and hermetic definition; middle because it struggles to escape the overdetermination of binarism; and ground because it is indeed grounded in the direct, empirical evidence of ethnography.

I situate that ground, too, in the difficulty of choices and of their consequences. These include choices for anthropologists to make about what stand to take on political issues that enfold them in tense arguments with their informants. They also include the binary choices—official versus intimate, normative versus performative, "real" versus "rhetorical"—that shape informants' daily lives and that an ethnographic account must recognize. This is a position that recognizes the reality and the importance of binarism and other forms of essentialism in social life, particularly (but not exclusively) in nation-state societies; but it is also one that rejects the classificatory necessity of essentialism to the business of analysis and description—a difficult balance that is perhaps best described as refusing to essentialize essentialism.

This approach records the dissonance between official and social perspectives, but it treats that dissonance as a product of both discourses—two discourses that are in practice a single rhetoric of community, family, even body, and both of which are therefore intensely entailed in each other. We treat them separately for analytical purposes, but at the risk of forgetting that radical commonality. Yet it is a commonality that encapsulates plural possibilities—pluralism, in a word. There is no single "national view"; to act as though such a thing existed beyond the strategic defense of cultural intimacy is unthinkingly to accept the essentialism of the nation-state and simultaneously to reject the lived experiences of its citizens.

In my earlier work, some of which is represented in this book, I focused heavily on what I saw as a contrast between the discourse of the state and that of ordinary people. This gave a binary emphasis to much of what I wrote: hence disemia. But the binarism that I have described is a culturally and historically specific phenomenon, and one that social agents have often manipulated for a huge variety of self-interested purposes.

To those who persist in seeing binary emphasis in the theoretical content of these arguments, I offer two suggestions. The first is to consider, as I do at length in *Anthropology through the Looking-Glass*, the common grounds on which the binary emphases of anthropology and nationalism developed. Most nationalisms, especially those located right on the fault line of the orientalist/occidentalist division of cultural labor, do indeed exhibit strongly binary divisions between insiders and outsiders; but that rhetoric, despite its own claims to rest on universal principles, does not commit the analyst to a universal theory of cognitive structures. Conversely, however, even the conviction that such structures are a figment of the scholarly imagination is no reason to throw out the baby of palpable rhetorical and symbolic dualism with the bathwater of discarded structuralist theories.

The second suggestion is that we ask why, in the face of an argument about the strategic uses of binarism, critics still persist in treating it as a complementary opposition of the old structuralist variety. The inference seems clear: the inability to recognize binarism as a strategy suggests that some of these critics, at least, may themselves be more prone to binary ways of thinking about the world than they admit. Theirs is the binarism of ideological nationalists as well as of scholars, some mentioned in this collection, who continue to insist on a radical division between the material and the symbolic, or the scientific and the moral. Again, it is precisely athwart these unreflexive binarisms that I would wish to situate the militant middle ground—that is, in the space of a choice between rigid formalism and an equally unthinking nihilism. In practice, few of those who take these extreme positions actually practice what they preach. Like nationalists, however, they cannot afford to recognize the strategic nature of their essentializing.

These essays, then, have largely addressed the strategic uses of these binary oppositions within the broader context of thinking about the complicated relationship between a nation-state and its people. I hope to have added here, however, a much more explicit acknowledgment of a fundamental paradox: the degree to which the idea of the nation-state succeeds in large measure because its formal ideology encapsulates, or, perhaps, incorporates, all the inward flaws and imperfections to which it is officially and ostensibly opposed. If the nation is credibly represented as a family, people are loyal to it because they know that families are flawed—that is part of love—and so they rally to the defense of its compromising but warmly familiar intimacy. That curious interdependence, which is perhaps not spelled out so explicitly in my earlier work, is the surest way of emphasizing, once and for all, that the ontology of binarism lies entirely in the processes of accommodation between intimacy and its defense—the protection of the secrets of the house from the glare of the public space by householders who are busily probing the defenses of their neighbors at the same time. This description, lifted straight from ethnographic accounts of Greek villages (e.g., du Boulay 1974), is itself an unveiling of cultural intimacy. Perhaps, too, it is true that the portrait that emerges applies to virtually all other societies as well. In that case, however, should we not recognize in the defense of social and cultural intimacy the mark of our common humanity? There is no excuse then for either exceptionalism or the refusal to recognize the cultural specificities that some may wish to stake out within a majoritarian nation-state.

Notes

NOTES TO INTRODUCTION

Acknowledgments: I am deeply grateful to those good friends whose critical comments on this introductory chapter have helped me define my position and clarify many aspects of the argument. They are mentioned by name in the preface. I trust that they will recognize their input, however imperfectly realized.

1. See especially Handler 1985, 1988; Kapferer 1988; Watson 1994.

2. I first coined this term in Herzfeld 1995. I would especially like to thank Richard Fardon, who, by including me in the project of that volume, gave me the first serious incentive to develop it beyond the formal model of *disemia*—the codified tensions between collective self-knowledge and collective self-presentation—with which I had hitherto been working (see especially Herzfeld 1987:95–122). Peter Pels (personal communication, 1995) has suggested that "*national* intimacy" might be a more apposite term. While I agree with him that this formulation heightens the conceptual tension—nations are not usually thought to be intimate entities—I am anxious to avoid the implication already associated with Anderson's (1983) "imagined community" (see below) that these are *exclusively* national-level phenomena.

3. This useful formulation comes from Blok 1981, and can be preserved independently of his central argument (see Herzfeld 1987a: 11–12, 95).

4. Indeed, the Nuer, taken by Evans-Pritchard (1940) as the very antithesis of a state society, knew perfectly well that patrilineal kinship

was a convenient way of expressing political alliances rather than the literal reason for the solidarity of an entire tribe. See below, chapter 5.

5.   Baudrillard's commentary addresses the more general phenomenon of "simulation" in modern culture; but whose "real" does he mean? Is the ardent nationalist merely a dupe? Do people have no ironic capacity to recognize how stretched the metaphors of immediate experience have become? And is that experience *literally* im-mediate (that is, not mediated by signs at all)? Or, to take another example, is the Nuer use of agnatic kinship to *express* political relationships more real than the paternalism of the modern state? Such formulations beg a crucial question of ontology by reducing gradated differences of scale to a binary opposition: real versus metaphorical.

6.   See especially, and variously: Abélès 1989; Bellier 1993; Faubion 1993; Horn 1994; Rabinow 1989; Traweek 1988; Verdery 1991; Zabusky 1995.

7.   See Beidelman 1995. But my approach in fact recognizes that bureaucrats may interpret their work as a civic duty rather than as a personal goldmine and that, in so doing, they make ethical choices; they are social agents. The extent to which they may deviate from the prevailing civic morality varies culturally and situationally, but even the most socially conscientious bureaucracies must engage in activities that exclude people defined as outsiders. When bureaucrats and other citizens agree in blaming "the system," the idiom of self-exoneration in which they share channels both the failures and the successes of the official ethic in its day-to-day application to real issues and dilemmas, and the fact that many bureaucrats do exactly what they are supposed to do in no way reduces the likelihood that their more disappointed clients, in particular, will seek culturally appropriate explanations for these actions. In arguing thus I reject the view of symbolism as an interesting but distracting epiphenomenon of political reality and address it as the malleable material of social engagement. For a similar but more grounded critique, see Heyman 1994 and my response.

8.   In countries like Greece, the relevant social history has been dominated by economic issues, to which a newly arrived but energetic anthropological presence offers greater depth and richer contexts, as Papataxiarchis (1993: 60) remarks. His comment is especially significant in that it appears in a volume of essays that emerged from the 1986 conference he coorganized in Mytilene to mark the launching of Greece's first university program in social anthropology (at the University of the Aegean).

9.   The constant refrain in Greek appraisals of the U.S. attitude to Greco-Turkish disputes is one of American ingratitude and pro-Turkish favoritism. I am prepared to argue that there is much substance to these charges. By representing U.S. one-sidedness as the stance of a bad parent, however, and specifically as that of unfair property distribution, those who level this charge must accept some degree of responsibility for the

persistence of U.S. paternalism, as it is so aptly named, in the geopolitics of the region. Indeed, this would appear to be a classic example of the way in which a discourse of resistance may actually serve to confirm and perpetuate the hegemony against which it is directed—a point that has been suggested with regard to my own (Herzfeld 1991b) attempt to sketch a "poetics of womanhood" (see e.g., Loizos and Papataxiarchis 1991b: 13). On the rhetoric of self-exoneration in international relations, see Herzfeld 1992a; on the conceptual limits and possibilities of "resistance" see Comaroff and Comaroff 1989; Gutmann 1993; Mbembe 1991, 1992; Reed-Danahay 1993. Diamandouros (1994) poses an interesting contrast in Greek political culture between "underdog" and "reformist" positions, in which the latter represents precisely the desire to relocate responsibility for Greek political actions within Greek society itself rather than relying on the status of perennial underdog in international affairs.

10.　See especially Herzfeld 1982b; Kenna 1976; Vernier 1991. The affective relationship between naming and property is also briefly and anecdotally explored in Herzfeld 1991a: 133, 136.

11.　For an excellent early account of the politics of cartography in the Balkans, see Wilkinson 1951.

12.　Some of this discussion is foreshadowed in Bakhtin 1981 and Lotman and Uspenskii 1985, but these theorists do not satisfactorily engage with the role of agency in the selective deployment of official and subversive codes, and they tend to reify the distinction between official and nonofficial codes (see also Mbembe 1992: 4). On musical disemia see Dorn 1991, Turino 1993; on disemia in conflicting economic ideologies (the formal market versus bargaining and other socially embedded idioms), see Herzfeld 1991a: 160–163. For a more extended general discussion of disemia, see Herzfeld 1987a: 95–122.

13.　Lee Drummond (personal communication) has suggested the perceptive pun "dys-semia" here. The pun has a somewhat pejorative sense ("dys" is derived from the Greek root *dus*, badly), however, whereas the original formulation was not intended to carry such negative implications (Greek *di-*, double, twice, is ostensibly value-neutral). Ferguson's (1959) original formulation of diglossia as pairing an "H" (high) and an "L" (low) register encountered similar difficulties.

14.　Greeks today usually call themselves *Ellines*, Hellenes. This was the official term adopted by the Greek state from the start, despite the fact that it had long been an unfamiliar designation for most of the population until shortly before independence; the more usual term was *Romii*, which alluded to the Byzantine (i.e., East Roman) heritage and its Ottoman successors. Greeks often call themselves *Romii* when they want to emphasize their disrespect for the formal culture and its values; the term also has left-wing connotations (see Herzfeld 1982a:141). Those who complain that this binary opposition omits the other terms that Greeks have sometimes used of themselves, or that people rarely still call themselves *Romii*, are missing the point that the *Ellines-Romii* distinction provides a basic model of disemia on which infinite variations are possible in social and linguistic practice.

15. On Turkish self-designation, see Delaney 1995.

16. Cf. Fabian 1983, on the relationship between exoticizing "denials of coevalness" and hegemony.

17. On the relationship between nostalgia and interiority or intimacy, see S. Stewart 1984.

18. Elsewhere (Herzfeld 1992a: 5–10, 1996) I have called this cosmology a "secular theodicy."

19. On Tinos the pilgrimage to the shrine of the Virgin Mary has taken on powerful nationalist overtones. I owe this example to Jill Dubisch (personal communication, 1995), whose book on the Tinos pilgrimage, *In a Different Place* (Dubisch 1995), should be consulted.

20. On the complex links between narrative and architecture in the construction of conficting histories, see Gable, Handler, and Lawson 1992; Herzfeld 1991a.

21. See the discussion in Herzfeld 1987: 189–191, and passim.

22. See Handler 1985, 1988; Herzfeld 1987a, 1991c. On racial stereotypes, see Wade 1995; Wallman 1978; and several of the essays in Bond and Gilliam 1994.

23. There is some irony in this, inasmuch as Charles Sanders Peirce, whose tripartite division of signs into icons, indexes, and symbols animates this discussion, has been the focus of a certain amount of American scholastic nationalism. Among the most useful discussions of the Peircean schema are Deely 1990 and, for a specifically anthropological application, Parmentier 1994.

24. Freedberg offers this comment specifically in the context of discussing the Iconoclast movement in Byzantine Christianity, but its logic also fits the populist appeal of nationalism. The Iconoclasts feared precisely this power of images, which can occlude their divine referent (see also Baudrillard 1988: 169). In nationalism, however, this occlusion may be desirable in that it can mask the social heterogeneity underlying the premise of cultural unity; representations of social harmony—in bromides about a "classless society" and "our brothers and sisters" (and in those airline courtesies again!)—hide the social alienation against which people build the escape I have called "structural nostalgia."

25. Again I am incorporating terms and ideas to which I have already given some play; see Herzfeld 1991a: 16, 1995: 128.

26. The picture is beginning to change with the passing of the generation that was active in politics both before and after the 1967–74 period of military dictatorship. It is not entirely clear how far the shepherds' ties with politicians actually influenced the course of national politics, but it is at least certain that the pastoral tail did wag the parliamentary dog to a surprising degree.

27. On the constitution of society, see especially Giddens 1984; Lincoln 1989.

28. See Herzfeld 1987a: 77–78. Norman (1994) argues that Swedish working-class women may ironically challenge the conditions of their subordination through obscene joking about their own bodies.

29. See, for example, the intense discussion that occurred in the pages of the Greek glossy biweekly *Ikonomikos Takhidhromos* on precisely this topic in 1993. In this debate I was both a target and a contributor. For defending a colleague's right to explore the minoritarian identity claims of Slavic speakers in Greek Macedonia, I was vilified as creating a school of thought whose sole focus was to deny the Greeks' ancient heritage while concealing the political implications of such a move. For the main discussion, see Herzfeld 1993 and Kargakos 1993; for a detailed exposé of the methodological devices employed to support the nationalist position, see especially Karakasidou 1994b. For a revealing defense of national interests, partly in terms of what I am calling cultural intimacy, see Georgakas 1996; at the time of going to press, responses to this piece appeared in the May/June 1996 issue of *Odyssey* (pp. 7–9); see also Gudeman and Herzfeld 1996. The positivistic defense of supposedly traditional *methods* lends a scientific gloss to the nationalistic defense of perceived ethnonational *interests*. The rhetoric provides a fine illustration of Lloyd's (1990) point about the socially embedded character of the literal-metaphorical and rational-irrational polarities, discussed later in this book.

Notes to Chapter Two

1. For a useful analysis of this issue from a semiotic perspective, see Handler and Linnekin 1984.

2. *Anthellinas*, anti-Greek, is a term much favored by extreme nationalists for those who criticize the Greek claim to a Classical heritage or who in other ways attack the nationalist position. It was extensively used by the military régime of 1967–74 to describe its enemies—a clear case of a government's identification of itself with polity and nation. But, in times of extreme international tension, it is sometimes trotted out against any foreigner who is thought not to be totally committed to the current Greek political line.

3. *Politismos* is derived from *polis*, city-state; cf. the derivation of "civilization" from *civis*, "inhabitant of a *civitas*."

4. *Koultoura* is a term sometimes used by left-wing social commentators. A sarcastic derivative of this term is the newly coined *koultouriaris*, "one who makes a profession out of knowing about culture, a member of the intellectual establishment."

5. At the time I spoke fluent Athenian Greek, but was not warmly encouraged to learn the local dialect by the villagers. This reaction stood in sharp contrast to what I experienced in the Cretan mountains.

6. "A shoe from your own place, even if it is patched,/but where you know the craftsman who made it!" The Panhellenic variant uses only the first line; the second would not necessarily make much sense in

the wider context, although "knowledge" is a formal definition of the insider (*dhikos mas*) at all levels of social differentiation, including the mass national and religious, and provides a major key to the metonymical relationship between local and national identities.

7.   The pun depends on a common transference of the terminal prevocalic *n* of the masculine accusative definite article to the succeeding noun. *Omos* is the usual term for shoulder, *nomos* for law. Such transferences have generated well-known forms, especially in toponymy (for example, Nidhra from ldhra [Hydra]).

Notes to Chapter Three

Acknowledgments: In preparing the essay on which this chapter was based, I was greatly helped by the critical commentary of John N. Deely, Ivan Karp, and Greg N. Mahnke.

1.   Indeed, the literalism that can be attacked so effectively in verbal or cultural translation (Beidelman 1980, 1981; Crick 1976; Goldstein 1976: Willis 1980) creeps up on us much more easily when the question of similarity arises, especially, but by no means exclusively, in the visual arena.

2.   As Hamnett's (1967: 387) discussion of riddles demonstrates, category reification obstructs insight into any mode of discourse. To adopt Goldstein's (1976) terminology, academic disciplines are constituted by the practice of scholarship.

3.   Although I have found the term "reversibility" convenient here, this use of it should not be confused with the more usual anthropological sense (akin to "symbolic inversion") found, for example, in Babcock 1978.

4.   This is what Shapiro and Shapiro (1976; see also Shapiro 1980) mean by "hierarchy."

5.   Indeed, the point was unfairly made in early criticism of Vico (see Battistini 1975: 103). Vico does not appear to have entertained the kind of irredentist politics in support of which his work later came to be cited. But such artifactual territoriality, in which scholars used "monuments of the word" to mark politicocultural boundaries, did eventually prove durable; see Nisbet 1969: 100; Herzfeld 1982a: 10–11.

Note to Chapter Four

1.   Note that Tambiah's account of ethnonationalism nevertheless avoids the charge of irrationality with which Connor (1993: 383) charges it. Connor's remark that ethnonationalist rhetoric works "not through appeals to *reason* but through appeals to *emotions* (appeals not to the mind but to the blood)" is analytically unhelpful but ethnographically illuminating: by using the opposition between mind and body

through the imagery of blood as opposed to rationality, he demonstrates both the symbolic basis of rationalist rhetoric and the degree to which scholarly analyses of these phenomena may become permeated—even amid an otherwise perceptive discussion—by the very imagery that they seek to objectify and dissect.

Notes to Chapter Five

1. As an example of this discourse played out in foreign policy terms, see especially Huntington 1993.
2. These critiques notably include Asad 1973; Clifford 1983; Clifford and Marcus 1986; and Fabian 1983; and see also Said 1989. On anthropology as contested by virtual caricatures of science and morality, see D'Andrade 1995.
3. This, in respect of economics, is also the position articulated by Carrier 1995b and 1995c: 202.
4. For an outstanding early demonstration see Loizos 1975.
5. I discuss this justification for the classic focus on small, remote communities in Herzfeld 1985a: xvi, and Herzfeld 1987a: 63; for a measured critical response see Bakalaki 1993. The urgent search for "relevance" may partially explain why it is becoming increasingly unfashionable to conduct such field research, but this in turn risks reproducing precisely the occidentalist-nationalist discourse I discuss in this chapter; and, as far as Greece is concerned, it overlooks the excellent point made in the most plausibly urban of all published Greek ethnographies that in fact the invention of a separate sphere of urban anthropology violates cultural categories and social experience (Hirschon 1989: 233).
6. This is the logical development of the theoretical position laid out in Herzfeld 1987a. Bakalaki (1993: 53) notes that anthropologists working in Greece have had to contend with a double-sided attack—for focusing on small communities on the one hand, and for overgeneralizing on the other—and concludes (1993: 56) that these are two aspects of a common problem, that of assuming that the local and national of social identity are mutually congruent. The criticism seems entirely fair—and is equally applicable to ideologues who imagine the national community in the idiom of the local. Note that the equation of anthropologists with a category of foreigners fortunately no longer applies. Indeed, a Greek nonanthropologist who found himself criticized in Alaska for "ask[ing] too many questions" has noted that "*all* Greeks who go abroad to work or study are ardent anthropologists" because, he thinks, this is essential to their survival (Baloglou 1995); his plea for anthropologists to turn to more modern and literate aspects of Greek society will not fall on deaf ears in the profession today. His genial (and truly comparative) observation about ordinary Greeks abroad deserves serious reflection for the new research angles it could recommend. Foreign anthropologists who work in Greece must be immensely grateful that

their Greek colleagues have largely rejected the easy option of dismissing foreign anthropologists' perceptions as necessarily ignorant or malign (see especially Gefou-Madianou 1993a, 1993b).

7. See the discussion of Anderson 1983 in the introduction; see also Herzfeld 1992a: 76.

8. See the introduction, especially note 4. I have argued elsewhere that the practices of social relativity that Evans-Pritchard called "segmentation" (Fortes and Evans-Pritchard 1940) are no less true of modern nation-states than they are of Nilotic tribes (Herzfeld 1987a: 152–157; 1992a: 101–104).

9. It would probably be impossible to trace this connection with anything more than intuition, but it is true that clothing plays a very important role in less ambiguous or derivative cases of that symbolic connection. In Glendi, the one place a thief could hide meat from a stolen animal was among his virginal sister's underclothes: he knew that the police would never risk the violence that searching among them would provoke (Herzfeld 1985a: 48).

10. See the balanced discussion by Stavros (1995). Official policy recognizes two groups (Jews and Muslims) as religious minorities, none as ethnic minorities. The distinction, which in the case of the Muslims (many but not all of whom are Turkish-speaking) primarily reflects territorial anxieties, has embroiled the Greek authorities in several international confrontations.

11. Whatever one thought about the executions, British reaction was comparable to that evinced by the Iranian edict against Salman Rushdie, on which Asad's (1994) controversial account demonstrates the Eurocentrism of British liberal ideology. Blok's (1981) observation that emergent nation-states may appropriate the discourse of honor and remove it from the sphere of interpersonal or local-level relations, is pertinent to my argument about the sources of cultural intimacy; but his view of a homogeneous Mediterranean moral code not only conflates numerous different concepts (Herzfeld 1984b) but also reproduces an evolutionist perspective similar to that which Asad (1994) finds directed at the Muslim world in British political discourse; it is thus important to disaggregate the two strands of his argument, detaching the historicity of particular nation-states' appropriation of local values from the unilineal schema in terms of which Blok has—unfortunately, in my view— couched his otherwise very useful insight.

12. See also Faubion 1993. The outrage that Faubion's book appears to have provoked in some Greek circles appears, in part, to derive from the converse of the elite reaction to anthropology that I am discussing here, the sense that intellectuals should be immune to the ethnographer's analytic interest.

13. This was the position of the two towering figures of grand nineteenth-century historiography in Greece, Spyridon Zambelios (1828–1881) (1852) and Konstantinos Paparrhegopoulos (1815–1891) (1932).

14. Especially relevant are: Clogg 1987, 1993; Diamandouros 1994; Spourdalakis 1988; Kharalambis 1989.

15. Similar arguments have been extensively aired in the U.S. and Western Europe, showing clearly that the storm of protest in Greece belongs to a far wider ideological debate, of which it is nonetheless both diagnostic and, doubtless because of the Greeks' more immediate geopolitical worries, something of a caricature.

16. See Herzfeld 1987a: 45, 51, 115.

17. There is no point in claiming that Greek fears about the territorial ambitions of their nearest neighbors are necessarily either unrealistic or paranoid. Indeed, I would argue that such crass psychological stereotypes are part of the problem, not a serious contribution to solving it. But it is true that the tendency to blame others for Greece's predicament, while grounded in painful historical experience (Couloumbis, Petropulos, and Psomiades 1976), is often couched in a culturally distinctive style (Herzfeld 1992a: 127–157) that can simply invite ridicule.

Notes to Chapter Six

Acknowledgments: In addition to support acknowledged in Herzfeld 1985a for research done in the Upper Milopotamos village of Glendi, I would like to express my gratitude to the Wenner-Gren Foundation for Anthropological Research for a grant-in-aid that enabled me to conduct the subsequent fieldwork in the summer of 1987 on which this article is principally based. The foundation is not responsible for the opinions expressed here. I similarly absolve those who reviewed a version of this chapter for *Man*, as well as several other colleagues whose generous criticism has helped me greatly in revising it: Joëlle Bahloul, Richard Bauman, Loring M. Danforth, Michael Jackson, Martha B. Kendall, Jerome R. Mintz, C. Nadia Seremetakis, Charles Stewart, Lawrence J. Taylor, and Richard R. Wilk. John M. Hollingsworth rendered my crude cartography intelligible (fig. 1). To the many, often necessarily anonymous Cretan friends whose voices inform this analysis, I owe a special gratitude that is both personal and intellectual.

1. The structural nostalgia that orthodox structuralism shares with so many of the world's cultures suggests that the attempt to distinguish the "unconscious models" of the latter from the anthropologists' own analytical models (Lévi-Strauss 1963; cf. Herzfeld 1987a: 60) may have been too ambitious, not to say ethnocentric.

2. See Black-Michaud (1975) for a useful review of the definitional problems associated with the concept of feud and of the attendant issues of duration and conclusion.

3. See Gellner (1988: 149) for an interesting analogue from an Islamic society and especially for Ibn Khaldûn's anticipation of this type of argument.

4.   On the conventions of animal-theft, see Herzfeld (1985a: 163–231, especially 183–189 on alliances). Spiritual kin, notably when the link is created through baptism rather than marriage, should not raid one another.

5.   Standard Greek *ghrousouzia*. Its Turkish root form means "being unlucky, banishing fortune"; see Herzfeld (1987a: 178).

6.   Shepherds prefer total indirection where possible. The victim's kinsman seeks his spiritual kinsmen in villages where he suspects that the theft originated; the latter leave him in their homes while they check with likely prospects among their own kin.

7.   Campbell (1964: 344) adopts the same metaphor to describe the significance of family icons.

8.   Being *Khrist(h)ianos* (Christian) signifies social acceptability in a community of sinners, rather than devotion. Calling someone *Khristianos* may thus imply roguery rather than religiosity.

9.   "Eating," a common metaphor for theft, also implies the (dishonest) acquisition of wealth.

10.   The Classical name of the court (*Areopagos*, hill of Ares) dates from the earliest years of the Greek state.

11.   Needham (1972) argues against describing psychological inner states for entire peoples; Loizos (1975: 301, n. 2) extends this to secular, political conviction.

12.   *Pistemenos* (literally, believed) implies a mutuality of trust that the English "persuaded" does not really capture. It may be taken as a tiny shred of evidence for the desire for a restoration of perfect balance implicit in the concept of structural nostalgia.

13.   Cutting off these bells (*sklaveria*), which are distinctive to each animal and flock, graphically affronts the victim's masculinity. See Herzfeld (1985a: 191–2); Stewart (1991: 71–72).

14.   Usually translated as dishonor, this term implies especially acts of sexual dishonesty or violence.

15.   Bailey (1971: 17) similarly identifies "concentric circles of trust" with Greek data from Campbell (1964). On segmentation as the key organizing principle, see Herzfeld (1987a: 173–179).

16.   Theft of the ram, practically a threat to flock reproduction, is another symbolic emasculation of the shepherd (cf. n. 13, above).

17.   On the theological foundations of gender ideology in Greece, see particularly du Boulay (1974: 100–120; 1986).

18.   Deformation of conventional forms is basic to the "poetics of social interaction" (Herzfeld 1985a: 16; and see chapter 7).

19.   In English and related languages, there is a complex etymological relationship between "love" and "belief." At least two anthropologists have made use of this connection: Needham (1972: 41–44) suggests that these terms represent inaccessible psychological inner states, while Hart (1988: 186–187) connects the notion of trust to the "evidence of the senses." Whatever the consequences of either position,

most recent writers (e.g., Gambetta 1988b) would accept that trust and its near synonyms can only be analyzed with confidence as representations. This, however, is no small or trivial undertaking.

20.   *Timi* also means price. Despite problems about the supposed equivalence of *timi* and honor, the *loghos timis* does seem to have precisely the force of the word of honor in English.

21.   For the corollary of the shepherd's role as divine, see Campbell 1964: 26).

22.   The Classical and Koinē Greek is usually transliterated as *logos.* According to the conventions for transliterating modern Greek that I have adopted here, this word, spelled the same way in Greek, emerges as *loghos;* the respective plural forms are *logoi* and *loyi.* Cretan shepherds frequently emphasize a surprising piece of information with the exclamation *logho timis* ([on my] word of honor), much as we might in English (cf. "scout's honor").

23   See also Stewart (1985a: 1991) for further, detailed explorations of this relationship.

Notes to Chapter Seven

Acknowledgments: A version of one part of this paper was presented on October 24, 1987, at the Annual Meeting of the Semiotic Society of America at Pensacola, Florida. I am indebted to Eric Schwimmer for his helpful reading of that version. A further version was circulated by the Center as #22 in its series of Working Papers and Proceedings under the title, "Rhetoric and the Constitution of Social Relations" (1988), and I have benefited from many subsequent discussions of the argument.

1.   See the varied contributions of Carrier (1995a, 1995c); Fabian (1983), Kuper (1988); Sahlins (1976); and Tambiah (1990); as well as my own discussion of Western claims to rationality in bureaucratic practice (Herzfeld 1992a).

2.   Historiography has proved more sensitive to this issue than have many other social epistemologies, and there are several accounts of the rhetoric of history (e.g., Goldstein 1976). Richard Harvey Brown (1977, 1991) has done a great deal to advance this cause in sociology, and in the social sciences generally; see also the essays collected in Clifford and Marcus 1986.

3.   There is an irony in citing Bourdieu in such a context, in that Bourdieu (1977: 18) himself sees indigenous exegesis as only "semi"-theoretical, and as generated only by outsiders' questions. This restricts the concept of social theory to a level that denies the intellectual creativity of the indigenous actor and so undermines the attribution of agency precisely at the moment of otherwise acknowledging it. For a more detailed elaboration of this point see Herzfeld 1987a: 82–87; see also Karp 1986: 133–134. On indigenous notions of meaning in Greece,

see the discussions in Herzfeld 1981 and 1985a, and Caraveli's (1982) treatment of related concepts. On "emergence," see Bauman 1977; Giddens 1984; Karp 1980. While anthropologists have recognized the illogic in automatically subordinating symbolism to social structure (e.g., Needham 1963), they have been less generous to the encompassing category of rhetoric. In the past two decades, anthropologists in the Kenneth Burke tradition (e.g., Sapir and Crocker 1977; Fernandez 1986), have focused on the performative aspects of language in social life and to treat the play of tropes as constitutive of cultural life.

4. This should provide reassurances in the light of George's (1996: 136) concerns about the potential of Jakobson's model for generating an excessively static and formal analysis.

5. Cowan (1990), building on several papers on the rhetoric of embodiment, offers an outstanding contribution to the analysis of the embodiment of ideology that develops the work of Bourdieu and Gramsci. For another perspective that also uses Bourdieu's concepts of habitus and bodily hexis, see Jackson 1983. On the relationship between embodiment, clothing, continence, and disemia, see Herzfeld 1987a: 96–101.

6. Bakalaki's criticism of earlier formulations, including some of my own, is as well-taken as it is balanced. She makes the crucial point that, while dualisms such as "West-East" certainly do play a prominent role in Greek social discourse, their schematic association with contrasted, fixed ideologies is reductionist in that they ignore certain forms of social agency—such as that of women who internalize the "European" model to which public discourse supposedly debars their access. She also sees the mechanistic quality of the earlier formulations as partly grounded in the extremely restrictive orientation of most ethnographic work to community-level studies (although it should be said that, beginning with Campbell 1964, many ethnographers have examined the sometimes successful attempts of the village tail to wag the governmental dog). In that her critique calls for a more flexible understanding of the uses to which such ideological formalisms are put—in my terms, the essentializing strategies that activate them—I would argue that a poetics of social life, considerably expanded beyond the limits of my first attempt to apply it in *The Poetics of Manhood*, is fully compatible, and mutually reinforcing, with the nuanced and historically grounded analytic approach she proposes. See also, for a serious critique of quite general import, Handelman 1994: 370–2; the shift of analytic focus from disemia to the less formal concept of cultural intimacy (see pp. 14–16, above) should address some key concerns.

References Cited

Aarsleff, Hans
  1975   *From Locke to Saussure*. Madison: University of Wisconsin Press.
Abélès, Marc
  1989   *Jours tranquilles en 89: Ethnologie politique d'un département français*. Paris: Odile Jacob.
  1990   *Anthropologie de l'état*. Paris: A. Colin.
Alexakis, Elefth. P.
  1990   *Ta yeni ke i ikoyenia stin paradhosiaki kinonia tis Manis*. Athens: privately published.
Alexiou, Margaret B.
  1974   *The Ritual Lament in Greek Tradition*. Cambridge: Cambridge University Press.
Almeida, Miguel Vale de
  1995   *Senhores de si: Uma interpretação antropologica da masculinidade*. Lisbõa: Fim de Século.
Althusser, Louis
  1971   Ideology and Ideological State Apparatuses, Notes toward an Investigation. In *Lenin and Philosophy and the Other Essays*. Trans. Ben Brewster, 121–73. London: New Left Books.
Anderson, Benedict
  1983   *Imagined Communities: Reflections on the Origin and Spread of Nationalism*. London: Verso.
Andromedas, John N.
  1976   Maniat Folk Culture and the Ethnic Mosaic in the Southeast Peloponnese. In *Regional Variation in Modern Greece and Cyprus: Toward a Perspective on the Ethnography of Greece*.

Annals of the New York Academy of Sciences 268:1–465. Ed.
Muriel Dimen and Ernestine Friedl, 268: 1–465. 99–206.

Appadurai, Arjun
1981 The Past as a Scarce Resource. *Man*, n.s., 16:201–19.
1988 How to Make a National Cuisine: Cookbooks in Contemporary India. *Comparative Studies in Society and History* 30:3–24.

Ardener, Edwin W.
1971a Introductory Essay. In *Social Anthropology and Language*. Ed. Edwin Ardener, ix–cii. A.S.A. Monographs, 10. London: Tavistock.
1971b Social Anthropology and the Historicity of Historical Linguistics. In *Social Anthropology and Language*. Ed. Edwin Ardener, 209–41. A.S.A. Monographs, 10. London: Tavistock.
1975 The Problem Revisited. In *Perceiving Women*. Ed. Shirley Ardener, 19–27. London: J.M. Dent.
1978 Some Outstanding Problems in the Analysis of Events. *The Yearbook of Symbolic Anthropology* 1:103–21.

Asad, Talal
1973 (ed.) *Anthropology and the Colonial Encounter*. London: Ithaca Press.
1979 Anthropology and the Analysis of Ideology. *Man*, n.s., 14:607–627.
1987 On Ritual and Discipline in Medieval Christian Monasticism. *Economy and Society* 16:159–203.
1994 *Genealogies of Religion: Discipline and Reasons of Power in Christianity and Islam*. Baltimore: Johns Hopkins University Press.

Austin, J. L.
[1956–57]1971 A Plea for Excuses. In *Philosophy and Linguistics*. Ed. Colin Lyas, 79–101. London: Macmillan.
[1962] 1975 *How to Do Things with Words*. Eds. J. O. Urmson and Marina Sbisà, Cambridge, MA: Harvard University Press.

Babcock, Barbara A., ed.
1978 *The Reversible World*. Ithaca: Cornell University Press.

Badone, Ellen
1991 Ethnography, Fiction, and the Meanings of the Past in Brittany. *American Ethnologist* 18:518–545.

Bailey, F. G.
1971 Gifts and Poison. In *Gifts and Poison: the Politics of Reputation*. Ed. F. G. Bailey, Oxford: Blackwell.
1973 Losa. *In* Debate and Compromise. Ed. F. G. Bailey, 164–99. Oxford: Basil Blackwell.

Bakalaki, Alexandra
1993 Anthropoloyikes prosengisis tis sinkhronis ellinikis kinonias. *Dhiavazo* 323:52–58.

1994   Gender-Related Discourses and Representations of Cultural
        Specificity in Nineteenth-Century and Twentieth-Century
        Greece. *Journal of Modern Greek Studies* 12:75–112.
Bakhtin, Mikhail
    1981   *The Dialogic Imagination.* Trans. Carol Emerson and J.
            Michael Holmquist, Austin: University of Texas Press.
Baloglou, George
    1995   Just Anthropology. Internet messages in MGSA-List. 8 June
            and 15 June.
Banfield, E. C.
    1958   *The Moral Basis of a Backward Society.* Glencoe: Free
            Press.
Barthes, Roland
    1964   *Eléments de sémiologie.* Paris: Seuil.
Battistini, Andrea
    1975   *La degnità della retorica: studi su G.B. Vico.* Pisa: Pacini.
Baudrillard, Jean
    1988   *Selected Writings.* Ed. M. Poster. Stanford: Stanford Univer-
            sity Press.
Bauman, Richard
    1977   *Verbal Art as Performance.* Rowley, MA: Newbury House.
    1986   *Story, Performance, and Event: Contextual Studies of Oral
            Narrative. Cambridge Studies in Oral and Literate Culture*
            10. Cambridge: Cambridge University Press.
    1987   The Role of Performance in the Ethnography of Speaking. In
            *Performance, Speech Community, and Genre, Working Pa-
            pers and Proceedings of the Center for Psychosocial Studies,*
            no. 11, 3–12. Chicago: Center for Psychosocial Studies.
Bauman, Richard, and Charles L. Briggs
    1990   Poetics and Performance as Critical Perspectives on Language
            and Social Life. *Annual Review of Anthropology* 19:59–88.
Beidelman, Thomas O.
    1980   The Moral Imagination of the Kaguru: Some Thoughts on
            Tricksters, Translation, and Comparative Analysis. *American
            Ethnologist* 7:27–42.
    1981   The Nuer Concept of *Thek* and the Meaning of Sin: Explana-
            tion, Translation, and Social Structure. *History of Religions*
            21:126–55.
    1995   Bureaucracy and the Public: Accenting the Negative. *Current
            Anthropology* 36:533–34.
Bellier, Irène
    1993   *L'ENA comme si vous y étiez.* Paris: Seuil.
Bernal, Martin
    1987   *Black Athena: The Afroasiatic Roots of Classical Civilization.*
            Vol. 1: *The Fabrication of Ancient Greece 1785–1985.* New
            Brunswick, NJ: Rutgers University Press.

Bertarelli, Achille
  1938   L'iconografia popolare italiana: sue caratteristiche: come deve essere studiata. *Lares* 9:28–32.
Black-Michaud, J.
  1975   *Cohesive Force: Feud in the Mediterranean and the Middle East.* Oxford: Blackwell.
Blok, Anton
  1974   *The Mafia of a Sicilian Village, 1860–1960: A Study of Violent Peasant Entrepreneurs.* Oxford: Basil Blackwell.
  1981   Rams and Billy-Goats: A Key to the Mediterranean Code of Honour. *Man*, n.s., 16:427–40.
Boehm, Christopher
  1984   *Blood Revenge: The Enactment and Management of Conflict in Montenegro and Other Tribal Societies.* Lawrence: University Press of Kansas.
Bogatyrev, Petr G.
  [1937] 1971 *The Functions of Folk Costume in Moravian Slovakia.* Trans. Richard G. Crum. The Hague: Mouton.
Bolinger, Dwight
  1975   *Aspects of Language.* 2d ed. New York: Harcourt Brace Jovanovich.
Bona, Emma
  1940   Arti popolari e artigianato. *Lares* 11:475–77.
Bond, George C., and Angela Gilliam, eds.
  1994   *Social Construction of the Past: Representation as Power.* London: Routledge.
Boon, James
  1982   *Other Tribes, Other Scribes: Symbolic Anthropology in the Comparative Study of Cultures, Histories, Religions, and Texts.* Cambridge: Cambridge University Press.
Bottomley, Gill, and John Lechte
  1990   Nation and Diversity in France. *Journal of Intercultural Studies* 11: 49–63.
Bourdieu, Pierre
  1977   *Outline of a Theory of Practice.* Trans. Richard Nice. Cambridge: Cambridge University Press.
  1984   *Distinction: Critique of the Judgement of Taste.* Trans. Richard Nice. Cambridge, MA: Harvard University Press.
Bourdieu, Pierre, and P. Lamaison
  1985   De la règle aux stratégies: entretiens avec Pierre Bourdieu. *Terrain* 4:93–100.
Brandes, Stanley E.
  1980   Metaphors of Masculinity: Sex and Status in Andalusian Folklore. *Publications of the American Folklore Society*, n.s., 1. Philadelphia: University of Pennsylvania Press.

Brenneis, Donald
  1987   Performing Passions Aesthetics and Politics in an Occa-
          sionally Egalitarian Community. *American Ethnologist* 14:
          236–250.
Bringa, Tone
  1995   *Being Muslim the Bosnian Way: Identity and Community in a
          Central Bosnian Village.* Princeton: Princeton University Press.
Brown, Peter
  1971   The Rise and Function of the Holy Man in Late Antiquity.
          Journal of Roman Studies 61: 80–101.
Brown, Richard Harvey
  1977   *A Poetic for Sociology: Towards a Logic of Discovery for the
          Human Sciences.* Cambridge: Cambridge University Press.

  1991   (ed.) *Writing the Social Text: Poetics and Politics in Social Sci-
          ence Discourse.* New York: Aldine de Gruyter.
Brown, Roger, and Albert Gilman
  1960   The Pronouns of Power and Solidarity. In *Style in Language.*
          Ed. Thomas A. Sebeok, 253–276. Cambridge: MIT Press.
Broyard, Anatole
  1986   Sadder Music and Stronger Poetics. *New York Review of
          Books* (April 27):14–15.
Bruner, Edward M., and Phyllis Gorfain
  1984   Dialogic Narration and the Paradoxes of Masada. In *Text,
          Play, and Story: The Construction and Reconstruction of Self
          and Society.* Ed. Edward M. Bruner, 56–79. Washington, DC:
          American Ethnological Society.
Buttitta, Antonio
  1971   *Ideologie e folklore.* Palermo: Flaccovio.
Byrnes, Robert F., ed.
  1976   *Communal Families in the Balkans: The Zadruga.* Notre
          Dame: University of Notre Dame Press.
Campbell, J. K.
  1964   *Honour, Family, and Patronage: A Study of Institutions and
          Moral Values in a Greek Mountain Community.* Oxford:
          Clarendon Press.

  1976   Regionalism and Local Community. In *Regional Variation in
          Modern Greece and Cyprus: Toward a Perspective on the
          Ethnography of Greece.* Ed. Muriel Dimen and Ernestine
          Friedl, 18–27. *Annals of the New York Academy of Sciences*
          268:1–465.
Caraveli, Anna
  1982   The Song Beyond the Song: Aesthetics and Social Interac-tion
          in Greek Folksong. *Journal of American Folklore* 95:129–58.
Carrier, James
  1992   Occidentalism: The World Turned Upside-Down. *American
          Ethnologist* 19:195–212.

1995a (ed.) *Occidentalism: Images of the West*. Oxford: Clarendon Press.

1995b Maussian Occidentalism: Gift and Commodity Systems. In *Occidentalism: Images of the West*. Ed. James Carrier, 85–108. Oxford: Clarendon Press.

1995c *Gifts and Commodities: Exchange and Western Capitalism since 1700*. London and New York: Routledge.

Cartledge, Paul
1994 The Greeks and Anthropology. *Anthropology Today* 10(3):3–6.

Ceram, C. W.
1957–58 *A Picture History of Archaeology*. London: Thames and Hudson.

Chock, Phyllis Pease
1987 The Irony of Stereotypes: Toward an Anthropology of Ethnicity. *Cultural Anthropology* 2:347–68.

Clark, Grahame
1939 *Archaeology and Society*. London: Methuen.
1966 The Invasion Hypothesis in British Archaeology. *Antiquity* 40:172–89.

Clarke, David L.
1962 Matrix Analysis and Archaeology with Particular Reference to British Beaker Pottery. *Proceedings of the Prehistoric Society*, n.s., 28:371–83.
1968 *Analytical Archaeology*. London: Methuen.

Classen, Constance
1993 *Worlds of Sense: Exploring the Senses in History and Across Cultures*. London and New York: Routledge.

Clifford, James
1983 On Ethnographic Authority. *Representations* 2 (Spring): 118–46.

Clifford, James, and George Marcus, eds.
1986 *Writing Culture: The Poetics and Politics of Ethnography*. Berkeley: University of California Press.

Clogg, Richard
1987 *Parties and Elections in Greece: The Search for Legitimacy*. London: C. Hurst.
1993 *Greece 1981–93: The Populist Decade*. New York: St. Martin's Press.

Cocchiara, Giuseppe
1952 *Storia del foklore in Europa*. Torino: Einaudi.

Cohen, Colleen Ballerino, Richard Wilk, and Beverly Stoeltje
1996 Introduction. In *Beauty Queens on the Global Stage: With Gender, Contests, and Power*. Ed. Colleen Ballerino Cohen, Beverly Stoeltje, and Richard Wilk, 1–11. New York and London: Routledge.

Cohen, Erik
  1971   Arab Boys and Tourist Girls in a Mixed Jewish-Arab Community. *International Journal of Comparative Sociology* 12:217–33.
Cohen, Jonathan
  1975   *Spoken and Unspoken Meanings*. Lisse: Peter de Ridder Press.
Collard, Anna
  1989   Investigating "Social Memory" in a Greek Context. In *History and Ethnicity*. Ed. Elizabeth Tonkin, Maryon McDonald, and Malcolm Chapman, 89–103. London and New York: Routledge.
Collingwood, R. G.
  1939   *An Autobiography*. London: Oxford University Press.
  1965   *Essays in the Philosophy of History*. Ed. William Debbins. Austin: University of Texas Press.
Comaroff, Jean, and John L. Comaroff
  1989   The Colonization of Consciousness in South Africa. *Economy and Society* 18:267–95.
Connor, Walker
  1993   Beyond Reason: The Nature of the Ethnonational Bond. *Ethnic and Racial Studies* 16: 373–89.
Coufoudakis, Evangelos
  1985   Greek-Turkish Relations, 1973–1983: The View from Athens. *International Security* 9:185–217.
Couloumbis, T. A., John A. Petropulos, and H. J. Psomiades, eds.
  1976   *Foreign Interference in Greek Politics: An Historical Perspective*. New York: Pella.
Couroucli, Maria
  1985   *Les oliviers du lignage*. Paris: Maisonneuve et Larose.
Cowan, Jane K.
  1990   *Dance and the Body Politic in Northern Greece*. Princeton: Princeton University Press.
Crick, Malcolm
  1976   *Explorations in Language and Meaning: Towards a Semantic Anthropology*. London: Malaby.
Dakin, Douglas
  1973   *The Greek Struggle for Independence, 1821–1833*. London: Batsford.
Damer, Seán
  1986   Poetics or Posturing? *Critique of Anthropology* 7(1):71–75.
  1988   Legless in Sfakia: Drinking and Social Practice in Western Crete. *Journal of Modern Greek Studies* 6:291–310.
D'Andrade, Roy
  1995   Moral Models in Anthropology (and Reply). *Current Anthropology* 36:399–408, 433–38.

Danforth, Loring M.
  1982   *The Death Rituals of Rural Greece*. Princeton: Princeton University Press.
de Certeau, Michel de
  1984   *The Practice of Everyday Life*. Trans. Steven F. Rendall. Berkeley: University of California Press.
Deely, John
  1982   *Introducing Semiotic: Its History and Doctrine*. Bloomington: Indiana University Press.
  1990   *Basics of Semiotics*. Bloomington: Indiana University Press.
Delaney, Carol
  1995   Father State, Motherland, and the Birth of Turkey. In *Naturalizing Power: Essays in Feminist Cultural Analysis*. Ed. Sylvia Yanagisako and Carol Delaney, 177–99. New York: Routledge.
Detienne, Marcel
  1986   *The Creation of Mythology*. Trans. Margaret Cook. Chicago: University of Chicago Press.
Diamandouros, P. Nikiforos
  1994   *Cultural Dualism and Political Change in Postauthoritarian Greece*. Madrid: Centro Juan March de Estudios Avanzados en Ciencias Sociales, Estudio no. 50.
Dorn, Paméla
  1991   Change and Ideology: The Ethnomusicology of Turkish Jewry. Ph.D. diss., Indiana University.
Douglas, Mary
  1966   *Purity and Danger: An Analysis of Concepts of Pollution and Taboo*. London: Routledge & Kegan Paul.
  [1970] 1973 *Natural Symbols: Explorations in Cosmology*. Harmondsworth, UK: Penguin.
  1975   *Implicit Meanings: Essays in Anthropology*. London: Routledge & Kegan Paul.
Douglass, Carrie B.
  1995   "Europe," "Spain," and the Bulls. *Journal of Mediterranean Studies* 2:69–79.
Doxiadis, Constantinos
  1968   *Ekistics: An Introduction to the Science of Human Settlements*. London: Hutchinson.
Dresch, Paul
  1986   The Significance of the Course Events take in Segmentary Systems. *American Ethnologist* 13:309–32.
Drummond, Lee
  1980a   The Cultural Continuum: A Theory of Intersystems. *Man*, n.s., 15:352–74.
  1980b   The Analysis of Ideology. *Man*, n.s., 15:738.

1981   The Serpent's Children: Semiotics of Cultural Genesis in Arawak and Trobriand Myth. *American Ethnologist* 8:633–60.

1996   *American Dreamtime: A Cultural Analysis of Popular Movies and Their Implications for a Science of Humanity.* Lanham, MD: Rowman & Littlefield.

Dubisch, Jill

1988   Golden Oranges and Silver Ships: An Interpretive Approach to a Greek Holy Shrine. *Journal of Modern Greek Studies* 6:117–34.

1995   *In a Different Place: Pilgrimage, Gender, and Politics at a Greek Island Shrine.* Princeton: Princeton University Press.

du Boulay, Juliet

1974   *Portrait of a Greek Mountain Village.* Oxford: Clarendon Press.

1986   Women—Images of their Nature and Destiny in Rural Greece. In *Gender and Power in Rural Greece.* Ed. J. Dubisch, 199–68. Princeton: Princeton University Press.

Dundes, Alan

1985   Nationalistic Inferiority Complexes and the Fabrication of Fakelore: A Reconsideration of Ossian, the *Kinder und Hausmarchen,* the *Kalevala,* and Paul Bunyan. *Journal of Folklore Research* 22:5–18.

Eco, Umberto

1976   *A Theory of Semiotics.* Bloomington: Indiana University Press.

Elias, Norbert

1978   *The History of Manners. The Civilizing Process.* Vol. 1. Trans. Edmund Jephcott. New York: Pantheon.

Eriksen, Thomas Hylland

1993   *Ethnicity and Nationalism: Anthropological Perspectives.* London: Pluto Press.

Evans-Pritchard, E. E.

1940   *The Nuer: A Description of the Modes of Livelihood and Political Institutions of a Nilotic People.* Oxford: Clarendon Press.

1956   *Nuer Religion.* Oxford: Clarendon Press.

Fabian, Johannes

1983   *Time and the Other: How Anthropology Makes Its Object.* New York: Columbia University Press.

Fardon, Richard

1985   Introduction: A Sense of Relevance. In *Power and Knowledge: Anthropological and Sociological Approaches.* Ed. Richard Fardon, 1–20. Edinburgh: Scottish Academic Press.

Farnell, Brenda

1994   Ethno-graphics and the Moving Body. *Man,* n.s., 29:930–74

1995a Introduction. In *Action Sign Systems in Cultural Context: The Visible and the Invisible in Movement and Dance.* Ed. Brenda Farnell, 1–28. Edinburgh: Scottish Academic Press.

1995b *Do You See What I Mean? Plains Indians Sign Talk and the Embodiment of Action.* Austin: University of Texas Press.

Faubion, James
1993 *Modern Greek Lessons: A Primer in Historical Constructivism.* Princeton: Princeton University Press.

Feely-Harnik, Gillian
1978 Divine Kingship and the Meaning of History among the Sakalava of Madagascar. *Man,* n.s., 13:402–17.

Feld, Steven
1982 *Sound and Sentiment: Birds, Weeping, Poetics, and Song in Kaluli Expression.* Philadelphia: University of Pennsylvania Press.

Femia, Joseph V.
1981 *Gramsci's Political Thought: Hegemony, Consciousness and the Revolutionary Process.* Oxford: Clarendon Press.

Ferguson, Charles A.
1959 Diglossia. *Word* 15:325–40.

Ferguson, Kathy E.
1984 *The Feminist Case Against Bureaucracy.* Phildelphia: Temple University Press.

Fernandez, James W.
1974 The Mission of Metaphor in Expressive Culture. *Current Anthropology* 15:119–45.

1986 *Persuasions and Performances.* Bloomington: Indiana University Press.

1988 Andalusia on Our Minds: Two Contrasting Places in Spain as Seen in a Vernacular Poetic Duel of the Late 19th Century. *Cultural Anthropology* 3:21–35.

Fletcher, Sheila
1980 *Feminists and Bureaucrats.* Cambridge: Cambridge University Press.

Forge, Anthony
1968 Learning to See in New Guinea. In *Socialization: The Approach from Social Anthropology.* Ed. Philip Mayer. A.S.A. Monographs. vol. 8, 269–91. London: Tavistock.

Fortes, M., and E. E. Evans-Pritchard, eds.
1940 *African Political Systems.* Milford Haven: Oxford University Press/International Institute of African Languages and Cultures.

Foster, George M.
1965 Peasant Society and the Image of Limited Good. *American Anthropologist* 67:293–315.

Foucault, Michel
  1966   *Les mots et les choses: une archéologie des sciences humaines.*
         Paris: Gallimard.
Freedberg, David
  1989   *The Power of Images: Studies in History and Theory of Response.* Chicago: University of Chicago Press.
Friedl, Ernestine
  1962   *Vasilika: A Village in Modern Greece.* New York: Holt, Rinehart & Winston.
  1964   Lagging Emulation in Post-Peasant Society. *American Anthropologist* 66:569–85.
Furth, Charlotte
  1995   Theory and Local Knowledge in the History and Anthropology of the Body. *American Ethnologist* 22:997–99.
Gable, Eric, Richard Handler, and Anna Lawson
  1992   On the Uses of Relativism: Fact, Conjecture, and Black and White Histories of Colonial Williamsburg. *American Ethnologist* 19:791–805.
Gajek, Esther
  1990   Christmas under the Third Reich. *Anthropology Today* 6(4):4–9.
Galaty, John G.
  1982   Being "Maasai": Being "People-of-Cattle": Ethnic Shifters in East Africa. *American Ethnologist* 9:1–20.
Gambetta, Diego
  1988a Can We Trust Trust? In *Trust: Making and Breaking Cooperative Relations.* Ed. D. Gambetta, 213–37. Oxford: Blackwell.
  1988b ed., *Trust: Making and Breaking Cooperative Relations.* Oxford: Blackwell
Gardin, Jean-Claude
  1980   *Archaeological Constructs: An Aspect of Theoretical Archaeology.* Cambridge: Cambridge University Press.
Geertz, Clifford
  1973   *The Interpretation of Cultures.* New York: Basic Books.
  1983   *Local Knowledge: Further Essays in Interpretive Anthropology.* New York: Basic Books.
Gefou-Madianou, Dimitra
  1993a Mirroring Ourselves through Western Texts: The Limits of an Indigenous Anthropology. In *The Politics of Ethnographic Reading and Writing: Confrontation of Western and Indigenous Views.* Ed. Henk Driessen, 160–81. Saarbrucken and Fort Lauderdale: Breitenbach.
  1993b Anthropoloyiki Iki: Ya mia kritiki tis "Yiyenous Anthropoloyias." *Dhiavazo* (323):44–51.

Gelles, Paul
1995   Equilibrium and Extraction: Dual Organization in the Andes. *American Ethnologist* 22:710–42.

Gellner, Ernest
1983   *Nations and Nationalism.* Ithaca, NY: Cornell University Press.
1988   Trust, Cohesion and the Social Order. In *Trust: Making and Breaking Cooperative Relations.* Ed. D. Gambetta. Oxford: Blackwell.

Georgakas, Dan.
1996   Don't Believe the Hype, Please. *Odyssey*, March/April, 1996, 49–51.

George, Kenneth M.
1996   *Showing Signs of Violence: The Cultural Politics of a Twentieth-Century Headhunting Ritual.* Berkeley: University of California Press.

Gewertz, Deborah B., and Frederick K. Errington
1995   Duelling Currencies in East New Britain: The Construction of Shell Money as National Cultural Property. In *Occidentalism: Images of the West.* Ed. James Carrier, 161–91. Oxford: Clarendon Press.

Giannuli, Dimitra
1995   Greeks or "Strangers at Home": The Experience of Ottoman Greek Refugees during their Exodus to Greece, 1922–1923. *Journal of Modern Greek Studies* 13:271–87.

Giddens, Anthony
1984   *The Constitution of Society: Introduction to the Theory of Structuration.* Berkeley: University of California Press.

Gilsenan, Michael
1976   Lying, Honor, and Contradiction. In *Transaction and Meaning: Directions in the Anthropology of Exchange and Symbolic Behavior.* Ed. B. Kapferer. A.S.A. Essays. Vol. 1, pp. 191–219. Philadelphia: Institute for the Study of Human Issues.
1986   Review of Herzfeld 1985a. *American Ethnologist* 14:393–94.

Gluckman, Max
1955   *Custom and Conflict in Africa.* Oxford: Basil Blackwell.

Goffman, Erving
1959   *The Presentation of Self in Everyday Life.* Garden City, NY: Doubleday.

Goldschläger, Alain
1982   Towards a Semiotics of Authoritarian Discourse. *Poetics Today* 3:11–20.

Goldstein, Leon J.
1976   *Historical Knowing.* Austin: University of Texas Press.

Gombrich, Ernst H.
  1961   *Art and Illusion: A Study in the Psychology of Pictorial Rep-
         resentation.* 2d ed. Princeton: Princeton University Press.
  1979   *The Sense of Order : A Study in the Psychology of Decorative
         Art.* Ithaca, NY: Cornell University Press.
Goody, Jack
  1977   *The Domestication of the Savage Mind.* Cambridge: Cam-
         bridge University Press.
Grillo, R. D., ed.
  1980   *"Nation" and "State" in Europe: Anthropological Perspec-
         tives.* London: Academic Press.
Greenwood, Davydd J.
  1977   Culture by the Pound: An Anthropological Perspective on
         Tourism as Commoditization. In *Hosts and Guests: The An-
         thropology of Tourism.* Ed. Valene L. Smith, 129–38.
         Philadelphia: University of Pennsylvania Press.
  1984   *The Taming of Evolution: The Persistence of Nonevolutionary
         Views in the Study of Humans.* Ithaca: Cornell University Press.
Gudeman, Stephen, and Michael Herzfeld
  1996   When an Academic Press Bows to a Threat. *Chronicle of
         Higher Education,* 12 April 1996, p. A56.
Gupta, Akhil
  1995   Blurred Boundaries: The Discourse of Corruption, the Cul-
         ture of Politics, and the Imagined State. *American Ethnologist*
         22:375–402.
Gutmann, Matthew C.
  1993   Rituals of Resistance: A Critique of the Theory of Everyday
         Forms of Resistance. *Latin American Perspectives* 20(2):
         74–92.
Halpern, Joel
  1967   *A Serbian Village: Social and Cultural Change in a Yugoslav
         Community.* Rev. ed. New York: Harper.
Hamilakis, Yannis, and Eleana Yalouri
  1995   Antiquities as Symbolic Capital in Modern Greek Society. *An-
         tiquity* 70: 117–29.
Hammel, Eugene A.
  1968   *Alternative Social Structures and Ritual Relations in the
         Balkans.* Englewood Cliffs, NJ: Prentice-Hall.
Hamnett, Ian
  1967   Ambiguity, Classification and Change: The Function of Rid-
         dles. *Man,* n.s., 2:379–92.
Handelman, Don
  1990   *Models and Mirrors: Towards an Anthropology of Public
         Events.* Cambridge: Cambridge University Press.
  1994   Critiques of Anthropology: Literary Turns, Slippery Bends.
         Poetics Today 15:341–81.

198

Handler, Richard
   1985a On Dialogue and Destructive Analysis: Problems in Narrating
         Nationalism and Ethnicity. *Journal of Anthropological Re-
         search* 41:171–82.
   1988 *Nationalism and the Politics of Culture in Quebec.* Madison:
         University of Wisconsin Press.
Handler, Richard, and Jocelyn Linnekin
   1984 Tradition, Genuine or Spurious. *Journal of American Folk-
         lore* 97:273–90.
Hannerz, Ulf
   1987 The World in Creolisation. *Africa* 57:546–59.
Hanson, F. Allan
   1979 Does God Have a Body? Truth, Reality and Cultural Rela-
         tivism. *Man*, n.s., 14:515–29.
Harris, Roy
   1980 *The Language-Makers.* Ithaca, NY: Cornell University Press.
Hart, Janet
   1996 *New Voices in the Nation: Women and the Greek Resistance,
         1941–1964.* Ithaca, NY: Cornell University Press.
Hart, Keith
   1988 Kinship, Contract, and Trust: the Economic Organization of
         Migrants in an African City Slum. In *Trust: Making and Break-
         ing Cooperative Relations.* Ed. Diego Gambetta, 176–93. Ox-
         ford: Blackwell.
Hasluck, Margaret M.
   1954 *The Unwritten Law in Albania.* Cambridge: Cambridge Uni-
         versity Press.
Hawkes, Terence
   1977 *Structuralism and Semiotics.* Berkeley: University of Califor-
         nia Press.
Hegel, G.W.F.
   1977 *Phenomenology of the Spirit.* Translated by A.V. Miller. Ox-
         ford: Clarendon Press.
Herzfeld, Michael
   1980a The Dowry in Greece: Terminological Usage and Historical
         Reconstruction. *Ethnohistory* 27:225–241.
   1980b Honour and Shame: Some Problems in the Comparative
         Analysis of Moral Systems. *Man*, n.s., 15:339–51.
   1980c On the Ethnography of "Prejudice" in an Exclusive Commu-
         nity. *Ethnic Groups* 2:283–305.
   1981 An Indigenous Theory of Meaning and its Elicitation in Per-
         formative Context. *Semiotica* 34:113–41.
   1982a *Ours Once More: Folklore, Ideology, and the Making of
         Modern Greece.* Austin: University of Texas Press.

1982b When Exceptions Define the Rules: Greek Baptismal Names and the Negotiation of Identity. *Journal of Anthropological Research* 38:288–302.

1983a Interpreting Kinship Terminology: The Problem of Patriliny in Rural Greece. *Anthropological Quarterly* 56:157–66.

1983b Semantic Slippage and Moral Fall: the Rhetoric of Chastity in Rural Greece. *Journal of Modern Greek Studies* 1:161–72.

1984a The Significance of the Insignificant: Blasphemy as Ideology. *Man*, n.s., 19:653–64.

1984b The Horns of the Mediterraneanist Dilemma. *American Ethnologist* 11:439–54.

1985a *The Poetics of Manhood: Contest and Identity in a Cretan Mountain Village.* Princeton: Princeton University Press.

1985b Lévi-Strauss in the Nation-State. *Journal of American Folklore* 98:191–208.

1985c "Law" and "Custom": Ethnography *in* and *of* Greek National Identity. *Journal of Modern Greek Studies* 3:167–85.

1986 Within and Without: The Category of "Female" in the Ethnography of Rural Greece. In *Gender and Power in Rural Greece*. Ed. Jill Dubisch, 215–33. Princeton: Princeton University Press.

1987a *Anthropology through the Looking-Glass: Critical Ethnography in the Margins of Europe.* Cambridge: Cambridge University Press.

1987b "As in Your Own House": Hospitality, Ethnography, and the Stereotypes of Mediterranean Society. In *Honour and Shame and the Unity of the Mediterranean*. Ed. David D. Gilmore, 75–89. Washington, DC: American Anthropological Association (Special Publication #22).

1990 Pride and Perjury: Time and the Oath in the Mountain Villages of Crete. *Man*, n.s., 25:305–22.

1991a *A Place in History: Social and Monumental Time in a Cretan Town.* Princeton: Princeton University Press.

1991b Silence, Submission, and Subversion: Towards a Poetics of Womanhood. In *Contested Identities: Gender and Kinship in Modern Greece*. Ed. Peter Loizos and Evthymios Papataxiarchis, 79–97. Princeton, NJ: Princeton University Press.

1991c Textual Form and Social Formation in Evans-Pritchard and Lévi-Strauss. In *Writing the Social Text: Poetics and Politics in Social Science Discourse*. Ed. Richard Harvey Brown, 53–70. New York: Aldine de Gruyter.

1992a *The Social Production of Indifference: Exploring the Symbolic Roots of Western Bureaucracy.* Oxford: Berg.

1992b On Mediterraneanist Performances. *Journal of Mediterranean Studies* 2:141–47.

1992c History in the Making: National and International Politics in a Rural Cretan Community. In *Europe Observed*. Ed. João de Pina-Cabral and John Campbell, 93–122. London: Macmillan.

1993   Erevnitiko kathikon ke mistikopathia. *Ikonomikos Takhidhromos*, 12 August 1993, pp. 42–43.

1995   It Takes One to Know One: Collective Resentment and Mutual Recognition among Greeks in Local and Global Contexts. In *Counterworks*. Ed. Richard Fardon, 124–42. London and New York: Routledge.

1996   Les enjeux du sang: La production officielle des stéréotypes dans les Balkans. Le cas de la Grèce. *Anthropologie et Sociétés* 19(3):37–51.

Heyman, Josiah McC.
1994   Putting Power in the Anthropology of Bureaucracy: The Immigration and Naturalization Service at the Mexico-United States Border. *Current Anthropology* 36:261–87.

Hill, Jane H.
1992   "Today There Is No Respect": Nostalgia, "Respect" *Pragmatics* 2: 263–280.

Hill, Jonathan D.
1988   Introduction: Myth and History. In *Rethinking History and Myth: Indigenous South American Perspectives on the Past*. Ed. Jonathan D. Hill, 1–18. Chicago: University of Illinois Press.

1990   Poetic Transformations of Narrative Discourse in an Amazonian Society. In *Native Latin American Cultures through their Discourse*. Ed. Ellen B. Basso, 115–31. Special Publications of the Folklore Institute, no. 1.

1993   *Keepers of the Sacred Chants: The Poetics of Ritual Power in an Amazonian Society*. Tucson: University of Arizona Press.

Hirschon, Renée
1978   Open Body/Closed Space: The Transformation of Female Sexuality. In Shirley Ardene, ed., *Defining Females* (London: Croom Helm), pp. 66–88.

1989   *Heirs of the Greek Catastrophe: The Social Life of Asia Minor Refugees in Paris*. Oxford: Clarendon Press.

Hobsbawm, Eric
1959   *Primitive Rebels: Studies in Archaic Forms of Social Movement in the 19th and 20th Centuries*. Manchester: Manchester University Press.

1969   *Bandits*. London: Weidenfeld and Nicolson.

1990   *Nations and Nationalism since 1780: Programme, Myth, Reality*. Cambridge: Cambridge University Press.

1983b Introduction: Inventing Traditions. In *The Invention of Tradition*. Ed. Eric Hobsbawm and Terence Ranger, 1–14.

Hochschild, Arlie Russell.
   1983   *The Managed Heart: Commercialization of Human Feeling.*
          Berkeley: University of California Press.
Hodgen, Margaret T.
   1936   *The Doctrine of Survivals: A Chapter in the History of Scientific Method in the Study of Man.* London: Allenson.
Holden, David
   1972   *Greece Without Columns: The Making of the Modern Greeks.* London: Faber and Faber.
Horn, David G.
   1994   *Social Bodies: Science, Reproduction, and Italian Modernity.*
          Princeton: Princeton University Press.
Humphreys, S. C.
   1978   *Anthropology and the Greeks.* London, Henley, and Boston:
          Routledge & Kegan Paul.
Huntington, Samuel P.
   1993   The Clash of Civilizations? *Foreign Affairs* 72(3):22–50.
Jackson, Michael
   1983   Thinking through the Body: An Essay on Understanding Metaphor. *Social Analysis* 14:127–49.
Jakobson, Roman
   1960   Linguistics and Poetics. In *Style in Language.* Ed. Thomas A.
          Sebeok, 350–77. Cambridge: MIT Press.
Jervis, Robert
   1970   *The Logic of Images in International Relations.* Princeton:
          Princeton University Press.
Joseph, Brian D.
   1992   Intellectual Awareness as a Reflex of Linguistic Dimensions of Power: Evidence from Greek. *Journal of Modern Greek Studies* 10:71–85.
Just, Roger
   1989   Triumph of the Ethnos. In *History and Ethnicity* (*A.S.A. Monographs* 27). Ed. Elizabeth Tonkin, Malcolm Chapman, and Maryon McDonald, 71–88. London: Routledge.
Kamenetsky, Christa
   1977   Folktale and Ideology in the Third Reich. *Journal of American Folklore* 90:168–78.
Kapferer, Bruce
   1988   *Legends of People, Myths of State: Violence, Intolerance, and Political Culture in Sri Lanka and Australia.* Washington, DC: Smithsonian Institution Press.
Karakasidou, Anastasia
   1993a Politicizing Culture: Negating Ethnic Identity in Greek Macedonia. *Journal of Modern Greek Studies* 11:1–28.
   1994a Reply to Zahariadis. *Journal of Modern Greek Studies* 12:168–70.

Kargakos, Sarandos
1993   Ellinismos ke kanivalismos. *Ikonomikos Takhidhromos*, 1
        July 1993, pp. 44–5.
Karp, Ivan
1978   *Fields of Change among the Iteso of Kenya.* London: Rout-
        ledge & Kegan Paul.
1980   Beer Drinking and Social Experience in an African Society:
        An Essay in Formal Sociology. In *Exploration in African Sys-
        tems of Thought.* Ed. Ivan Karp and Charles S. Bird, 83–119.
        Bloomington: Indiana University Press.
1986a   Agency and Social Theory: A Review of Giddens. *American
        Ethnologist* 13:131–37.
1986b   Anthropology. In *Encyclopaedic Dictionary of Semiotics.* Ed.
        Thomas A. Sebeok, 30–35. New York: Plenum.
Kendon, Adam
1995   Sociality, Social Interaction, and Sign Language in Aboriginal
        Australia. In *Action Sign Systems in Cultural Context: The
        Visible and the Invisible in Movement and Dance.* Ed. Brenda
        Farnell, 112–23. Metuchen: Scarecrow Press.
Kenna, Margaret
1976   Houses, Fields, and Graves: Property and Ritual Obligation
        on a Greek Island. *Ethnology* 15:21–34.
1992   An Ironic Mirror: Michael Herzfeld on Greece, Anthropology
        and the Anthropology of Greece. *Journal of Mediterranean
        Studies* 2:135–40.
Kharalambis, Dimitrios
1989   *Pelatiakes skhesis ke laïkismos: I eksothesmiki sinenesi sto
        elliniko politiko sistima.* Athens: Eksandas.
Kleinman, Arthur M.
1995   *Writing at the Margin: Discourse Between Anthropology and
        Medicine.* Berkeley: University of California Press.
Kligman, Gail
1981   *Căluş: Symbolic Transformation in Romanian Ritual.*
        Chicago: University of Chicago Press.
1989   *The Wedding of the Dead: Ritual, Poetics, and Popular Cul-
        ture in Transylvania.* Berkeley: University of California
        Press.
1990   Reclaiming the Public: A Reflection on Creating Civil Society
        in Romania. *East European Politics and Societies* 4: 393–438.
Koliopoulos, Yannis
1979   *Listes: I kendriki Elladha sta mesa tou 19ou eona.* Athens:
        Ermis.
Kozyris, P. John
1993   Reflections on the Impact of Membership in the European
        Economic Community on Greek Legal Culture. *Journal of
        Modern Greek Studies* 11:29–49.

Kuper, Adam
   1988   *The Invention of Primitive Society: Transformations of an Illusion*. London: Routledge.
Kyriakidis, Stilpon P.
   1955   *The Northern Ethnological Boundaries of Hellenism*. Thessaloniki: Institute for Balkan Studies.
Lane, Eugene N.
   1975   The Italian Connection: An Aspect of the Cult of Men. *Numen* 22:235–39.
Lawson, John Cuthbert
   [1910] 1964 *Modern Greek Folklore and Ancient Greek Religion: A Study of Survivals*. Foreword by Al. N. Oikonomides. New Hyde Park, NY: University Books.
Legg, Keith R.
   1969   *Politics in Modern Greece*. Stanford: Stanford University Press.
Legrand, Emile
   1881   *Bibliothèque grecque vulgaire*. Vol. 2. Paris: Maisonneuve.
Lehmann, W. P.
   1975   Saussure's Dichotomy Between Descriptive and Historical Linguistics. In *Directions for Historical Linguistics*. Ed. W. P. Lehmann and Yacov Malkiel, 3–20. Austin: University of Texas Press.
Lévi-Strauss, Claude
   1962   *La pensée sauvage*. Paris: Plon.
   1963   *Structural Anthropology*. Vol. 1. Trans. C. Jacobson and B. G. Schoepf. New York: Basic Books.
Li Causi, Luciano
   1995   Ridimensionare l'etnia? Note metodologiche sul fenomeno etnico (*with* interventi). *Ossimori* 6:13–28.
Lincoln, Bruce
   1989   *Discourse and the Construction of Society: Comparative Studies of Myth, Ritual, and Classification*. Oxford: Oxford University Press.
Linke, Uli
   1985   Blood as Metaphor in Proto-Indo-European. *Journal of Indo-European Studies* 13:333–76.
Lloyd, G.E.R.
   1990   *Demystifying Mentalities*. Cambridge: Cambridge University Press.
Loizos, Peter
   1975   *The Greek Gift: Politics in a Cypriot Village*. Oxford: Blackwell.
   1988   Intercommunal Killing in Cyprus. *Man*, n.s., 23: 639–53.
Loizos, Peter, and Evthymios Papataxiarchis, eds.
   1991a *Contested Identities: Gender and Kinship in Modern Greece*. Princeton: Princeton University Press.

1991b Introduction: Gender and Kinship in Marriage and Alternative Contexts. In *Contested Identities: Gender and Kinship in Modern Greece*. Ed. Peter Loizos and Evthymios Papataxiarchis, 5–25. Princeton: Princeton University Press.

Lotman, Iurii M. and Boris A. Uspenskii
1985 Binary Models in the Dynamics of Russian Culture. In *The Semiotics of Russian Cultural History*. Ed. and trans. Alexander D. Nakhimovsky and Alice Stone Nakhimovsky, 30–66. Ithaca, NY: Cornell University Press.

Machin, Barrie
1983 Cultural Codes, Religion and Attitudes to the Body in a Cretan Mountain Village. *Social Analysis* 14:107–62.

Mackridge, Peter
1985 *The Modern Greek Language: A Descriptive Analysis of Standard Modern Greek*. Oxford: Clarendon Press.

Maddox, Richard F.
1993 *El Castillo: The Politics of Tradition in an Andalusian Town*. Urbana: University of Illinois Press.

Mauss, Marcel
1968 *Sociologie et anthropologie*. Paris: P.U.F.

Mbembe, Achille
1991 Domaines de la nuit et autorité onirique: dans les maquis du Sud-Cameroun (1955–1958). *Journal of African History* 31:89–121.
1992 Provisional Notes on the Postcolony. *Africa* 62:3–37.

McDonald, Maryon
1996 "Unity in Diversity": Some Tensions in the Construction of Europe. *Social Anthropology* 4: 47–60.

Meeker, Michael E.
1979 *Literature and Violence in North Arabia*. Cambridge: Cambridge University Press.

Megas, Georgios A.
1946 *I Voulghari ekhoun ethnikon epos?* Athens: Society of the Propagation of Hellenic Letters.
1951 *The Greek House: Its Evolution and its Relation to the Houses of the Other Balkan Peoples*. Publication no. 37. Athens: Ministry of Reconstruction.

Mercouri, Melina
1971 *I Was Born Greek*. Garden City, NY: Doubleday.

Mintz, Jerome R.
1982 *The Anarchists of Casas Viejas*. Chicago: University of Chicago Press.

Moore, Sally Falk
1993 *Introduction: Moralizing States and the Ethnography of the Present*. Ed. Sally Falk Moore, 1–16. Arlington, VA: Ameri-

can Anthropological Association, American Ethnological Society Mongraph Series, #5.

Morison, Stanley
1972   *Politics and Script*. Ed. N. Barker. Oxford: Clarendon Press.

Moss, David
1979   Bandits and Boundaries in Sardinia. *Man*, n.s., 14:477–96.

Mosse, George L.
1985   *Nationalism and Sexuality*. New York: Basic Books.

Myrsiades, Linda S., and Kostas Myrsiades
1992   *Karagiozis: Culture and Comedy in Greek Puppet Theater*. Lexington: University Press of Kentucky.

Nadel-Klein, Jane
1992   Reweaving the Fringe: Localism, Tradition, and Representation in British Ethnography. *American Ethnologist* 18:500–17.

Needham, Rodney
1963   Introduction. In *Primitive Classification*. By Emile Durkheim and Marcel Mauss, vii–xlviii. London: Cohen and West.
1972   *Belief, Language, and Experience*. Chicago: University of Chicago Press.

Nisbet, Robert A.
1969   *Social Change and History: Aspects of the Western Theory of Development*. London and New York: Oxford University Press.

Norman, Karin
1994   The Ironic Body: Obscene Joking Among Swedish Working-Class Women. *Ethnos* 59:187–211.

Okely, Judith
1994   Thinking Through Fieldwork. In *Analyzing Qualitative Data*. Ed. Alan Bryman and Robert G. Burgess, 18–34. London and New York: Routledge.

Ong, Walter J.
1982   *Orality and Literacy: The Technologizing of the Word*. London: Methuen.

Orlove, Benjamin S., and Arnold J. Bauer
1996   Giving Importance to Imports. In *The Allure of the Foreign: Imported Goods in Post-Colonial Latin America*. Ed. Benjamin S. Orlove, 3ff. Ann Arbor: University of Michigan Press.

Ortner, S. B.
1984   Theory in Anthropology Since the Sixties. *Comparative Studies in Social History* 26:126–66.

Paparrhegopoulos, Konstantinos
1932   *Istoria tou ellinikou ethnous apo ton arkheoteron khronon mekhri tou 1930*. Ed. and updated by Pavlos Karolidis. Athens: Eleftheroudakes.

Papataxiarchis, Evthymios
 1991 Friends of the Heart: Male Commensal Solidarity, Gender, and Kinship in Aegean Greece. In *Contested Identities: Gender and Kinship in Modern Greece*. Ed. Peter Loizos and Evthymios Paptaxiarchis, 156–79. Princeton: Princeton University Press.
 1993 Isaghoyi: To parelthon sto paron: Anthropoloyia, istoria ke i meleti tis neoellinikis kinonias. In *Anthropoloyia ke parelthon: Simvoles stin kinoniki istoria tis neoteris Elladhas*. Ed. Evthymios Papataxiarchis and Theodoros Paradellis, 12–74. Athens: Alexandria.
Parmentier, Richard
 1994 *Signs in Society: Studies in Semiotic Anthropology*. Bloomington: Indiana University Press.
Peirce, Charles Sanders
 1960–66 *Collected Papers*. Ed. Charles Hartshorne and Paul Weiss. Cambridge, MA: Bellknap Press of Harvard University Press.
Pels, Peter
 1996 The Pidginization of Luguru Politics: Administrative Ethnography and the Paradoxes of Indirect Rule. *American Ethnologist* 23: forthcoming.
Peradotto, John
 1983 Texts and Unrefracted Facts: Philology. Hermeneutics and Semiotics. *Arethusa* 16:15–33.
Peristiany, J. C.
 1965 *Honour and Shame: The Values of Mediterranean Society*. London: Weidenfeld and Nicolson.
Pollis, Adamantia
 1987 The State, the Law, and Human Rights in Modern Greece. *Human Rights Quarterly* 9:587–614.
 1992 Greek National Identity: Religious Minorities, Rights, and European Norms. *Journal of Modern Greek Studies* 10:171–95.
Preziosi, Donald
 1979 *The Semiotics of the Built Environment: An Introduction to Architectonic Analysis*. Bloomington: Indiana University Press.
Rabinow, Paul
 1989 *French Modern: Norms and Forms of the Social Environment*. Cambridge: MIT Press.
Reed-Danahay, Deborah
 1993 Talking about Resistance: Ethnography and Theory in Rural France. *Anthropological Quarterly* 66:221–29.

Richards, I. A.
1936 *The Philosophy of Rhetoric*. London: Oxford University Press.

Rogers, Susan Carol
1987 Good to Think: The "Peasant" in Contemporary France. *Anthropological Quarterly* 60:56–63.

Rosaldo, Michelle Z.
1982 The Things We Do with Words: Ilongot Speech Acts and Speech Act Theory in Philosophy. *Language in Society* 11:203–37.

Roseman, Sharon
1996 "How We Built the Road": The Politics of Memory in Rural Galicia. *American Ethnologist*, 23(4).

Royce, Anya Peterson
1982 *Ethnic Identity: Strategies of Diversity*. Bloomington: Indiana University Press.

Safilios-Rothschild, Constantina
1969 Honour Crimes in Contemporary Greece. *British Journal of Sociology* 20: 205–18.

Sahlins, Marshall
1976 *Culture and Practical Reason*. Chicago: University of Chicago Press.

Said, Edward
1978 *Orientalism*. New York: Basic Books.
1989 Representing the Colonized: Anthropology's Interlocutors. *Critical Inquiry* 15:205–26.

Sapir, J. David, and J. Christopher Crocker, eds.
1977 *The Social Use of Metaphor: Essays in the Anthropology of Rhetoric*. Philadelphia: University of Pennsylvania Press.

Sassoon, Jean
1994 *Princess Sultana's Daughters*. New York: Doubleday.

Schein, Muriel Dimen
1975 When is an Ethnic Group? Ecology and Class Structure in Northern Greece. *Ethnology* 14:83–97.

Schneider, David M.
1968 *American Kinship: A Cultural Account*. Englewood Cliffs, NJ: Prentice-Hall.

Schneider, Jane, and Peter Schneider
1994 Mafia, Antimafia, and the Question of Sicilian Culture. *Politics and Society* 22:237–58.

Schwimmer, Eric
1990 La genèse du discours nationaliste chez les Maoris. *Culture* 10:23–34.
1992 La spirale dédoublée et l'identité nationale: L'art abstrait traditionnel maori a-t-il une signification? *Anthropologie et Sociétés* 16:59–72.

Scott, James C.
  1985   *Weapons of the Weak.* New Haven: Yale University Press.
Sebeok, Thomas A.
  1979   *The Sign and Its Masters.* Austin: University of Texas Press.
Shalinsky, Audrey C.
  1980   Group Prestige in Northern Afghanistan: The Case of an In-
         terethnic Wedding. *Ethnic Groups* 2:269–82.
Shapiro, Michael
  1980   Toward a Global Theory of Style (A Peircian Exposé). *Ars se-
         meiotica* 3:241–47.
Shapiro, Michael, and Marianne Shapiro
  1976   *Hierarchy and the Structure of Tropes.* Bloomington: Indiana
         University, Research Center for Language and Semiotic Studies.
Showalter, Elaine
  1986   Piecing and Writing. In *The Poetics of Gender.* Ed. Nancy K.
         Miller, 222–47. New York: Columbia University Press.
Simeone, William E.
  1978   Fascists and Folklorists in Italy. *Journal of American Folklore*
         91:543–57.
Simmel, Georg
  [1908] 1971 The Stranger. In *On Individuality and Social Forms.* Ed.
         Donald N. Levine, 145–49. Chicago: University of Chicago
         Press.
Slavenkoff, Pencho
  1904   The Folk-Song of the Bulgars. In *The Shade of the Balkans.*
         Ed. Pencho Slavenkoff, Henry Bernard, and E. J. Dillon,
         23–87. London: Nutt.
Sobo, Elisa Janine
  1993   *One Blood: The Jamaican Body.* Albany: State University of
         New York Press.
Sotiropoulos, Dimitri
  1977   Diglossia and the National Language Question in Modern
         Greece. *Linguistics* 197:5–31.
Soysal, Yasemin Nuhoğlu
  1994   *Limits of Citizenship: Migrants and Postnational Member-
         ship in Europe.* Chicago: University of Chicago Press.
Spicer, Edward H.
  1992   The Nations of a State. In *Boundary 2* 19(2): 26–48.
Spivak, Gayatri
  1989   In a Word. Interview with Ellen Rooney. *Differences*
         1(2):124–56.
Spourdalakis, Michalis
  1988   *The Rise of the Greek Socialist Party.* London and New York:
         Routledge.

Stacy, R. H.
  1977   *Defamiliarization in Language and Literature.* Syracuse, NY: Syracuse University Press.
Stavros, Stephanos
  1995   The Legal Status of Minorities in Greece Today: The Adequacy of their Protection in the Light of Current Human Rights Perceptions. *Journal of Modern Greek Studies* 13:1–32.
Stephen, Lynn
  1995   Women's Rights are Human Rights: The Merging of Feminine and Feminist Interests Among El Salvador's Mothers of the Disappeared. *American Ethnologist* 22:807–827.
Stewart, Charles
  1985a Exotika: Greek Values and their Supernatural Antitheses. *Scandinavian Yearbook of Folklore* 41:37–64.
  1985b Nymphomania: Sexuality, Insanity and Problems in Folklore Analysis. In *The Text and Its Margins: Post-Structuralist Approaches to Twentieth-Century Greek Literature.* Ed. M. Alexiou & V. Lambropoulos. New York: Pella.
  1989   Hegemony or Rationality? The Position of the Supernatural in Modern Greece. *Journal of Modern Greek Studies* 7:77–104.
  1991   *Demons and the Devil: Aspects of the Moral Imagination of Modern Greek Culture.* Princeton: Princeton University Press.
  1994   Honour and Sanctity: Two Levels of Ideology on a Greek Island. *Social Anthropology* 2:205–208.
Stewart, Susan
  1984   *On Longing: Narratives of the Miniature, the Gigantic, the Souvenir, the Collection.* Baltimore: Johns Hopkins University Press.
Strathern, Andrew
  1996   Review of Carrier 1995a. *American Ethnologist,* 23:136–37.
Sutton, David E.
  in press Local Names, Foreign Claims: Family Inheritance and National Heritage on a Greek Island. *American Ethnologist.*
Symonds, Richard
  1986   *Oxford and Empire: The Last Lost Cause?* New York: St. Martin's Press.
Talbott, Strobe
  1992   America Abroad: Greece's Defense Seems Just Silly. *Time,* 12 October; 64.
Tambiah, Stanley J.
  1989   Ethnic Conflict in the World Today. *American Ethnologist* 16:335–49.
  1990   *Magic, Science, Religion, and the Scope of Rationality.* Cambridge: Cambridge University Press.

Traweek, Sharon
  1988   *Dreamtimes and Lifetimes: The World of High Energy Physi-
         cists*. Cambridge: Harvard University Press.
Tsitsipis, Lukas D.
  1983   Narrative Performance in a Dying Language: Evidence from
         Albanian in Greece. *Word* 34: 25–36.
Tsoucalas, Constantine
  1991   "Enlightened" Concepts in the "Dark": Power and Freedom,
         Politics and Society. *Journal of Modern Greek Studies* 9: 1–22.
Turino, Thomas
  1993   *Moving Away from Silence: Music of the Peruvian Altiplano
         and the Experience of Urban Migration*. Chicago: University
         of Chicago Press.
Turner, Victor
  1974   *Dramas, Fields, and Metaphors: Symbolic Action in Human
         Society*. Ithaca, NY: Cornell University Press.
Urla, Jacqueline
  1993   Cultural Politics in an Age of Statistics: Numbers, Nations,
         and the Making of Basque Identity. *American Ethnologist*
         20:818–43.
  1995   Outlaw Language: Creating Alternative Public Spheres in
         Basque Free Radio. *Pragmatics* 5:245–61.
Verdery, Katherine
  1991   *National Ideology under Socialism: Identity and Cultural
         Politics in Ceauşescu's Romania*. Berkeley: University of Cal-
         ifornia Press.
  1996   *What Was Socialism, and What Comes Next?* Princeton:
         Princeton University Press.
Vernier, Bernard
  1991   *La genèse sociale des sentiments: aînés et cadets dans l'île
         grecque de Karpathos*. Paris: Editions de l'Ecole des Hautes
         Etudes en Sciences Sociales.
Vico, Giambattista
  [1728] 1977 *Autobiografia*. NUE, n.s., 37. Torino: Einaudi.
  1744   *Principij di Scienza Nuova*. 3d ed. Naples: Stamperia Muziana.
Vidal, Denis
  1988   A Propos des bergers crétois. *Etudes rurales* 97–98:242–48.
Wace, A. J. B. and Maurice Thompson
  1913   *Nomads of the Balkans*. London: Methuen.
Wade, Peter
  1995   The Cultural Politics of Blackness in Colombia. *American
         Ethnologist* 22:341–357.
Wallis, Mieczyslaw
  1975   *Arts and Signs*. Bloomington: Indiana University, Research
         Center for Language and Semiotic Studies.

Wallman, Sandra
  1978   The Boundaries of "Race": Processes of Ethnicity in England. *Man*, n.s., 13:200–217.
Watson, Rubie S., ed.
  1994   *Memory, History, and Opposition under State Socialism.* Santa Fe: School of American Research Press.
Waugh, Linda
  1980   The Pacific Function in Jakobson's Theory. *Poetics Today* 2: 57–82.
Wilhelm, Kathy
  1996   Vietnam's Internet Interruption. *Boston Globe*, 5 January: 2.
Wilkinson, Henry Robert
  1951   *Maps and Politics: A Review of the Ethnographic Cartography of Macedonia.* Liverpool: Liverpool University Press.
Willis, Roy
  1980   The Literalist Fallacy and the Problem of Oral Tradition. *Social Analysis* 4:28–37.
Wilson, William A.
  1976   *Folklore and Nationalism in Modern Finland.* Bloomington: Indiana University Press.
Zabusky, Stacia E.
  1995   *Launching Europe: An Ethnography of European Cooperation in Space Science.* Princeton: Princeton University Press.
Zahariadis, Nikolaos
  1994   Reply to Karakasidou. *Journal of Modern Greek Studies* 12:167–68.
Zambelios, Spyridon
  1852   *Asmata dhimotika tis Elladhos, ekdhothendos meta meletis istorikis peri Meseonikou Ellinismou.* Kerkira: Ermis.

Index

Cultural Intimacy